THE SIGNET CLASSIC POETRY SERIES is under the general editorship of poet, lecturer, and teacher JOHN HOLLANDER. Mr. Hollander's first book, *A Crackling of Thorns*, won the Yale Series of Younger Poets Awards for 1958. He was a recipient of a National Institute of Arts and Letters grant (1963) and has been a member of the Wesleyan University Press Poetry Board and the Bollingen Poetry Translation Prize Board. Mr. Hollander is Professor of English at Yale University.

JOHN ARTHOS, editor of SELECTED POETRY OF DRYDEN, is Professor of English at the University of Michigan. He was a Fullbright Research Professor in Florence, Italy, and has held Guggenheim and A. C. L. S. Fellowships in Paris and Florence. He is the author of various studies of seventeenth and eighteenth century poetry, among them *Dante, Michelangelo and Milton, The Art of Shakespeare*, and *Milton and the Italian Cities*. Professor Arthos is the editor of the Signet Shakespeare edition of *Love's Labours Lost*.

John Dryden

SELECTED POETRY

Edited by John Arthos

The Signet Classic Poetry Series
GENERAL EDITOR: JOHN HOLLANDER

A SIGNET CLASSIC from
NEW AMERICAN LIBRARY
TIMES MIRROR
New York and Toronto
The New English Library Limited, London

Library of Congress Catalog Card Number: 79–106043

SIGNET TRADEMARK REG. U.S. PAT. OFF. AND FOREIGN COUNTRIES
REGISTERED TRADEMARK—MARCA REGISTRADA
HECHO EN CHICAGO, U.S.A.

SIGNET, SIGNET CLASSICS, MENTOR and
PLUME BOOKS are published *in the United States* by
The New American Library, Inc.,
1301 Avenue of the Americas, New York, New York 10019,
in Canada by The New American Library of Canada Limited,
295 King Street East, Toronto 2, Ontario,
in the United Kingdom by The New English Library Limited,
Barnard's Inn, Holborn, London, E.C. 1, England

First Printing, April, 1970

PRINTED IN THE UNITED STATES OF AMERICA

Contents

Introduction

Of all England's poets Dryden is the one for whom the manner of grandeur counts the most. He masters it in a hundred ways—in passion, in thought, in mockery, even in joy. He brings grandeur into the light of common day, and it is still itself.

There is a fine simplicity in him too: no egotism ever offends us, and condescension is alien to him. The grandeur is sustained by this simplicity, even sometimes by the air of familiarity, as it can only be by those who set as right a value upon honesty as they do upon greatness. And together with that splendid ease there are times when his words have the sound, in Saintsbury's wonderful phrase, of a great bronze coin thrown down upon marble.

He is the least well valued of English poets nowadays although in the past he has been sufficiently admired. Changes of taste; the need for poetry to speak to the heart's affections, and for the music of passion and intuition; the disposition to put aside the attractions of reason and judgment—all this has caused more than one generation to miss the excellences that may again force themselves upon our recognition and admiration. Then, too, Dryden took politics and theology rather too seriously for tastes that are formed in cultivating introspection. Many of us have given up trying to follow the complexities he lays out for us so marvellously both in celebrating and mocking the disputes of Royalists and Puritans and libertines. We have too often disposed of as superior journalism what is in fact literature. But perhaps the times are changing and perhaps he is again taking a place of well-lit honor.

Everywhere in Dryden there is an intelligence as vigorous as it is supple, unresting in penetration and eager to turn to every form. There was never to be any doubt about either the independence of his spirit or the free play of his judgment. He may have been so given to the cultivation of the grand that he could be misled into efforts at magnificence that was not in his power to realize. But whatever his deficiencies, he never lagged in energy and in experiment. It was in his nature to combine the heroic and the satiric, and on occasion he so joined them—in *Absalom and Achitophel* and in *Mac Flecknoe*—that he seems to have created unique forms. At other times, the burlesque and the mock-heroic merely weave in and out of a prologue or an epistle. But even in the most outrageous mockery he prefers to keep the measure. He would not have it said of him what he said of Collier, "that he is too much given to horseplay in his raillery."

A man of the theater when the theater was entertaining a highly limited society, when the people of the theater were almost as absorbed in themselves and in gossip about themselves as in their audience, he inevitably took to easy manners. In the Restoration this commonly meant the style of men and women on familiar terms with the Court. But other things, too, went to form Dryden's public style, for there was now current among writers in London a continuous give-and-take, a continuous business in the discussion of literary matters. The history of *Mac Flecknoe* well illustrates this influence. Here is, on the face of it, a poem about very little of anything: a mockery of a negligible man, a personality so vague that research can hardly define it, but like many small men obviously wading beyond his depth. And so as a *jeu d'esprit,* having the time of his life in metamorphosing the gnat into an eagle, Dryden works out this beautifully sustained comic masterpiece. What begins as a slight mockery of a trivial matter sooner or later becomes a comic turning upside-down of much of literary London. But through the penetration of the wit, and the resonance of the words, it also comes to take into view the most serious literary concerns and the deepest rooted interests of society.

This wonderful production Dryden permitted to circulate in manuscript for some years as a kind of semi-public jest. After a while a pirate publisher got hold of it, but it was still some years before Dryden saw to it that a good text was printed, although without his name, and it was not until 1692 that he publicly acknowledged it.

Coming of age during the Commonwealth Dryden found employment with the government, and he even wrote a poem honoring Cromwell. But it was upon the restoration of the monarchy that he found the atmosphere and the encouragement his talents would flourish in. On good terms with the Court, favored by the King, granted a pension, before long made Poet Laureate and Historiographer Royal, he turned to almost every kind of writing.

He wrote a variety of occasional poems and comedies in prose and in verse, and he soon found himself attracted to the heroic drama. Davenant, who like Dryden was greatly interested in opera, had been an innovator of this form in England, and in addition there was the example of the heroic drama of Corneille and Racine. The French had helped form the tastes of many of the English who had spent the years of the Puritan exile in their country, and their influence upon English drama after the Restoration was increasingly acknowledged.

But it was not only in the drama, through whatever intermediaries, that classical theory and classical modes were making their way. In narrative verse, in translations, in critical discourses, as indeed in the very temper of much of intellectual life, classicism was everywhere strengthening its hold. In the *Annus Mirabilis* Dryden undertook an ambitious subject in a modified form of the epic, and in his satires he would also be exploiting epic conventions. The manner of his writing was in fact saturated with the influence of Virgil. And about the same time that he was composing the *Annus Mirabilis* he was putting down his thoughts on the values of classicism for the English. On leave from London, as it were, to escape the menace of the plague of 1665, he composed his famous *Essay on Dramatic Poesy*. By representing conversation among men who obviously delighted to talk about literature, Dryden laid out a series of arguments. Among them were propositions arguing for the need of the English to recognize the authority of the claims for classicism. Dryden's own reasonings in the essay did not go so far, but it is clear that he was profoundly engaged in reflecting upon the importance of the neo-classical movement, both in itself and for what it signified in the history of English literature. In his superbly judicious and easy way, proceeding so unpretentiously in the recording of talk, Dryden was in fact composing one of the finest surveys of the substantial literary issues of the age.

By the time he was thirty-five, then, he was practised in many forms of the craft of writing and he had been initiated into the complex skills of holding an audience in the theater. But however much Dryden insisted that writers must please to live, he conceived of the profession as embracing the widest responsibilities. The age was electric with controversy in religion and politics and philosophy. The very existence of the theater, and the character of the one he served, depended upon political and social agreements. For him the life of thought led everywhere and the most pressing responsibilities he accepted with great satisfaction. So we find that for him heroic drama, mock-heroic satire, literary criticism, lead directly into political and religious controversy.

The pretensions of bad poets, extremities of opinion in the controversies surrounding the Popish Plot, arguments disputing the claims of the churches of Rome and of England and of the dissenters, disputes over the relative authority of reason and revelation, the advances of skepticism and of science—all these matters were to be fused in a coherently articulated understanding. The life of the mind was to be all of a piece, the manners of expression were to depend on that single coherence. It was his labor to demonstrate that the issues exercising him in sounding the nature of classicism were those that engaged him in outlining the role he believed a man of sense must play on the larger stages of the world.

There is some confusion with respect to the consequences of Dryden's absorption in ideas about classicism. In the preface to *Troilus and Cressida* he adopted as extreme a position as he was ever to express, and in the work itself I suppose he thought he was bringing Shakespeare's play not only into a purer form but into the compass of the theater in a more worthy way. I suppose he believed he was doing this as much through clarifying the issues of the play as in simplifying the action. There are other plays as well, most famously *All for Love* and *Don Sebastian,* where the clarity of the theme, the concentration of the action, and the nature of the verse evidently are indebted to classical theory. Such works belong to a quite different category than dramas of the stamp of *The Conquest of Granada.* But if we look at *All for Love* as a work illustrating Dryden's subscription to neo-classical ideas, we observe that it holds our attention through the intricacy of the relations that entangle the persons of the play, by means of surprises in the involutions of the plot, and by the pathos of the resolution. It offers us persons we are already disposed to credit —out of our knowledge of history or of Shakespeare— but as characters they barely come alive. They do not carry the play along, the play carries them. There is a continuing creation of situations and of encounters, and there is an exciting tension in the debates. The play, in fact, moves us primarily through its intellection. It moves us with the thought that this is the way an articulate work of art is articulated. At the very end it may achieve a truly enthralling effect, but on the whole we feel that we have been placed outside the world of the play and held there by our awareness of how ingeniously things have been arranged.

In the re-workings of *The Tempest* and *Paradise Lost* the spirit is anything but impious, and there are passages that are splendid. While Dryden and others might from time to time have used the word "improved," as if to account for their endeavors, I think there was nothing invidious in their intention, however inferior the new work may seem to us. And this points to what is most noteworthy about the classicism of Dryden and indeed of his contemporaries, and not only in drama: their works lack the imaginative power, the conviction of ethical involvement, and most especially the depth of religiousness, that characterize the success of the French classical writers. For all the thoughtfulness of his speculation about love and honor and glory and resignation, for all the brilliance of his gifts, Dryden succeeds hardly better than Davenant in what he appears to be aiming at. Certainly he does not enrich English poetry with the power that seems to be almost within easy reach when the prescriptions of classical doctrine are not setting the terms.

To put it perhaps too bluntly, classical ideals helped him restrain the extravagance he himself was attracted to as much as his nation itself habitually is, and nearly as much as were his predecessors in the English drama. There is in fact something as legitimate and affecting in the extravagance that degenerates so quickly into bombast as there is in the tempered intensity of *All for Love* or in the grand adaptations of Horace and Chaucer. And indeed I think it is in the *Fables,* and especially in the translation of Boccaccio, that Dryden strikes the vein that calls upon his finest and strongest gifts. I think we must say that for all that is justified in the demands he makes upon himself in taking to neo-classical ways, he is most himself, and best, when he does not stifle the Elizabethan, the "gothic," the "barbarous." He lacks the energy of Marlowe and of Shakespeare but something of their splendor is still in his blood.

The classical temper served Dryden well in satirical writing. In *Absalom and Achitophel* he displayed the strength of his mind at its fullest in embedding a satire on contemporary politics in an Old Testament story nar-

rated half in the manner of the Roman epic poets, half
in the manner of a sermon. Apparently his aim was at
once to enlarge and demean the issues of contemporary
strife by bringing forward episodes out of the tumultuous
lives of David and Absalom and Achitophel—to enlarge
this strife by inflating his contemporaries into ancient
Hebrew warriors and the chosen of God, and to demean
it by reducing it all to the stupidity of barbarism and
the pathos of the inept. He casts a hundred different
lights upon the acts of those who would subvert a monarchy; and in the coolest and most justly measured way
(part of the joy of the work is the apparent extravagances
that are in fact so carefully measured), he judges and con-
demns and discards, while, at the same time, through
allusion and analogy he establishes a claim for sanity in
religion and politics alike. In *Absalom and Achitophel* he
can be unsparing—

> He could not live by God, but changed his master;
> Inspired by want, was made a factious tool,
> They got a villain, and we lost a fool.
> (Absalom and Achitophel, II)

He can reduce an ignoramus to even less—

> Now stop your noses, readers, all and some,
> For here's a tun of midnight work to come,
> Og, from a treason-tavern rolling home.
> Round as a globe, and liquored every chink,
> Goodly and great he sails behind his link,
> With all his bulk there's nothing lost in Og,
> For every inch that is not fool is rogue.
> (Absalom and Achitophel, II)

He holds back, however, from mere rage or outrage
or fear or contempt. No matter how deeply moved, he
maintains the tone of address agreeable to the few that
take delight "in that which reasonable men should write."
Even so, the grand almost always maintains its ascendancy
over the familiar. The satire, the railing, even the play
with the grotesque and hideous—"fretted the pigmy body

to decay"—express not only a feeling of simplicity, but are the reverse of the love of the grand, even while they continue to keep the accent of the grand. We see also in the translations of the Roman satirists that Dryden is imposing heroics upon words that in the original were almost familiar. What begins simply enough in Horace—

Tyrrhena regum progenies . . . [1]

is, as Dryden himself announces, "Paraphrased in Pindaric verse"—

> Descended of an ancient line,
> That long the Tuscan scepter swayed.

But the grandeur in Dryden is also in the humanity of the sentiment. Honoring Ben Jonson, and adapting and imitating Molière, Dryden accepted the Renaissance view of comedy as the ridiculing of folly and vice. But in these writings, as in the satires, even when he is hitting hardest, Dryden keeps the manner of one whose chief care is to retain respect for what is good. And it is through this poise, as much as through his gifts, that again and again he elevates the comic into the enchanted world of the imagination.

It is properly said that satire at its most powerful exploits righteous indignation, but there are many ways of being righteous. The way of Jeremiah was not Dryden's. He honored truth and candor and loyalty, he revered the institutions of church and state, but he held as firmly to the claims of good sense and humility. He may have been incapable of white-hot rage; but in any event, he was too much affected by the currents of skepticism and the advances of science to take to the mantle of a prophet. And by contrast with many satirists, he was too much a man of the world, a man of affairs, too sociable for the role of public preacher. When he rails he also laughs. Dr. Johnson made him too sober-sided when he said that his genius "was not very fertile of merriment, nor ductile to humor, but acute, argumentative, comprehensive, and sublime." This makes too little of the fun Dryden takes in his own wit, and in his tolerance.

[1] Literally, "scion of Tuscan kings" (*Odes III, 29*).

He is always amusing himself, and he is also always taking
pleasure in letting us in on his amusement—

> O poet, damned dull poet, who could prove
> So senseless! to make Nelly die for love!
> Nay, what's yet worse, to kill me in the prime
> Of Easter term, in tart and cheese-cake time!
> > (Epilogue to *Tyrannic Love*)

> A double noose thou on thy neck dost pull,
> For writing treason, and for writing dull;
> To die for faction is a common evil,
> But to be hanged for nonsense is the devil.
> > (*Absalom and Achitophel*, II)

He enjoys sharing laughter as he enjoys sharing his
judgments and condemnations. But even in the mockery of
Shaftesbury and Monmouth and all the trouble-makers,
all who could do such irreparable harm, he means for his
readers not to give up hope, as if even the corrupt might
be induced to laugh at their grotesqueness, and as if in
the mockery of the petty he would reassure us of the
existence of greatness. He does not rail except when he
wants to tease the gallant and the vicious and the know-it-
alls in the theater, and then, too, he almost always blunts
the edge of satire, aiming still to please. And possibly
even hoping to reform.

> Of all the tyrannies of humankind,
> The worst is that which persecutes the mind.
> Let us but weigh at what offense we strike;
> 'T is but because we cannot think alike,
> In punishing of this, we overthrow
> The laws of nations and of nature too.
> Beasts are the subjects of tyrannic sway,
> Where still the stronger on the weaker prey;
> Man only of a softer mold is made,
> Not for his fellow's ruin, but their aid;
> Created kind, beneficent, and free,
> The noble image of the Deity.
> > (*The Hind and the Panther*, I)

Dryden took to translation as, he said, young men take to love and rhyming. In the 1680's he had translated specimens of poets that were dear to him—Virgil and Theocritus—but it was apparently not until the 1690's that he gave himself to translating the whole of Virgil, the work that would crown his career. And even after that was finished, in 1697, he went on to some of the finest of all his writings, the translations of Chaucer and Ovid and Boccaccio that were to be assembled under the title of *Fables,* published in the year of his death, 1700. He had proposed translating Homer, and had completed a few passages, and indeed there were many others he translated in whole or in part—most notably Juvenal, Persius, and Lucretius.

In these creative translations his poetry took on an assured imaginative power, reaching sometimes, I think, a quality of poetic movement he did not sustain as well elsewhere. In *The Knight's Tale,* Chaucer's marvellous climax is full of the tears of things and full also of joy in life. It has the quality also of the simply beautiful. What Chaucer handed over to Dryden was a story full of the nuances of the mingling of lives, and of suspense in the contrivance of events that follow from that mingling; he also gave him ideas about fate and the way fate controls even the passions. Chaucer subordinated his very subtle exploitation of the dramatic and the melodramatic to the play of irony. Dryden took all this, avoided the comparison with beauty, and spilled over into the delights of argument. It is the new style of the couplet that gave him his chance to exult in the inspiration he meant to transform, and the poem caught up his fire.

But there was an inspiration of another kind also. Somewhere in the second part of *Palamon and Arcite* the suspense of the story takes hold and we cannot put it down, and in the third part Dryden hits his stride and there is a still greater surge of power. The marvellous declamatory speech of Palamon pours out. Half defying the gods, half pathetic, the defeated hero takes comfort in his thoughts, even in his faultless rhetoric, and there

arises out of the words and the joy in the display of
artifice the throb of defeat itself:

> This I may say, I only grieve to die,
> Because I lose my charming Emily:
> To die, when Heav'n had put you in my power,
> Fate could not choose a more malicious hour!
> What greater curse could envious Fortune give,
> Than just to die when I began to live!
> Vain men, how vanishing a bliss we crave,
> Now warm in love, now withering in the grave!
> Never, O never more to see the sun!
> Still dark, in a damp vault, and still alone!
> This fate is common; but I lose my breath,
> Near bliss, and yet not blest before my death.
> Farewell; but take me dying in your arms,
> 'Tis all I can enjoy of all your charms;
> This hand I cannot but in death resign.
> Ah, could I live! but while I live 'tis mine.

And then there is the equally marvellous conclusion, as
unlike Chaucer's as anything could be—the great series
of apostrophes and declaimings on the nature of fortune,
on vicissitude, on the inevitable uncertainty of human
affairs. Whatever the character of the ending in Chaucer,
in Dryden it is staged and framed, and the curtain comes
down to the sound of the orchestra dominated by the
clash of cymbals.

> And speaking thus, he gave Emilia's hand.
> Smiled Venus, to behold her own true knight
> Obtain the conquest, though he lost the fight;
> And blessed with nuptial bliss the sweet laborious night.
> Eros and Anteros, on either side,
> One fired the bridegroom, and one warmed the bride;
> And long-attending Hymen from above
> Showered on the bed the whole Idalian grove.
> All of a tenor was their after-life,
> No day discolored with domestic strife;
> No jealousy, but mutual truth believed,

Secure repose, and kindness undeceived.
Thus Heav'n, beyond the compass of his thought,
Sent him the blessing he so dearly bought.
So may the Queen of Love long duty bless,
And all true lovers find the same success.

Dryden speaks of the character of translation more modestly than quite fits his practice:

> For, after all, a translator is to make his author appear as charming as possibly he can, provided he maintains his character, and makes him not unlike himself. Translation is a kind of drawing after the life; where every one will acknowledge there is a double sort of likeness, a good one and a bad. 'Tis one thing to draw the outlines true, the features like, the proportions exact, the coloring itself perhaps tolerable; and another thing to make all these graceful, by the posture, the shadowings, and, chiefly, by the spirit which animates the whole. I cannot, without some indignation, look on an ill copy of an excellent original. Much less can I behold with patience Virgil, Homer, and some others, whose beauties I have been endeavoring all my life to imitate, so abused, as I may say, to their faces, by a botching interpreter. What English readers, unacquainted with Greek or Latin, will believe me, or any other man, when we commend those authors, and confess we derive all that is pardonable in us from their fountains, if they take those to be the same poets, whom our Ogilbys have translated? But I dare assure them, that a good poet is no more like himself, in a dull translation, than his carcass would be to his living body.
>
> (*Preface* to *Sylvæ*)

He had spoken of Shakespeare as one who did not need books, who was naturally learned. But he himself needed them: they helped him see, and they did not get in his way. And his way is to assure us that, when he is translating, it is he himself writing about what his author writes about, the experiences and the world he himself knows. He is in fact setting out to rival his original.

Virgil was his model throughout his life, he had always emulated him, now he might even replace him.

It may be thought that translation was his truest vein because he lacked inventiveness. And the record points that way—the number of the translations, the adaptations of the plays of others, the satires built on other's narratives —all this seems to testify how much he required the kindling of other's minds. Whatever the truth here is, in the *Fables* certainly the poetry takes on a living movement of its own and charms as only works of the imagination can.

Dryden's criticism is one of his many glories and one of the glories of English literature. In a famous passage, Dr. Johnson praises his critical prose as follows:

> . . . none of his prefaces was ever thought tedious. They have not the formality of a settled style, in which the first half of the sentence betrays the other. The clauses are never balanced, nor the periods modelled; every word seems to drop by chance, though it falls into its proper place. Nothing is cold or languid; the whole is airy, animated, and vigorous: what is little is gay; what is great is splendid.

His prose expresses almost as perfectly as his verse the full-blooded and generous character of his mind. And it shows even more clearly how in the presence of anything lively he is perfectly perceptive and freely discriminating, unimpeded by pre-judgments. This quick life shows itself most wonderfully in the *Essay on Dramatic Poesy* where he is so adept at presenting the views of others not merely fairly but winningly, so that we have the added pleasure of knowing that we are being led through these winding ways by a genuinely alert mind.

Perhaps the greatest value of his criticism is that he speaks of particular writers in the light of the whole history of literature. The whole of it was, as he would say, "ever present to him," and the points he is making get their force from his mastery of the context. When he praises Congreve, for example, we are learning how much Congreve's excellence derives from his understanding of the comic tradition, but we are learning even more from Dryden's own knowledge of the tradition and from his own mastery of what comedy does indeed consist in.

The prose of his disputations is equally fine although it does not give quite so vivid an impression of informality. The long preface to *Religio Laici* is as remarkable as the poem; it is perhaps even more persuasive, and as argumentative prose I think it rivals Hooker's. And when he turns to narrative and biography and history—translating Maimbourg or Plutarch—he is still writing with the ease and assurance of the writer who is thinking as he goes.

The more one looks at the range and variety of Dryden's achievement the more it looks all of a piece—as it says in the concluding song of the marvellous *Secular Masque,* at the very end of the long career—"All, all of a piece throughout."

It is as if fate let him play out his gifts, let him spend himself exactly as the vigor and health of his mind urged, let him do what he could. There were of course interruptions—driven from London and the theater by the plague, excluded toward the end from an alien court—but there seems on the whole to have been little of the turmoil that has troubled and deflected the careers of so many. He took to comedy, to prose, to the heroic; to pamphleteering, to translation, to criticism; yet he was never merely following fashion. There were times when he may have inaugurated it. But mostly he approached the new challenge with zest: he had many arrows to his bow and he would shoot them all.

He has the manner of greatness and so he is careless of small faults. He has of course the conscience of his craft, and he aspires often enough to perfection, but he makes no great matter of neatness. His mind is masculine. When the matter is worthy he is without fault. But there are also notoriously times when he lets things slide, when he has lost touch with what is truly fine, and when he asks us to accept a mere shell. There are also times when the verse does not so much resound as clatter. Too often he does not rise far enough above the jokes a vulgar aristocracy takes for wit. But he never mistakes his aim, and if he writes to please he also writes to raise.

In a few sentences he has left us the finest praise we have of Chaucer and of Shakespeare, and it would have been such a pleasure for him to know that he was to be honored equally finely, as generously and as rightly, by Dr. Johnson:

> Perhaps no nation ever produced a writer that enriched his language with such variety of models. To him we owe the improvement, perhaps the completion of our meter, the refinement of our language, and much of the correctness of our sentiments. By him we were taught *sapere et fari*, to think naturally and express forcibly. Though Davies has reasoned in rhyme before him, it may be perhaps maintained that he was the first who joined argument with poetry. He showed us the true bounds of a translator's liberty. What was said of Rome, adorned by Augustus, may be applied by an easy metaphor to English poetry embellished by Dryden, *lateritiam invenit, marmoream reliquit*, he found it brick, and he left it marble.

JOHN ARTHOS
Ann Arbor, Michigan

A General Note on the Text

The overall textual policy for the Signet Classic Poetry series attempts to strike a balance between the convenience and dependability of total modernization, on the one hand, and the authenticity of an established text on the other. Starting with the Restoration and Augustan poets, the General Editor has set up the following guidelines for the individual editors:

Modern American spelling will be used, although punctuation may be adjusted by the editor of each volume when he finds it advisable. In any case, syllabic final "ed" will be rendered with grave accent to distinguish it from the silent one, which is written out without apostrophe (e.g. "to gild refinèd gold," but "asked" rather than "ask'd"). Archaic words and forms are to be kept, naturally, whenever the meter requires it.

In the case of poets from earlier periods, the text is more clearly a matter of the individual editor's choice, and the type and degree of modernization has been left to his decision. But in any event, archaic typographical conventions ("i," "j," "u," "v," etc.) have all been normalized in the modern way.

JOHN HOLLANDER

A Note on this Edition

The text is modernized in accord with the principles governing the printing of works in this series. The earliest printings of Dryden's works have been the basis of the text, with the invaluable aid of the editions of Sir Walter Scott, G. R. Noyes, and James Kinsley. The texts present remarkably few problems. The punctuation, however, sometimes resists modernization. Dryden's use of colons, and to a lesser degree of semi-colons, is very unlike modern practice, and very often his punctuation reveals an idea of sentence structure quite alien to modern thinking. It is often possible to satisfy modern expectations by substituting commas and periods, but I have often followed Dryden's punctuation quite conservatively.

Chronology

1631	August 9. John Dryden, son of Mary Pickering and Erasmus Dryden, born at Aldwinkle All Saints, Northamptonshire.
1644–50	At Westminster School, London, under Dr. Busby.
1649	Publishes first poem, *Upon the Death of Lord Hastings,* a school fellow.
1650–54	At Trinity College, Cambridge. Receives B. A. degree.
1654	Dryden's father dies, leaving him an annual income of £40.
1657–58	In London in the service of the Commonwealth.
1658	*Heroic Stanzas to the Glorious Memory of . . . Oliver, Late Lord Protector.* (Printed 1659)
1660	*Astræa Redux, A Poem on the Happy Restoration and Return of . . . Charles II.*
1662	Fellow of the Royal Society.
1663	Production of his first play, a prose comedy, *The Wild Gallant.*
1663	Marries Lady Elizabeth Howard, daughter of the Earl of Berkshire.
1664	*The Rival Ladies,* Dryden's first verse drama. Collaborates with Sir Robert Howard on *The Indian Queen.*
1665	*The Indian Emperor,* in which Dryden establishes rhyme as the verse appropriate for heroic drama. Driven from London by the

Selected Bibliography

Editions of the Works:

The Works of John Dryden. Sir Walter Scott and George Saintsbury (eds.). London: William Paterson, 1882–93.

Essays of John Dryden. W. P. Ker (ed.). Oxford: The Clarendon Press, 1900.

The Letters of John Dryden, With Letters Addressed to Him. C. E. Ward (ed.). Durham, North Carolina: Duke University Press, 1942.

The Poetical Works of John Dryden. George R. Noyes (ed.). Cambridge, Massachusetts: Houghton, Mifflin, 1909; revised edition, 1950.

The Works of John Dryden. E. N. Hooker and others (eds.). Berkeley and Los Angeles: University of California Press, 1956.

The Poems of John Dryden. James Kinsley (ed.). Oxford: The Clarendon Press, 1958.

Biographies:

Johnson, Samuel. "Life of Dryden," in *The Lives of the English Poets,* G. B. Hill (ed.). Oxford: The Clarendon Press, 1905.

Osborn, J. M. *John Dryden: Some Biographical Facts and Problems.* New York: Columbia University Press, 1940.

Saintsbury, George. *Dryden.* New York: Harper & Brothers, 1881.

Scott, Sir Walter. *The Life of Dryden.* In *Works,* vol. 1.

Ward, Charles E. *The Life of John Dryden.* Chapel Hill: University of North Carolina, 1961.

Criticism:

Bredvold, L. I., *The Intellectual Milieu of John Dryden.* Ann Arbor: The University of Michigan Press, 1934.

Eliot, T. S., *Homage to John Dryden.* London: L. and Virginia Woolf, 1924.

———— *John Dryden: The Poet, the Dramatist, the Critic.* New York: T. & Elsa Holliday, 1932.

Frost, William. *Dryden and the Art of Translation.* New Haven: Yale University Press, 1955.

Harth, J. P. *Contexts of Dryden's Thought.* Chicago: University of Chicago Press, 1968.

Kirsch, A. C. *Dryden's Heroic Drama.* Princeton: Princeton University Press, 1965.

Miner, E. R. *Dryden's Poetry.* Bloomington: University of Indiana Press, 1967.

Roper, Alan. *Dryden's Poetic Kingdoms.* London: Routledge & Kegan Paul, 1961.

Schilling, B. N. *Dryden, A Collection of Critical Essays.* Englewood Cliffs, N. J.: Prentice-Hall, 1963.

Sutherland, J. R. *John Dryden: The Poet as Orator.* Glasgow: Jackson, 1963.

Swedenberg, H. T., Jr. *Essential Articles for a Study of John Dryden.* Hamden, Connecticut: Archon Books, 1966.

Van Doren, Mark. *John Dryden: A Study of His Poetry.* New York: Henry Holt, 1924.

Waith, E. M. *The Herculean Hero in Marlowe, Chapman, Shakespeare, and Dryden.* London: Chatto & Windus, 1962.

Upon the Death of the Lord Hastings

Must noble Hastings immaturely die,
The honor of his ancient family?
Beauty and learning thus together meet,
To bring a *winding* for a *wedding sheet?*
Must Virtue prove Death's harbinger? must she,   5
With him expiring, feel mortality?
Is death, sin's wages, grace's now? shall art
Make us more learned, only to depart?
If merit be disease; if virtue death;
To be good, not to be; who'd then bequeath   10
Himself to discipline? who'd not esteem
Labor a crime, study self-murther deem?
Our noble youth now have pretense to be
Dunces securely, ignorant healthfully.
Rare linguist! whose worth speaks itself, whose praise,   15
Though not his own, all tongues besides do raise!
Than whom great Alexander may seem less,
Who conquered men, but not their languages.
In his mouth nations speak; his tongue might be
Interpreter to Greece, France, Italy.   20
His native soil was the four parts o' th' earth;
All Europe was too narrow for his birth.
A young apostle; and (with reverence may
I speak 'it) inspired with gift of tongues, as they.
Nature gave him, a child, what men in vain   25
Oft strive, by art though furthered, to obtain.
His body was an orb, his sublime soul
Did move on virtue's and on learning's pole:

Whose regular motions better to our view,
30 Than Archimedes'° sphere, the heavens did show.
Graces and virtues, languages and arts,
Beauty and learning, filled up all the parts.
Heav'n's gifts, which do, like falling stars, appear
Scattered in others; all, as in their sphere,
35 Were fixed and conglobate in 's soul and thence
Shone through his body, with sweet influence;
Letting their glories so on each limb fall,
The whole frame rendered was celestial.
Come, learned Ptolemy, and trial make,
40 If thou this hero's altitude canst take:
But that transcends thy skill; thrice happy all,
Could we but prove thus astronomical.
Lived Tycho° now, struck with this ray, which shone
More bright i' th' morn, than others' beam at noon,
45 He'd take his *astrolabe,* and seek out here
What new star 'twas did gild our hemisphere.
Replenished then with such rare gifts as these,
Where was room left for such a foul disease?
The nation's sin hath drawn that veil, which shrouds
50 Our day-spring in so sad benighting clouds.
Heaven would no longer trust its pledge; but thus
Recalled it; rapt its Ganymede° from us.
Was there no milder way but the smallpox,
The very filthiness of Pandora's box?°
55 So many spots, like *næves,°* our Venus soil?
One jewel set off with so many a foil?
Blisters with pride swelled, which through 's flesh did
        sprout,
Like rose-buds, stuck i' th' lily skin about.
Each little pimple had a tear in it,
60 To wail the fault its rising did commit:
Who, rebel-like, with their own lord at strife,
Thus made an insurrection 'gainst his life.
Or were these gems sent to adorn his skin,

---

30 **Archimedes'** Greek mathematician and astronomer   43 **Tycho**
Tycho Brahe, a Danish astronomer   52 **Ganymede** beautiful youth
taken by Zeus to become cup-bearer for the gods   54 **Pandora's box**
according to legend, a chest containing all human ills   55 **næves**
blemishes

The cabinet of a richer soul within?
No comet need foretell his change drew on,   65
Whose corpse might seem a *constellation*.
O, had he died of old, how great a strife
Had been, who from his death should draw their life?
Who should, by one rich draught, become whate'er
Seneca, Cato, Numa, Cæsar, were;   70
Learned, virtuous, pious, great; and have by this
An universal *metempsuchosis*.°
Must all these aged sires in one funeral
Expire? all die in one so young, so small?
Who, had he lived his life out, his great fame   75
Had swollen 'bove any Greek or Roman name.
But hasty winter, with one blast, hath brought
The hopes of autumn, summer, spring, to nought.
Thus fades the oak i' th' sprig, i' th' blade the corn;
Thus without young, this Phœnix° dies, new-born.   80
Must then old three-legged graybeards° with their
        gout,
Catarrhs, rheums, aches, live three ages out?
Time's offal, only fit for th' hospital,
Or t' hang an antiquary's room withal!
Must drunkards, lechers, spent with sinning, live   85
With such help as broths, possets,° physic give?
None live, but such as should die? shall we meet
With none but ghostly fathers in the street?
Grief makes me rail: sorrow will force its way;
And showers of tears tempestuous sighs best lay.   90
The tongue may fail, but overflowing eyes
Will weep out lasting streams of elegies.
    But thou, O *virgin-widow*,° left alone,
Now thy beloved, heaven-ravished *spouse* is gone,
(Whose skilful sire in vain strove to apply   95
Medicines, when thy balm was no remedy,)
With greater than Platonic love, O wed
His soul, though not his body, to thy bed:

72 **metempsuchosis** transmigration of a soul (here accented on third
syllable)   80 **Phœnix** legendary Arabian bird born from the ashes
of its predecessor   81 **three-legged graybeards** old men supported
by canes   86 **possets** hot milk   93 **virgin-widow** surviving fiancée

Let that make thee a mother; bring thou forth
100 Th' *ideas*° of his virtue, knowledge, worth;
Transcribe th' original in new copies; give
Hastings o' th' better part: so shall he live
In 's nobler half; and the great grandsire be
Of an heroic divine progeny;
105 An issue, which t' eternity shall last,
Yet but th' irradiations which he cast.
Erect no *mausoleums,* for his best
Monument is his spouse's marble° breast.

100 ideas eternal types   108 **marble** white, shining

Astræa Redux:°

A Poem on the Happy Restoration and Return of His Sacred Majesty Charles the Second

Now with a general peace the world was blest,
While ours, a world divided from the rest,
A dreadful quiet felt, and worser far
Than arms, a sullen interval of war:
Thus when black clouds draw down the laboring skies,   *5*
Ere yet abroad the winged thunder flies,
An horrid stillness first invades the ear,
And in that silence we the tempest fear.
Th' ambitious Swede,° like restless billows tossed,
On this hand gaining what on that he lost,   *10*
Though in his life he blood and ruin breathed,
To his now guideless kingdom peace bequeathed.
And Heaven, that seemed regardless of our fate,
For France and Spain did miracles create;
Such mortal quarrels to compose in peace,   *15*
As nature bred, and interest did increase.
We sighed to hear the fair Iberian bride
Must grow a lily to the lily's side,
While our cross stars denied us Charles his bed,
Whom our first flames and virgin love did wed.   *20*
For his long absence Church and State did groan;
Madness the pulpit, faction seized the throne:
Experienced age in deep despair was lost,
To see the rebel thrive, the loyal crossed:

° **Astræa Redux** the goddess of justice being returned to the earth
9 **Swede** Charles X

25 Youth, that with joys had unacquainted been,
     Envied gray hairs that once good days had seen;
     We thought our sires, not with their own content,
     Had, ere we came to age, our portion spent.
     Nor could our nobles hope their bold attempt,
30 Who ruined crowns, would coronets exempt:
     For when by their designing leaders taught
     To strike at power which for themselves they sought,
     The vulgar, gulled into rebellion, armed;
     Their blood to action by the prize was warmed.
35 The sacred purple then and scarlet gown,°
     Like sanguine dye, to elephants was shown.
     Thus when the bold Typhœus° scaled the sky,
     And forced great Jove from his own heaven to fly,
     (What king, what crown from treason's reach is free,
40 If Jove and Heaven can violated be?)
     The lesser gods, that shared his prosperous state,
     All suffered in the exiled Thunderer's° fate.
     The rabble now such freedom did enjoy,
     As winds at sea, that use it to destroy:
45 Blind as the Cyclops, and as wild as he,
     They owned a lawless savage liberty,
     Like that our painted ancestors so prized
     Ere empire's arts their breasts had civilized.
     How great were then our Charles his woes, who thus
50 Was forced to suffer for himself and us!
     He, tossed by fate, and hurried up and down,
     Heir to his father's sorrows, with his crown,
     Could taste no sweets of youth's desired age;
     But found his life too true a pilgrimage.
55 Unconquered yet in that forlorn estate,
     His manly courage overcame his fate.
     His wounds he took, like Romans, on his breast,
     Which by his virtue were with laurels dressed.
     As souls reach heaven while yet in bodies pent,
60 So did he live above his banishment.

---

35 **sacred . . . gown** the purple garments worn by bishops, and the
scarlet worn by peers 37 **Typhœus** giant who temporarily de-
throned Jove 42 **Thunderer's** Jove's

That sun, which we beheld with cozened eyes
Within the water, moved along the skies.
How easy 'tis, when Destiny proves kind,
With full-spread sails to run before the wind!
But those that 'gainst stiff gales laveering° go,   65
Must be at once resolved and skilful too.
He would not, like soft Otho,° hope prevent,
But stayed and suffered Fortune to repent.
These virtues Galba° in a stranger sought,
And Piso to adopted empire brought.   70
How shall I then my doubtful thoughts express,
That must his sufferings both regret and bless!
For when his early valor Heav'n had crossed,
And all at Worcester° but the honor lost,
Forced into exile from his rightful throne,   75
He made all countries where he came his own;
And viewing monarchs' secret arts of sway,
A royal factor for their kingdoms lay.
Thus banished David spent abroad his time,
When to be God's anointed was his crime;   80
And, when restored, made his proud neighbors rue
Those choice remarks he from his travels drew.
Nor is he only by afflictions shown
To conquer others' realms, but rule his own:
Recovering hardly what he lost before,   85
His right endears it much; his purchase more.
Inured to suffer ere he came to reign,
No rash procedure will his actions stain.
To business ripened by digestive thought,
His future rule is into method brought;   90
As they who first proportion understand,
With easy practice reach a master's hand.
Well might the ancient poets then confer
On Night the honored name of *Counselor,*
Since struck with rays of prosperous fortune blind,   95
We light alone in dark afflictions find.

---

65 **laveering** beating to windward   67 **Otho** a degenerate Roman
emperor   69 **Galba** Roman emperor who chose Piso as his successor instead of Otho   74 **Worcester** crucial battle

In such adversities to scepters trained,
The name of *Great* his famous grandsire° gained;
Who yet a king alone in name and right,
100 With hunger, cold, and angry Jove did fight;
Shocked by a Covenanting League's° vast powers,
As holy and as catholic as ours:
Till Fortune's fruitless spite had made it known,
Her blows not shook but riveted his throne.
105   Some lazy ages, lost in sleep and ease,
No action leave to busy chronicles:
Such, whose supine felicity but makes
In story *chasms*, in *epoches*° mistakes:
O'er whom Time gently shakes his wings of down,
110 Till with his silent sickle they are mown.
Such is not Charles his too too active age,
Which, governed by the wild distempered rage
Of some black star infecting all the skies,
Made him at his own cost like Adam wise.
115 Tremble, ye nations, who, secure before,
Laughed at those arms that 'gainst ourselves we bore:
Roused by the lash of his own stubborn tail,
Our lion now will foreign foes assail.
With *alga*° who the sacred altar strows?
120 To all the sea-gods Charles an offering owes:
A bull to thee, Portunus,° shall be slain,
A lamb to you, the tempests of the main:
For those loud storms that did against him roar
Have cast his shipwracked vessel on the shore.
125 Yet as wise artists mix their colors so,
That by degrees they from each other go:
Black steals unheeded from the neighboring white,
Without offending the well-cozened sight:
So on us stole our blessed change, while we
130 Th' effect did feel, but scarce the manner see.
Frosts that constrain the ground, and birth deny
To flowers that in its womb expecting lie,

98 **Great . . . grandsire** Henry IV   101 **Covenanting League's** the
Solemn League and Covenant of 1643   108 **epoches** (here pronounced as three syllables)   119 **alga** a weed   121 **Portunus** god
of harbors

Do seldom their usurping power withdraw,
But raging floods pursue their hasty thaw.
Our thaw was mild, the cold not chased away,   135
But lost in kindly heat of lengthened day.
Heav'n would no bargain for its blessings drive,
But what we could not pay for, freely give.
The Prince of Peace would, like himself, confer
A gift unhoped without the price of war: 140
Yet, as he knew his blessing's worth, took care,
That we should know it by repeated prayer;
Which stormed the skies, and ravished Charles from
      thence,
As Heav'n itself is took by violence.
Booth's forward valor° only served to show   145
He durst that duty pay we all did owe:
Th' attempt was fair; but Heav'n's prefixed hour
Not come: so, like the watchful travellor
That by the moon's mistaken light did rise,
Lay down again, and closed his weary eyes.   150
'T was MONK° whom Providence designed to loose
Those real bonds false freedom did impose.
The blessed saints that watched this turning scene,
Did from their stars with joyful wonder lean,
To see small clues draw vastest weights along,   155
Not in their bulk, but in their order strong.
Thus pencils can by one slight touch restore
Smiles to that changed face that wept before.
With ease such fond *chimæras*° we pursue
As fancy frames for fancy to subdue;   160
But when ourselves to action we betake,
It shuns the mint like gold that chymists make.°
How hard was then his task, at once to be
What in the body natural we see.
Man's architect distinctly did ordain   165
The charge of muscles, nerves, and of the brain,

---

145 **Booth's . . . valor** Sir George Booth advancing in support of
Charles 151 **Monk** General George Monk, powerful supporter of
the King 159 **chimæras** fire-breathing monsters, illusions 162 **gold
. . . make** simulated gold being unmalleable

Through viewless conduits spirits to dispense,
The springs of motion from the seat of sense.
'T was not the hasty product of a day,
170 But the well-ripened fruit of wise delay.
He, like a patient angler, ere he strook,
Would let them play a while upon the hook.
Our healthful food the stomach labors thus,
At first embracing what it straight doth crush.
175 Wise leeches will not vain receipts obtrude,
While growing pains pronounce the humors crude;
Deaf to complaints, they wait upon the ill,
Till some safe *crisis* authorize their skill.
Nor could his acts too close a vizard° wear,
180 To scape their eyes whom guilt had taught to fear,
And guard with caution that polluted nest,
Whence Legion twice before was dispossessed:°
Once sacred house; which when they entered in,
They thought the place could sanctify a sin;
185 Like those that vainly hoped kind Heav'n would wink,
While to excess on martyrs' tombs they drink.
And as devouter Turks first warn their souls
To part, before they taste forbidden bowls;
So these, when their black crimes they went about,
190 First timely charmed their useless conscience out.
Religion's name against itself was made;
The shadow served the substance to invade:
Like zealous missions, they did care pretend
Of souls in show, but made the gold their end.
195 Th' incensed powers beheld with scorn from high
An heaven so far distant from the sky,
Which durst, with horses' hoofs that beat the ground,
And martial brass, bely the thunder's sound.
'T was hence at length just Vengeance thought it fit
200 To speed their ruin by their impious wit.
Thus Sforza,° curst with a too fertile brain,
Lost by his wiles the power his wit did gain.

179 **vizard** mask   182 **Legion twice ... dispossessed** Cromwell twice
dispersed the Rump Parliament   201 **Sforza** Lodovico Sforza, tyrant
of Milan

Henceforth their fogue° must spend at lesser rate
Than in its flames to wrap a nation's fate.
Suffered to live, they are like Helots° set,   205
A virtuous shame within us to beget.
For by example most we sinned before,
And glass-like clearness mixed with frailty bore.
But since reformed by what we did amiss,
We by our sufferings learn to prize our bliss: 210
Like early lovers, whose unpracticed hearts
Were long the may-game of malicious arts,
When once they find their jealousies were vain,
With double heat renew their fires again.
'T was this produced the joy that hurried o'er   215
Such swarms of English to the neighboring shore,
To fetch that prize, by which Batavia° made
So rich amends for our impoverished trade.
O had you seen from Scheveline's° barren shore,
(Crowded with troops, and barren now no more,)   220
Afflicted Holland to his farewell bring
True sorrow, Holland to regret a king,
While waiting him his royal fleet did ride,
And willing winds to their lowered sails denied.
The wavering streamers, flags, and standart out,   225
The merry seamen's rude but cheerful shout;
And last, the cannons' voice that shook the skies,
And, as it fares in sudden ecstasies,
At once bereft us both of ears and eyes.
The Naseby,° now no longer England's shame,   230
But better to be lost in Charles his name,
(Like some unequal bride in nobler sheets)
Receives her lord; the joyful London meets
The princely York, himself alone a freight;
The Swift-sure groans beneath great Gloc'ster's weight.   235
Secure as when the halcyon breeds, with these
He that was born to drown might cross the seas.
Heav'n could not own a Providence, and take

203 **fogue** fury   205 **Helots** slaves among the Greeks   217 **Batavia**
capital of the Dutch East Indies   219 **Scheveline's** port in Holland
from which Charles embarked for England   230 **Naseby** the name
of the ship *Naseby* was changed to *Charles*

The wealth three nations ventured at a stake.
240 The same indulgence Charles his voyage blessed,
Which in his right had miracles confessed.
The winds that never moderation knew,
Afraid to blow too much, too faintly blew;
Or out of breath with joy, could not enlarge
245 Their straightened lungs, or conscious of their charge.
The British Amphitrite,° smooth and clear,
In richer azure never did appear;
Proud her returning prince to entertain
With the submitted fasces° of the main.

250 And welcome now, *great monarch,* to your own;
Behold th' approaching cliffs of Albion:
It is no longer motion cheats your view,
As you meet it, the land approacheth you.
The land returns, and in the white it wears
255 The marks of penitence and sorrow bears.
But you, whose goodness your descent doth show,
Your heav'nly parentage and earthly too;
By that same mildness which your father's crown
Before did ravish, shall secure your own.
260 Not tied to rules of policy, you find
Revenge less sweet than a forgiving mind.
Thus, when th' Almighty would to Moses give
A sight of all he could behold and live;
A voice before his entry did proclaim
265 *Long-suffering, goodness, mercy,* in his name.
Your power to justice doth submit your cause,
Your goodness only is above the laws;
Whose rigid letter, while pronounced by you,
Is softer made. So winds that tempests brew,
270 When through Arabian groves they take their flight,
Made wanton with rich odors, lose their spite.
And as those lees° that trouble it, refine
The agitated soul of generous wine:
So tears of joy, for your returning spilt,
275 Work out and expiate our former guilt.

246 **Amphitrite** goddess of the sea   249 **fasces** symbol of power of
the Roman magistrates   272 **lees** dregs

Methinks I see those crowds on Dover's strand,
Who, in their haste to welcome you to land,
Choked up the beach with their still growing store,
And made a wilder torrent on the shore;
While, spurred with eager thoughts of past delight,   280
Those who had seen you court a second sight;
Preventing° still your steps, and making haste
To meet you often, wheresoe'er you passed.
How shall I speak of that triumphant day
When you renewed th' expiring pomp of May!   285
(A month that owns an interest in your name:
You and the flowers are its peculiar claim.)°
That star that at your birth shone out so bright,
It stained the duller sun's meridian light,
Did once again its potent fires renew,   290
Guiding our eyes to find and worship you.

    And now Time's whiter° series is begun,
Which in soft centuries shall smoothly run:
Those clouds that overcast your morn shall fly,
Dispelled to farthest corners of the sky.   295
Our nation, with united interest blest,
Not now content to poise, shall sway the rest.
Abroad your empire shall no limits know,
But, like the sea, in boundless circles flow.
Your much-loved fleet shall with a wide command   300
Besiege the petty monarchs of the land;
And as old Time his offspring swallowed down,
Our ocean in its depths all seas shall drown.
Their wealthy trade from pirates' rapine free.
Our merchants shall no more adventurers be;   305
Nor in the farthest East those dangers fear
Which humble Holland must dissemble here.
Spain to your gift alone her Indies owes,
For what the powerful takes not he bestows:
And France, that did an exile's presence fear,   310
May justly apprehend you still too near.
At home the hateful names of parties cease,
And factious souls are wearied into peace.

282 **Preventing** anticipating   287 Charles returned to London in
triumph on his birthday   292 **whiter** more fortunate (a Latinism)

The discontented now are only they
315 Whose crimes before did your just cause betray:
Of those your edicts some reclaim from sins,
But most your life and blest example wins.
O happy prince, whom Heav'n hath taught the way,
By paying vows, to have more vows to pay!
320 O happy age! O times like those alone
By fate reserved for great Augustus' throne!
When the joint growth of arms and arts foreshew
The world a monarch, and that monarch *you*.

To my Honored Friend,
Dr. Charleton,
on his learned and useful Works; and more particularly this of Stonehenge, by him Restored to the true Founders.

The longest tyranny that ever swayed
Was that wherein our ancestors betrayed
Their free-born reason to the Stagirite,°
And made his torch their universal light.
So truth, while only one supplied the state,   5
Grew scarce, and dear, and yet sophisticate;
Until 't was bought, like empiric° wares, or charms,
Hard words sealed up with Aristotle's arms.
Columbus was the first that shook his throne,
And found a temperate in a torrid zone: 10
The feverish air fanned by a cooling breeze,
The fruitful vales set round with shady trees;
And guiltless men, who danced away their time,
Fresh as their groves, and happy as their clime.
Had we still paid that homage to a name,   15
Which only God and nature justly claim,
The western seas had been our utmost bound,
Where poets still might dream the sun was drowned:
And all the stars that shine in southern skies
Had been admired by none but savage eyes.   20
    Among th' asserters of free reason's claim,
Th' English are not the least in worth or fame.
The world to Bacon does not only owe
Its present knowledge, but its future too.

3 **Stagirite** Aristotle   7 **empiric** experimental

45

25 Gilbert° shall live, till loadstones° cease to draw,
    Or British fleets the boundless ocean awe;
    And noble Boyle, not less in nature seen,
    Than his great brother° read in states and men.
    The circling streams, once thought but pools, of blood
30 (Whether life's fuel, or the body's food)
    From dark oblivion Harvey's° name shall save;
    While Ent° keeps all the honor that he gave.
    Nor are *you,* learned friend, the least renowned;
    Whose fame, not circumscribed with English ground,
35 Flies like the nimble journeys of the light;
    And is, like that, unspent too in its flight.
    Whatever truths have been, by art or chance,
    Redeemed from error, or from ignorance,
    Thin in their authors, like rich veins of ore,
40 Your works unite, and still discover more.
    Such is the healing virtue of your pen,
    To perfect cures on books, as well as men.
    Nor is this work the least: you well may give
    To men new vigor, who make stones to live.
45 Through you the Danes, their short dominion lost,
    A longer conquest than the Saxons boast.
    Stonehenge, once thought a temple, you have found
    A throne, where kings, our earthly gods, were
        crowned;
    Where by their wondering subjects they were seen,
50 Joyed with their stature, and their princely mien.
    Our sovereign here above the rest might stand,
    And here be chose again to rule the land.
      These ruins sheltered once his sacred head,
    Then when from Wor'ster's fatal field he fled;
55 Watched by the genius of this royal place,
    And mighty visions of the Danish race.
    His refuge then was for a temple shown;
    But, he restored, 't is now become a throne.

---

25 **Gilbert** William Gilbert, who wrote on magnetism   25 **load-
stones** magnets   27–8 **Boyle . . . brother** Robert Boyle, the scientist,
was the brother of Roger Boyle, Earl of Orrery, the poet and statesman   31 **Harvey's** William Harvey, discoverer of the circulation of
the blood   32 **Ent** George Ent, a physician

Annus Mirabilis
The year of wonders, MDCLXVI

I

In thriving arts long time had Holland grown,
   Crouching at home, and cruel when abroad;
Scarce leaving us the means to claim our own.
   Our king they courted, and our merchants awed.

II

Trade, which like blood should circularly flow,   5
   Stopped in their channels, found its freedom lost:
Thither the wealth of all the world did go,
   And seemed but shipwracked on so base a coast.

III

For them alone the heav'ns had kindly heat,
   In eastern quarries ripening precious dew;°   10
For them the Idumæan balm° did sweat,
   And in hot Ceylon spicy forests° grew.

IV

The sun but seemed the laborer of their year;
   Each waxing moon supplied her watery store
To swell those tides,° which from the line did bear   15
   Their brim-full vessels to the Belgian shore.

10 In . . . dew "Precious stones at first are dew, condensed and
hardened by the warmth of the sun or subterranean fires." The
notes to this poem given in quotation marks are Dryden's own.
11 Idumæan balm Arabian spice   12 Ceylon . . . forests the Dutch
are trading in spices   14–15 Each waxing . . . tides "According to
their opinion, who think that great heap of waters under the line is
depressed into tides by the moon, towards the poles"

V

Thus mighty in her ships stood Carthage long,
    And swept the riches of the world from far;
Yet stooped to Rome, less wealthy, but more strong;
20   And this may prove our second Punic war.°

VI

What peace can be where both to one pretend?
    (But they more diligent, and we more strong)
Or if a peace, it soon must have an end;
    For they would grow too powerful were it long.

VII

25 Behold two nations then, engaged so far,
    That each seven years the fit must shake each land:
Where France will side to weaken us by war,
    Who only can his vast designs withstand.

VIII

See how he feeds th' Iberian° with delays,
30   To render us his timely friendship vain:
And while his secret soul on Flanders preys,
    He rocks the cradle of the babe of Spain.°

IX

Such deep designs of empire does he lay
    O'er them whose cause he seems to take in hand,
35 And, prudently, would make them lords at sea,
    To whom with ease he can give laws by land.

X

This saw our king, and long within his breast
    His pensive counsels balanced to and fro;

20 **second . . . war** the first being that waged under Cromwell against the Low Countries   29 **th' Iberian** "The Spaniard"   32 **babe of Spain** alluding to the supposed French plan of dividing the Spanish provinces in the Netherlands with Holland

He grieved the land he freed should be oppressed,
  And he less for it than usurpers do.   40

XI

His generous mind the fair ideas drew
  Of fame and honor, which in dangers lay;
Where wealth, like fruit on precipices, grew,
  Not to be gathered but by birds of prey.

XII

The loss and gain each fatally were great;   45
  And still his subjects called aloud for war;
But peaceful kings, o'er martial people set,
  Each other's poise and counterbalance are.

XIII

He, first, surveyed the charge with careful eyes,
  Which none but mighty monarchs could maintain;   50
Yet judged, like vapors that from limbecs° rise,
  It would in richer showers descend again.

XIV

At length resolved t' assert the watery ball,
  He in himself did whole armadoes bring:
Him aged seamen might their master call,   55
  And choose for general, were he not their king.

XV

It seems as every ship their sovereign knows,
  His awful summons they so soon obey;
So hear the scaly herd when Proteus° blows,
  And so to pasture follow through the sea.   60

XVI

To see this fleet upon the ocean move

51 **limbecs** distilling apparatus   59 **Proteus** "(Cerulean Proteus feeds
the great herds of the sea and the seals in the deep) — Virgil." English
translations of the Latin of Dryden's notes are given in parentheses.
Unattributed translations are by the editor

Angels drew wide the curtains of the skies;
And Heav'n, as if there wanted lights above,
  For tapers made two glaring comets° rise;

XVII

65 Whether they unctuous exhalations are,
  Fired by the sun, or seeming so alone;
Or each some more remote and slippery star
  Which loses footing when to mortals shown;°

XVIII

Or one, that bright companion of the sun,
70   Whose glorious aspect sealed our new-born king,
And now, a round of greater years begun,
  New influence from his walks of light did bring.

XIX

Victorious York° did first, with famed success,
  To his known valor make the Dutch give place:
75 Thus Heav'n our monarch's fortune did confess,
  Beginning conquest from his royal race.

XX

But since it was decreed, auspicious king,
  In Britain's right that thou shouldst wed the main,
Heav'n, as a gage, would cast some precious thing,
80   And therefore doomed that Lawson° should be
     slain.

XXI

Lawson amongst the foremost met his fate,
  Whom sea-green Sirens from the rocks lament:

---

64 **two . . . comets** two comets, of ill omen, had appeared in 1664
and 1665   65–8 **unctuous . . . shown** old theories on the composition
of comets   73 **York** the Duke of York, brother to the King
80 **Lawson** Sir John Lawson, admiral in command of a flying
squadron

Thus as an offering for the Grecian state,
 He first was killed who first to battle went.

XXII

Their chief° blown up, in air, not waves, expired,   *85*
 To which his pride presumed to give the law;
The Dutch confessed Heav'n present, and retired,
 And all was Britain the wide ocean saw.

XXIII

To nearest ports their shattered ships repair,
 Where by our dreadful cannon they lay awed: *90*
So reverently men quit the open air,
 When thunder speaks the angry gods abroad.

XXIV

And now approached their fleet from India, fraught
 With all the riches of the rising sun,
And precious sand from southern climates° brought,   *95*
 (The fatal regions where the war begun.)

XXV

Like hunted castors,° conscious of their store,
 Their waylaid wealth to Norway's coasts they
  bring;
There first the North's cold bosom spices bore,
 And winter brooded on the eastern spring.   *100*

XXVI

By the rich scent we found our perfumed prey,°
 Which, flanked with rocks, did close in covert lie;
And round about their murdering cannon lay,
 At once to threaten and invite the eye.

---

85 **Their chief** Admiral Opdam   95 **southern climates** "Guinea"
97 **castors** beavers   101 **we found . . . prey** the English attacked the
Dutch spice fleet in the harbor of Bergen

XXVII

105 Fiercer than cannon, and than rocks more hard,
　　The English undertake th' unequal war:
　　Seven ships alone, by which the port is barred,
　　　Besiege the Indies, and all Denmark dare.

XXVIII

　　These fight like husbands, but like lovers those;
110　　These fain would keep, and those more fain enjoy;
　　And to such height their frantic passion grows,
　　　That what both love, both hazard to destroy.

XXIX

　　Amidst whole heaps of spices lights a ball,
　　　And now their odors armed against them fly,
115 Some preciously by shattered porcelain fall,
　　　And some by aromatic splinters die.

XXX

　　And though by tempests of the prize bereft,
　　　In Heaven's inclemency some ease we find:
　　Our foes we vanquished by our valor left,
120　　And only yielded to the seas and wind.

XXXI

　　Nor wholly lost we so deserved a prey;
　　　For storms, repenting, part of it restored:
　　Which, as a tribute from the Baltic sea,
　　　The British ocean sent her mighty lord.

XXXII

125 Go, mortals, now, and vex yourselves in vain
　　　For wealth, which so uncertainly must come:
　　When what was brought so far, and with such pain,
　　　Was only kept to lose it nearer home.

XXXIII

　　The son, who twice three months on th' ocean tossed,
130　　Prepared to tell what he had passed before,

Now sees in English ships the Holland coast,
    And parents' arms in vain stretched from the shore.

XXXIV

This careful husband had been long away,
    Whom his chaste wife and little children mourn;
Who on their fingers learned to tell the day   *135*
    On which their father promised to return.

XXXV

Such are the proud designs° of humankind,
    And so we suffer shipwrack everywhere!
Alas, what port can such a pilot find,
    Who in the night of fate must blindly steer!   *140*

XXXVI

The undistinguished seeds of good and ill,
    Heav'n, in his bosom, from our knowledge hides;
And draws them in contempt of human skill,
    Which oft for friends mistaken foes provides.

XXXVII

Let Munster's prelate° ever be accurst,   *145*
    In whom we seek the German faith° in vain.
Alas, that he should teach the English first
    That fraud and avarice in the Church could reign!

XXXVIII

Happy, who never trust a stranger's will,
    Whose friendship's in his interest understood!   *150*
Since money given but tempts him to be ill,
    When power is too remote to make him good.

XXXIX

Till now, alone the mighty nations strove;

137 **Such ... designs** "From Petronius: (If you reckon up things well, there is shipwreck everywhere — Noyes)"   145 **Munster's prelate** German bishop who withdrew from the war   146 **German faith** "Tacitus saith of them: (None among mortals surpass the Germans in war or in keeping their pledge)"

The rest, at gaze, without the lists did stand:
155 And threatening France, placed like a painted Jove,
Kept idle thunder in his lifted hand.°

XL

That eunuch guardian of rich Holland's trade,
    Who envies us what he wants power t' enjoy;
Whose noiseful valor does no foe invade,
160   And weak assistance will his friends destroy:

XLI

Offended that we fought without his leave,
    He takes this time his secret hate to show;
Which Charles does with a mind so calm receive
    As one that neither seeks nor shuns his foe.

XLII

165 With France, to aid the Dutch, the Danes unite:
    France as their tyrant, Denmark as their slave.
But when with one three nations join to fight,
    They silently confess that one more brave.

XLIII

Lewis had chased the English from his shore,
170   But Charles the French as subjects does invite:
Would Heav'n for each some Solomon restore,
    Who, by their mercy, may decide their right!

XLIV

Were subjects so but only by their choice,
    And not from birth did forced dominion take,
175 Our prince alone would have the public voice,
    And all his neighbors' realms would deserts make.

XLV

He without fear a dangerous war pursues,
    Which without rashness he began before.
As honor made him first the danger choose,
180   So still he makes it good on virtue's score.

155–6 **threatening . . . hand** "War declared by France"

XLVI

The doubled charge his subjects' love supplies,°
    Who, in that bounty, to themselves are kind:
So glad Egyptians see their Nilus rise,
    And in his plenty their abundance find.

XLVII

With equal power he does two chiefs create,°   185
    Two such as each seemed worthiest when alone;
Each able to sustain a nation's fate,
    Since both had found a greater in their own.

XLVIII

Both great in courage, conduct, and in fame,
    Yet neither envious of the other's praise;   190
Their duty, faith, and interest too the same,
    Like mighty partners equally they raise.

XLIX

The prince long time had courted Fortune's love,
    But once possessed did absolutely reign:
Thus with their *Amazons* the *heroes* strove,   195
    And conquered first those beauties they would
        gain.

L

The duke beheld, like Scipio, with disdain,
    That Carthage which he ruined rise once more;
And shook aloft the fasces° of the main,
    To fright those slaves with what they felt before.   200

LI

Together to the watery camp they haste,
    Whom matrons passing to their children show;
Infants' first vows for them to Heav'n are cast,
    And future people° bless them as they go.

181 **charge ... supplies** Parliament supports the King with great sums
185 **two chiefs create** "Prince Rupert and Duke Albemarle sent to
sea"   199 **fasces** symbol of authority   204 **future people** "(Throngs
of children and the future people — Pliny"

LII

205 With them no riotous pomp, nor Asian train,
     T' infect a navy with their gaudy fears;
  To make slow fights, and victories but vain;
     But war, severely, like itself appears.

LIII

  Diffusive of themselves, where'er they pass
210   They make that warmth in others they expect;
  Their valor works like bodies on a glass,
     And does its image on their men project.

LIV

  Our fleet divides,° and straight the Dutch appear,
     In number, and a famed commander,° bold:
215 The narrow seas can scarce their navy bear,
     Or crowded vessels can their soldiers hold.

LV

  The duke, less numerous, but in courage more,
     On wings of all the winds to combat flies;
  His murdering guns a loud defiance roar,
220   And bloody crosses on his flagstaffs rise.

LVI

  Both furl their sails, and strip them for the fight,
     Their folded sheets dismiss the useless air;
  Th' Elean plains° could boast no nobler sight,
     When struggling champions did their bodies bare.

LVII

225 Borne each by other in a distant line
     The sea-built forts in dreadful order move;
  So vast the noise, as if not fleets did join,
     But lands unfixed° and floating nations strove.

---

213 **Our fleet divides** the flieet unwisely separated to meet two threats
214 **famed commander** "Duke of Albemarle's battle, first day"   223
Th' Elean plains "Where the Olympic games were celebrated"   228
lands unfixed "From Virgil: (It seems as if the Cyclades again Were
rooted up and justled in the main — Dryden)"

LVIII

Now passed, on either side they nimbly tack;
  Both strive to intercept and guide the wind: 230
And, in its eye, more closely they come back,
  To finish all the deaths they left behind.

LIX

On high-raised decks the haughty Belgians ride,
  Beneath whose shade our humble frigates go:
Such port the elephant bears, and so defied   235
  By the rhinoceros her unequal foe.

LX

And as the built, so different is the fight;
  Their mounting shot is on our sails designed:
Deep in their hulls our deadly bullets light
  And through the yielding planks a passage find.   240

LXI

Our dreaded admiral from far they threat,
  Whose battered rigging their whole war receives;
All bare, like some old oak which tempests beat,
  He stands, and sees below his scattered leaves.

LXII

Heroes of old, when wounded, shelter sought;   245
  But he, who meets all danger with disdain,
Even in their face his ship to anchor brought,
  And steeple-high stood propped upon the main.

LXIII

At this excess of courage, all amazed,
  The foremost of his foes a while withdraw.   250
With such respect in entered Rome they gazed,
  Who on high chairs the godlike fathers saw.

LXIV

And now, as where Patroclus' body lay,
  Here Trojan chiefs advanced, and there the Greek;

255 Ours o'er the duke their pious wings display,
    And theirs the noblest spoils of Britain seek.

LXV

Meantime his busy mariners he hastes,
    His shattered sails with rigging to restore;
And willing pines ascend his broken masts,
260   Whose lofty heads rise higher than before.

LXVI

Straight to the Dutch he turns his dreadful prow,
    More fierce th' important quarrel to decide.
Like swans, in long array his vessels show,
    Whose crests, advancing, do the waves divide.

LXVII

265 They charge, recharge, and all along the sea
    They drive, and squander the huge Belgian fleet.
Berkeley° alone, who nearest danger lay,
    Did a like fate with lost Creüsa° meet.

LXVIII

The night comes on, we eager to pursue
270   The combat still, and they ashamed to leave:
Till the last streaks of dying day withdrew,
    And doubtful moonlight did our rage deceive.

LXIX

In th' English fleet each ship resounds with joy,
    And loud applause of their great leader's fame:
275 In fiery dreams the Dutch they still destroy,
    And, slumb'ring, smile at the imagined flame.

LXX

Not so the Holland fleet, who, tired and done,
    Stretched on their decks like weary oxen lie;
Faint sweats all down their mighty members run
280   (Vast bulks, which little souls but ill supply.)

267 **Berkeley** Sir William Berkeley, vice-admiral   268 **Creüsa** Aeneas' wife, lost in the escape from Troy

LXXI

In dreams they fearful precipices tread,
  Or, shipwracked, labor to some distant shore;
Or in dark churches walk among the dead:
  They wake with horror, and dare sleep no more.

LXXII

The morn they look on with unwilling eyes,°   285
  Till from their maintop joyful news they hear
Of ships which by their mold bring new supplies,
  And in their colors Belgian lions bear.

LXXIII

Our watchful general had discerned from far
  This mighty succor which made glad the foe;   290
He sighed, but, like a father of the war,
  His face spake hope,° while deep his sorrows flow.

LXXIV

His wounded men he first sends off to shore
  (Never, till now, unwilling to obey.)
They not their wounds but want of strength deplore,   295
  And think them happy who with him can stay.

LXXV

Then to the rest: "Rejoice," said he, "today;
  In you the fortune of Great Britain lies:
Among so brave a people, you are they
  Whom Heav'n has chose to fight for such a prize.   300

LXXVI

"If number English courages could quell,
  We should at first have shunned, not met, our foes,
Whose numerous sails the fearful only tell:
  Courage from hearts, and not from numbers,
    grows."

---

285 **The morn ... eyes** "Second day's battle"   292 **His face ... hope**
"(His outward smiles concealed his inward smart — Virgil, Dryden)"

LXXVII

305 He said, nor needed more to say: with haste
        To their known stations cheerfully they go;
    And all at once, disdaining to be last,
        Solicit every gale to meet the foe.

LXXVIII

    Nor did th' encouraged Belgians long delay,
310   But bold in others, not themselves, they stood:
    So thick, our navy scarce could steer their way
        But seemed to wander in a moving wood.

LXXIX

    Our little fleet was now engaged so far,
        That, like the swordfish in the whale, they fought:
315 The combat only seemed a civil war,
        Till through their bowels we our passage wrought.

LXXX

    Never had valor, no, not ours, before
        Done aught like this upon the land or main,
    Where not to be o'ercome was to do more
320   Than all the conquests former kings did gain.

LXXXI

    The mighty ghosts of our great Harries rose,
        And armèd Edwards looked, with anxious eyes,
    To see this fleet among unequal foes,
        By which fate promised them their Charles should
            rise.

LXXXII

325 Meantime the Belgians tack upon our rear,
        And raking chase-guns° through our sterns they
            send;
    Close by, their fire-ships, like jackals, appear,
        Who on their lions for the prey attend.

326 **chase-guns** armament set in the bow or stem of a ship

LXXXIII

Silent in smoke of cannons they come on
   (Such vapors once did fiery Cacus° hide.)   *330*
In these the height of pleased revenge is shown,
   Who burn contented by another's side.

LXXXIV

Sometimes, from fighting squadrons of each fleet,
   (Deceived themselves, or to preserve some friend,)
Two grappling Ætnas on the ocean meet,   *335*
   And English fires with Belgian flames contend.

LXXXV

Now at each tack our little fleet grows less;
   And like maimed fowl swim lagging on the main;
Their greater loss their numbers scarce confess
   While they lose cheaper than the English gain.   *340*

LXXXVI

Have you not seen when, whistled from the fist,
   Some falcon stoops at what her eye designed,
And, with her eagerness the quarry missed,
   Straight flies at check, and clips it down the wind;°

LXXXVII

The dastard crow that to the wood made wing,   *345*
   And sees the groves no shelter can afford,
With her loud caws her craven kind does bring,
   Who, safe in numbers, cuff the noble bird?

LXXXVIII

Among the Dutch thus Albemarle did fare:
   He could not conquer, and disdained to fly;   *350*
Past hope of safety, 't was his latest care,
   Like falling Cæsar, decently to die.

LXXXIX

Yet pity did his manly spirit move

330 **Cacus** Vulcan's son who had the power of spewing fire   344 **flies**
. . . wind turns aside from quarry and flies swiftly down the wind

To see those perish who so well had fought;
355 And generously with his despair he strove,
Resolved to live till he their safety wrought.

XC

Let other Muses write his prosperous fate,
Of conquered nations tell, and kings restored;
But mine shall sing of his eclipsed estate,
360 Which, like the sun's, more wonders does afford.

XCI

He drew his mighty frigates all before,
On which the foe his fruitless force employs:
His weak ones deep into his rear he bore,
Remote from guns as sick men from the noise.

XCII

365 His fiery cannon did their passage guide,
And following smoke obscured them from the foe.
Thus Israel safe from the Egyptian's pride,
By flaming pillars, and by clouds did go.

XCIII

Elsewhere the Belgian force we did defeat,
370 But here our courages did theirs subdue;
So Xenophon once led that famed retreat,
Which first the Asian empire overthrew.

XCIV

The foe approached; and one, for his bold sin,
Was sunk (as he that touched the ark was slain;)
375 The wild waves mastered him and sucked him in,
And smiling eddies dimpled on the main.

XCV

This seen, the rest at awful distance stood,
As if they had been there as servants set,
To stay, or to go on, as he thought good,
380 And not pursue, but wait on his retreat.

XCVI

So Libyan huntsmen on some sandy plain,
　　From shady coverts roused, the lion chase:
The kingly beast roars out with loud disdain,
　　And slowly moves, unknowing to give place.°

XCVII

But if some one approach to dare his force,　　385
　　He swings his tail and swiftly turns him round;
With one paw seizes on his trembling horse,
　　And with the other tears him to the ground.

XCVIII

Amidst these toils succeeds the balmy night;
　　Now hissing waters the quenched guns restore;　　390
And weary waves,° withdrawing from the fight,
　　Lie lulled and panting on the silent shore.

XCIX

The moon shone clear on the becalmed flood,
　　Where, while her beams like glittering silver play,
Upon the deck our careful general stood,　　395
　　And deeply mused on the succeeding day.°

C

"That happy sun," said he, "will rise again,
　　Who twice victorious did our navy see;
And I alone must view him rise in vain,
　　Without one ray of all his star for me.　　400

CI

"Yet like an English general will I die,

383–4 **The kingly . . . place** "The simile is Virgil's: (The lordly lion
still maintains his ground, Grins horrible, retires, and turns again —
Dryden)"　391 **weary waves** "From Statius: (Fierce rivers have not
their wonted sound; the uproar of the deep declines, and the seas,
leaning on the lands, become calm — Noyes)"　396 **succeeding day**
"The third of June, famous for two former victories" — both over
the Dutch

And all the ocean make my spacious grave:
Women and cowards on the land may lie;
    The sea's a tomb that's proper for the brave."

CII

405 Restless he passed the remnants of the night,
    Till the fresh air proclaimed the morning nigh;
And burning ships, the martyrs of the fight,
    With paler fires beheld the eastern sky.

CIII

But now, his stores of ammunition spent,
410   His naked valor is his only guard;
Rare thunders are from his dumb cannon sent,
    And solitary guns are scarcely heard.

CIV

Thus far had Fortune power, here forced to stay,
    Nor longer durst with virtue be at strife:
415 This, as a ransom, Albermarle did pay
    For all the glories of so great a life.

CV

For now brave Rupert from afar appears,
    Whose waving streamers the glad general knows;
With full-spread sails his eager navy steers,
420   And every ship in swift proportion grows.

CVI

The anxious Prince had heard the cannon long,
    And from that length of time dire *omens* drew
Of English overmatched, and Dutch too strong,
    Who never fought three days, but to pursue.

CVII

425 Then, as an eagle who, with pious care,
    Was beating widely on the wing for prey,
To her now silent eyrie does repair,
    And finds her callow infants forced away;

CVIII

Stung with her love, she stoops upon the plain,
  The broken air loud whistling as she flies, 430
She stops and listens, and shoots forth again,
  And guides her pinions by her young ones' cries:

CIX

With such kind passion hastes the Prince to fight,
  And spreads his flying canvas to the sound;
Him, whom no danger, were he there, could fright, 435
  Now, absent, every little noise can wound.

CX

As in a drought the thirsty creatures cry,
  And gape upon the gathered clouds for rain;
And first the martlet meets it in the sky,
  And with wet wings joys all the feathered train: 440

CXI

With such glad hearts did our despairing men
  Salute th' appearance of the Prince's fleet;
And each ambitiously would claim the ken
  That with first eyes did distant safety meet.

CXII

The Dutch, who came like greedy hinds before, 445
  To reap the harvest their ripe ears did yield,
Now look like those, when rolling thunders roar,
  And sheets of lightning blast the standing field.

CXIII

Full in the Prince's passage, hills of sand
  And dangerous flats in secret ambush lay, 450
Where the false tides skim o'er the covered land,
  And seamen with dissembled depths betray.

CXIV

The wily Dutch, who, like fallen angels, feared
  This new *Messiah's* coming, there did wait,

455 And round the verge their braving vessels steered,
    To tempt his courage with so fair a bait.

CXV

But he, unmoved, contemns their idle threat,
    Secure of fame whene'er he please to fight:
His cold experience tempers all his heat,
460   And inbred worth doth boasting valor slight.

CXVI

Heroic virtue did his actions guide,
    And he the substance, not the appearance chose;
To rescue one such friend he took more pride
    Than to destroy whole thousands of such foes.

CXVII

465 But when approached, in strict embraces bound,
    Rupert and Albemarle together grow;
He joys to have his friend in safety found,
    Which he to none but to that friend would owe.

CXVIII

The cheerful soldiers, with new stores supplied,
470   Now long to execute their spleenful will,
And in revenge for those three days they tried,
    Wish one, like Joshua's, when the sun stood still.

CXIX

Thus reinforced, against the adverse fleet,
    Still doubling ours, brave Rupert leads the way;
475 With the first blushes of the morn they meet,
    And bring night back upon the new-born day.°

CXX

His presence soon blows up the kindling fight,
    And his loud guns speak thick like angry men:
It seemed as slaughter had been breathed all night,
480   And Death new pointed his dull dart again.

476 new-born day "Fourth day's battle"

CXXI

The Dutch too well his mighty conduct knew,
  And matchless courage, since the former fight;
Whose navy like a stiff-stretched cord did show,
  Till he bore in and bent them into flight.

CXXII

The wind he shares, while half their fleet offends   485
  His open side, and high above him shows;
Upon the rest at pleasure he descends,
  And, doubly harmed, he double harms bestows.

CXXIII

Behind, the general mends his weary pace
  And sullenly to his revenge he sails;   490
So glides some trodden serpent on the grass,
  And long behind his wounded volume trails.°

CXXIV

Th' increasing sound is borne to either shore,
  And for their stakes the throwing nations fear;
Their passions double with the cannons' roar,   495
  And with warm wishes each man combats there.

CXXV

Plied thick and close as when the fight begun,
  Their huge unwieldy navy wastes away;
So sicken waning moons too near the sun,
  And blunt their crescents on the edge of day.   500

CXXVI

And now reduced on equal terms to fight,
  Their ships like wasted patrimonies show;
Where the thin scattering trees admit the light,
  And shun each other's shadows as they grow.

491–2 **So glides . . . trails** "From Virgil: (He drags his tail, and for
his head provides, And in some secret cranny slowly glides; But
leaves exposed to blows his back and battered sides — Dryden)"

CXXVII

505 The warlike Prince had severed from the rest
       Two giant ships, the pride of all the main;
     Which with his one so vigorously he pressed,
       And flew so home they could not rise again.

CXXVIII

     Already battered, by his lee they lay;
510   In vain upon the passing winds they call;
     The passing winds through their torn canvas play,
       And flagging sails on heartless sailors fall.

CXXIX

     Their opened sides receive a gloomy light,
       Dreadful as day let in to shades below;
515 Without, grim Death rides barefaced in their sight,
       And urges entering billows as they flow.

CXXX

     When one dire shot, the last they could supply,
       Close by the board the Prince's mainmast bore.
     All three now, helpless, by each other lie,
520   And this offends not, and those fear no more.

CXXXI

     So have I seen some fearful hare maintain
       A course till tired before the dog she lay;
     Who, stretched behind her, pants upon the plain,
       Past power to kill, as she to get away.

CXXXII

525 With his lolled tongue he faintly licks his prey;
       His warm breath blows her flix° up as she lies;
     She, trembling, creeps upon the ground away,
       And looks back to him with beseeching eyes.

CXXXIII

     The Prince unjustly does his stars accuse,
530   Which hindered him to push his fortune on;

526 flix fur

For what they to his courage did refuse
    By mortal valor never must be done.

CXXXIV

This lucky hour the wise Batavian° takes,
    And warns his tattered fleet to follow home,
Proud to have so got off with equal stakes,   535
    Where 'twas a triumph not to be o'ercome.°

CXXXV

The general's force, as kept alive by fight,
    Now, not opposed, no longer can pursue:
Lasting till Heav'n had done his courage right,
    When he had conquered, he his weakness knew.   540

CXXXVI

He casts a frown on the departing foe,
    And sighs to see him quit the watery field;
His stern fixed eyes no satisfaction show
    For all the glories which the fight did yield.

CXXXVII

Though, as when fiends did miracles avow,   545
    He stands confessed ev'n by the boastful Dutch,
He only does his conquest disavow,
    And thinks too little what they found too much.

CXXXVIII

Returned, he with the fleet resolved to stay,
    No tender thoughts of home his heart divide;   550
Domestic joys and cares he puts away,
    For realms are households which the great must
    guide.

CXXXIX

As those who unripe veins in mines explore
    On the rich bed again the warm turf lay,

---

533 **wise Batavian** Admiral De Witt   536 **Where . . . o'ercome** "From
Horace: (For whom to err and to escape is a splendid triumph)"

555 Till time digests the yet imperfect ore,
     And know it will be gold another day:

CXL

So looks our monarch on this early fight,
   Th' essay and rudiments of great success
Which all-maturing time must bring to light,
560   While he, like Heav'n, does each day's labor bless.

CXLI

Heav'n ended not the first or second day,
   Yet each was perfect to the work designed:
God and kings work, when they their work survey,
   And passive aptness in all subjects find.

CXLII

565 In burdened vessels first, with speedy care,
     His plenteous stores do seasoned timber send.
Thither the brawny carpenters repair,
     And as the surgeons of maimed ships attend.°

CXLIII

With cord and canvas from rich Hamburg sent,
570   His navies' molted wings he imps° once more;
Tall Norway fir, their masts in battle spent,
     And English oak, sprung leaks and planks restore.

CXLIV

All hands employed, the royal work grows warm,°
   Like laboring bees on a long summer's day,
575 Some sound the trumpet for the rest to swarm,
     And some on bells of tasted lilies play;

CXLV

With gluey wax some new foundations lay
   Of virgin combs which from the roof are hung;

---

568 **surgeons . . . attend** "His Majesty repairs the fleet"   570 **imps**
grafts feathers to birds' wings to improve their flight   573 **work . . .
warm** *"Fervet opus:* the same similitude in Virgil"

Some armed within doors upon duty stay,
   Or tend the sick, or educate the young.   *580*

CXLVI

So here, some pick out bullets from the sides,
   Some drive old oakum through each seam and rift.
Their left hand does the calking-iron guide,
   The rattling mallet with the right they lift.

CXLVII

With boiling pitch another near at hand,   *585*
   From friendly Sweden brought, the seams instops:
Which well paid o'er,° the salt sea waves withstand,
   And shakes them from the rising beak in drops.

CXLVIII

Some the galled ropes with dauby marling° bind,
   Or searcloth° masts with strong tarpauling coats;   *590*
To try new shrouds one mounts into the wind,
   And one, below, their ease or stiffness notes.

CXLIX

Our careful monarch stands in person by,
   His new-cast cannons' firmness to explore;
The strength of big-corned powder loves to try,   *595*
   And ball and cartridge sorts for every bore.

CL

Each day brings fresh supplies of arms and men,
   And ships which all last winter were abroad;
And such as fitted since the fight had been,
   Or new from stocks were fallen into the road.   *600*

CLI

The goodly *London* in her gallant trim°
   (The Phœnix daughter of the vanished old)°

587 **paid o'er** coated with pitch   589 **marling** line used for winding
ropes   590 **searcloth** waxed material   601 **London . . . trim** "*Loyal
London* described"—a new ship built by the city of London to replace the old one   602 **Phœnix . . . old** like the legendary bird, the
new ship took form after the destruction of the other by fire

Like a rich bride does to the ocean swim,
  And on her shadow rides in floating gold.

CLII

605 Her flag aloft, spread ruffling to the wind,
  And sanguine streamers seem the flood to fire:
The weaver, charmed with what his loom designed,
  Goes on to sea, and knows not to retire.

CLIII

With roomy decks, her guns of mighty strength,
610 Whose low-laid mouths each mounting billow laves;
Deep in her draught, and warlike in her length,
  She seems a sea-wasp flying on the waves.

CLIV

This martial present, piously designed,
  The loyal city give their best-loved King,
615 And, with a bounty ample as the wind,
  Built, fitted, and maintained, to aid him bring.

CLV

By viewing Nature, Nature's handmaid, Art,°
  Makes mighty things from small beginnings grow:
Thus fishes first to shipping did impart
620 Their tail the rudder, and their head the prow.

CLVI

Some log, perhaps, upon the waters swam,
  An useless drift which, rudely cut within,
And hollowed, first a floating trough became,
  And cross some rivulet passage did begin.

CLVII

625 In shipping such as this, the Irish kern°
  And untaught Indian on the stream did glide
Ere sharp-keeled boats to stem the flood did learn,
  Or fin-like oars did spread from either side.

617 **Nature . . . Art** "Digression concerning shipping and navigation"
625 **kern** peasant

CLVIII

Add but a sail, and Saturn so appeared,
   When from lost empire he to exile went,°   *630*
And with the golden age to Tiber steered,
   Where coin and first commerce he did invent.

CLIX

Rude as their ships was navigation then,
   No useful compass or meridian known;
Coasting, they kept the land within their ken,   *635*
   And knew no North but when the pole-star shone.

CLX

Of all who since have used the open sea,
   Than the bold English none more fame have won;
Beyond the year,° and out of Heav'n's high way,
   They make discoveries where they see no sun.   *640*

CLXI

But what so long in vain, and yet unknown,
   By poor mankind's benighted wit is sought,
Shall in this age to Britain first be shown,
   And hence be to admiring nations taught.

CLXII

The ebbs of tides and their mysterious flow,   *645*
   We, as arts' elements, shall understand,
And as by line upon the ocean go,
   Whose paths shall be familiar as the land.

CLXIII

Instructed ships° shall sail to quick commerce,
   By which remotest regions are allied;   *650*
Which makes one city of the universe,
   Where some may gain, and all may be supplied.

629–30 **Saturn . . . went** banished by Jupiter, Saturn established civil-
ization in Italy   639 **Beyond . . . year** "Virgil: (Beyond the solar year,
without the starry way — Dryden)"   649 **Instructed ships** "By a
more exact measure of longitude"

CLXIV

Then we upon our globe's last verge shall go
    And view the ocean leaning on the sky;
655 From thence our rolling neighbors we shall know,
    And on the lunar world securely pry.

CLXV

This I foretell from your auspicious care,°
    Who great in search of God and Nature grow;
Who best your wise Creator's praise declare,
660   Since best to praise his works is best to know.

CLXVI

O truly Royal! who behold the law
    And rule of beings in your Maker's mind;
And thence, like limbecs,° rich ideas draw,
    To fit the levelled use of humankind.

CLXVII

665 But first the toils of war we must endure,
    And from th' injurious Dutch redeem the seas.
War makes the valiant of his right secure,
    And gives up fraud to be chastised with ease.

CLXVIII

Already were the Belgians on our coast,
670   Whose fleet more mighty every day became
By late success, which they did falsely boast,
    And now by first appearing seemed to claim.

CLXIX

Designing, subtile, diligent, and close,
    They knew to manage war with wise delay;
675 Yet all those arts their vanity did cross,
    And, by their pride, their prudence did betray.

CLXX

Nor stayed the English long, but, well supplied,

657 **your . . . care** "Apostrophe to the Royal Society"   663 **limbecs**
distilling apparatus

Appear as numerous as th' insulting foe.
The combat now by courage must be tried,
   And the success the braver nation show.   680

CLXXI

There was the Plymouth squadron now come in,
   Which in the Straits last winter was abroad;
Which twice on Biscay's working bay had been,
   And on the midland sea the French had awed.

CLXXII

Old expert Allen,° loyal all along,   685
   Famed for his action on the Smyrna fleet;
And Holmes,° whose name shall live in epic song,
   While music numbers, or while verse has feet;

CLXXIII

Holmes, the Achates° of the generals' fight,
   Who first bewitched our eyes with Guinea gold,   690
As once old Cato in the Romans' sight
   The tempting fruits of Afric did unfold.

CLXXIV

With him went Sprag,° as bountiful as brave,
   Whom his high courage to command had brought;
Harman, who did the twice-fired *Harry* save,°   695
   And in his burning ship undaunted fought;

CLXXV

Young Hollis, on a Muse by Mars begot,
   Born, Caesar-like, to write and act great deeds;
Impatient to revenge his fatal shot,
   His right hand doubly to his left succeeds.°   700

---

685 **Allen** Vice-Admiral Sir Thomas Allen   687 **Holmes** Sir Robert
Holmes, who had taken Dutch ships in prize   689 **Achates** follower
of Aeneas   693 **Sprag** Sir Edward Sprag   695 **Harman . . . save** Sir
John Harman brought the ship *Henry,* under his command, safely to
harbor although afire   697–700 **Hollis . . . succeeds** Sir Fresche-
ville Hollis continued the fight after the loss of his left arm

CLXXVI

Thousands were there in darker fame that dwell,
  Whose deeds some nobler poem shall adorn,
And though to me unknown, they, sure, fought well,
  Whom Rupert led, and who were British born.

CLXXVII

705 Of every size an hundred fighting sail,
  So vast the navy now at anchor rides,
That underneath it the pressed waters fail,
  And with its weight it shoulders off the tides.

CLXXVIII

Now, anchors weighed, the seamen shout so shrill,
710   That heav'n, and earth, and the wide ocean rings;
A breeze from westward waits their sails to fill,
  And rests in those high beds his downy wings.

CLXXIX

The wary Dutch this gathering storm foresaw,
  And durst not bide it on the English coast;
715 Behind their treacherous shallows they withdraw,
  And there lay snares to catch the British host.

CLXXX

So the false spider, when her nets are spread,
  Deep ambushed in her silent den does lie,
And feels far off the trembling of her thread,
720   Whose filmy cord should bind the struggling fly.

CLXXXI

Then, if at last she find him fast beset,
  She issues forth, and runs along her loom.
She joys to touch the captive in her net,
  And drags the little wretch in triumph home.

CLXXXII

725 The Belgians hoped that, with disordered haste,
  Our deep-cut keels upon the sands might run;

Or, if with caution leisurely were passed,
    Their numerous gross might charge us one by one.

CLXXXIII

But with a fore-wind pushing them above,
    And swelling tide that heaved them from below,   730
O'er the blind flats our warlike squadrons move,
    And with spread sails to welcome battle go.

CLXXXIV

It seemed as there the British Neptune stood,
    With all his hosts of waters at command,
Beneath them to submit th' officious flood,   735
    And with his trident shoved them off the sand.°

CLXXXV

To the pale foes they suddenly draw near,
    And summon them to unexpected fight;
They start like murderers when ghosts appear,
    And draw their curtains in the dead of night.   740

CLXXXVI

Now van to van the foremost squadrons meet,°
    The midmost battles hastening up behind;
Who view, far off, the storm of falling sleet,
    And hear their thunder rattling in the wind.

CLXXXVII

At length the adverse admirals appear   745
    (The two bold champions of each country's right;)
Their eyes describe the lists as they come near,
    And draw the lines of death before they fight.

CLXXXVIII

The distance judged for shot of every size,
    The linstocks touch, the ponderous ball expires;   750

733–6 **Neptune . . . sand** "Virgil: (The god himself with ready trident
stands, And opes the deep, and spreads the moving sands—Dryden)"
741 "Second battle"

The vigorous seaman every porthole plies,
    And adds his heart to every gun he fires.

CLXXXIX

Fierce was the fight on the proud Belgians' side
    For honor, which they seldom sought before;
755 But now they by their own vain boasts were tied,
    And forced at least in show to prize it more.

CXC

But sharp remembrance on the English part,
    And shame of being matched by such a foe,
Rouse conscious virtue up in every heart,
760   And seeming to be stronger makes them so.°

CXCI

Nor long the Belgians could that fleet sustain,
    Which did two generals' fates, and Cæsar's bear;
Each several ship a victory did gain,
    As Rupert or as Albermarle were there.

CXCII

765 Their battered admiral too soon withdrew,
    Unthanked by ours for his unfinished fight;
But he the minds of his Dutch masters knew,
    Who called that providence which we called flight.

CXCIII

Never did men more joyfully obey,
770   Or sooner understood the sign to fly;
With such alacrity they bore away,
    As if to praise them all the States stood by.

CXCIV

O famous leader of the Belgian fleet,
    Thy monument inscribed such praise shall wear,
775 As Varro,° timely flying, once did meet,
    Because he did not of his Rome despair!

760 **seeming . . . so** "Virgil: (They are able because they seem to be)"
775 **Varro** defeated general honored by the Roman Senate

CXCV

Behold that navy, which a while before
  Provoked the tardy English close to fight,
Now draw their beaten vessels close to shore,
  As larks lie dared to shun the hobby's° flight.   780

CXCVI

Whoe'er would English monuments survey,
  In other records may our courage know,
But let them hide the story of this day,
  Whose fame was blemished by too base a foe.

CXCVII

Or if too busily they will enquire   785
  Into a victory which we disdain,
Then let them know, the Belgians did retire
  Before the patron saint of injured Spain.°

CXCVIII

Repenting England this revengeful day
  To Philip's manes° did an offering bring;   790
England, which first, by leading them astray,
  Hatched up rebellion to destroy her king.

CXCIX

Our fathers bent their baneful industry
  To check a monarchy that slowly grew;
But did not France or Holland's fate foresee,   795
  Whose rising power to swift dominion flew.

CC

In fortune's empire blindly thus we go,
  And wander after pathless destiny;
Whose dark resorts since prudence cannot know,
  In vain it would provide for what shall be.   800

780 **hobby's** a small falcon's   788 **patron . . . Spain** "St. James, on
whose day this victory was gained"   790 **Philip's manes** "Philip the
Second of Spain, against whom the Hollanders, rebelling, were aided
by Queen Elizabeth" **manes** the ghost of Philip

CCI

But what'er English to the blest shall go,
    And the fourth Harry or first Orange meet,°
Find him disowning of a Bourbon foe,
    And him detesting a Batavian fleet.

CCII

805 Now on their coasts our conquering navy rides,
    Waylays their merchants, and their land besets;
Each day new wealth without their care provides;
    They lie asleep with prizes in their nets.

CCIII

So, close behind some promontory lie
810   The huge leviathans t' attend their prey;
And give no chase, but swallow in the fry
    Which through their gaping jaws mistake the way.

CCIV

Nor was this all: in ports and roads remote,
    Destructive fires among whole fleets we send;°
815 Triumphant flames upon the water float,
    And outbound ships at home their voyage end.

CCV

Those various squadrons, variously designed,
    Each vessel freighted with a several load,
Each squadron waiting for a several wind,
820   All find but one, to burn them in the road.

CCVI

Some bound for Guinea, golden sand to find,
    Bore all the gauds the simple natives wear;
Some, for the pride of Turkish courts designed,
    For folded turbans finest Holland bear.

801-2 **whate'er English . . . meet** the English in Heaven, meeting
Henry IV of France, would learn to oppose the war against Henry
III; and meeting the first Prince of Orange would learn to detest the
Dutch naval power on which they nevertheless depended (Scott)
814 **fires . . . send** "Burning of the fleet in the Vlie by Sir Robert
Holmes"

CCVII

Some English wool, vexed° in a Belgian loom,   825
   And into cloth of spongy softness made,
Did into France or colder Denmark doom,
   To ruin with worse ware our staple trade.

CCVIII

Our greedy seamen rummage every hold,
   Smile on the booty of each wealthier chest;   830
And, as the priests who with their gods make bold,
   Take what they like, and sacrifice the rest.

CCIX

But ah! how unsincere are all our joys!°
   Which, sent from Heav'n, like lightning make no
     stay;
Their palling taste the journey's length destroys,   835
   Or grief, sent post, o'ertakes them on the way.

CCX

Swelled with our late successes on the foe,
   Which France and Holland wanted power to cross,
We urge an unseen fate to lay us low,
   And feed their envious eyes with English loss.   840

CCXI

Each element his dread command obeys,
   Who makes or ruins with a smile or frown;
Who, as by one he did our nation raise,
   So now he with another pulls us down.

CCXII

Yet London, empress of the northern clime,   845
   By an high fate thou greatly didst expire:
Great as the world's, which at the death of time
   Must fall, and rise a nobler frame by fire.°

825 **vexed** drawn   833 **But . . . joys** "Transit to the Fire of London"
847–8 **Great . . . fire** "Ovid: (Remembering, in the Fates, a time when
fire Should to the battlements of heaven aspire, And all his blazing
worlds above should burn, And all th' inferior globe to cinders turn
— Dryden)"

CCXIII

As when some dire usurper Heav'n provides
850 To scourge his country with a lawless sway,
His birth perhaps some petty village hides,
 And sets his cradle out of fortune's way,

CCXIV

Till fully ripe his swelling fate breaks out,
 And hurries him to mighty mischiefs on;
855 His Prince, surprised at first, no ill could doubt,
 And wants the power to meet it when 't is known.

CCXV

Such was the rise of this prodigious fire,
 Which, in mean buildings first obscurely bred,
From thence did soon to open streets aspire,
860 And straight to palaces and temples spread.

CCXVI

The diligence of trades and noiseful gain,
 And luxury, more late, asleep were laid:
All was the Night's,° and in her silent reign
 No sound the rest of nature did invade.

CCXVII

865 In this deep quiet, from what source unknown,
 Those seeds of fire their fatal birth disclose;
And first, few scattering sparks about were blown,
 Big with the flames that to our ruin rose.

CCXVIII

Then, in some close-pent room it crept along,
870 And, smouldering as it went, in silence fed;
Till th' infant monster, with devouring strong,
 Walked boldly upright with exalted head.

CCXIX

Now, like some rich or mighty murderer,

863 **All . . . Night's** the fire commenced the night preceding September 2

Too great for prison, which he breaks with gold;
Who fresher for new mischiefs does appear,   *875*
    And dares the world to tax him with the old;

CCXX

So scapes th' insulting fire his narrow jail,
    And makes small outlets into open air;
There the fierce winds his tender force assail,
    And beat him downward to his first repair.   *880*

CCXXI

The winds, like crafty courtesans,° withheld
    His flames from burning, but to blow them more;
And, every fresh attempt, he is repelled
    With faint denials, weaker than before.

CCXXII

And now, no longer letted° of his prey,   *885*
    He leaps up at it with enraged desire;
O'erlooks the neighbors with a wide survey,
    And nods at every house his threatening fire.

CCXXIII

The ghosts of traitors° from the Bridge descend,
    With bold fanatic specters to rejoice;   *890*
About the fire into a dance they bend,
    And sing their sabbath notes° with feeble voice.

CCXXIV

Our guardian angel saw them where he sate
    Above the palace of our slumbering King:
He sighed, abandoning his charge to fate,   *895*
    And, drooping, oft looked back upon the wing.

CCXXV

At length the crackling noise and dreadful blaze

881 **like ... courtesans** "Terence: (She artfully managed the greedy
man, that privation might inflame his mind — Noyes)"   885 **letted**
hindered   889 **ghosts of traitors** heads of persons executed for
treason were affixed to London Bridge   892 **sabbath notes** infernal
hymns chanted at the Witches' Sabbath

Called up some waking lover to the sight;
   And long it was ere he the rest could raise,
900   Whose heavy eyelids yet were full of night.

CCXXVI

The next to danger, hot pursued by fate,
   Half-clothed, half-naked, hastily retire;
And frighted mothers strike their breasts too late
   For helpless infants left amidst the fire.

CCXXVII

905 Their cries soon waken all the dwellers near;
   Now murmuring noises rise in every street;
The more remote run stumbling with their fear,
   And in the dark men justle as they meet.

CCXXVIII

So weary bees in little cells repose;
910   But if night-robbers lift the well-stored hive,
An humming through their waxen city grows,
   And out upon each other's wings they drive.

CCXXIX

Now streets grow thronged and busy as by day:
   Some run for buckets to the hallowed choir;
915 Some cut the pipes, and some the engines play;
   And some more bold mount ladders to the fire.

CCXXX

In vain, for from the East a Belgian wind
   His hostile breath through the dry rafters sent;
The flames impelled soon left their foes behind,
920   And forward with a wanton fury went.

CCXXXI

A key of fire ran all along the shore,
   And lightened all the river with a blaze;°

---

922 **river . . . blaze** "Virgil: (The seas are bright with splendor not
their own — Dryden)"

The wakened tides began again to roar,
  And wondering fish in shining waters gaze.

CCXXXII

Old father Thames raised up his reverend head,   925
  But feared the fate of Simoeis° would return.
Deep in his ooze he sought his sedgy bed,
  And shrunk his waters back into his urn.

CCXXXIII

The fire, meantime, walks in a broader gross;
  To either hand his wings he opens wide;   930
He wades the streets, and straight he reaches cross,
  And plays his longing flames on th' other side.

CCXXXIV

At first they warm, then scorch, and then they take;
  Now with long necks from side to side they feed;
At length, grown strong, their mother-fire forsake,   935
  And a new colony of flames succeed.

CCXXXV

To every nobler portion of the town
  The curling billows roll their restless tide:
In parties now they straggle up and down,
  As armies, unopposed, for prey divide.   940

CCXXXVI

One mighty squadron, with a side-wind sped,
  Through narrow lanes his cumbered fire does haste,
By powerful charms of gold and silver led,
  The Lombard bankers and the Change to waste.

CCXXXVII

Another backward to the Tower would go,   945
  And slowly eats his way against the wind;
But the main body of the marching foe
  Against th' imperial palace is designed.

926 **Simoeis** Trojan river dried up by Hephæstus

CCXXXVIII

Now day appears, and with the day the King,
950   Whose early care had robbed him of his rest.
Far off the cracks of falling houses ring,
    And shrieks of subjects pierce his tender breast.

CCXXXIX

Near as he draws, thick harbingers of smoke
    With gloomy pillars cover all the place;
955 Whose little intervals of night are broke
    By sparks that drive against his Sacred Face.

CCXL

More than his guards his sorrows made him known,
    And pious tears, which down his cheeks did shower:
The wretched in his grief forgot their own
960   (So much the pity of a King has power.)

CCXLI

He wept the flames of what he loved so well,
    And what so well had merited his love,
For never Prince in grace did more excel,
    Or royal city more in duty strove.

CCXLII

965 Nor with an idle care did he behold
    (Subjects may grieve, but monarchs must redress;)
He cheers the fearful, and commends the bold,
    And makes despairers hope for good success.

CCXLIII

Himself directs what first is to be done,
970   And orders all the succors which they bring.
The helpful and the good about him run,
    And form an army worthy such a King.

CCXLIV

He sees the dire contagion spread so fast
    That, where it seizes, all relief is vain;

And therefore must unwillingly lay waste   975
    That country which would, else, the foe maintain.

CCXLV

The powder blows up all before the fire:°
    Th' amazed flames stand gathered on a heap;
And from the precipice's brink retire,
    Afraid to venture on so large a leap.   980

CCXLVI

Thus fighting fires a while themselves consume,
    But straight, like Turks, forced on to win or die,
They first lay tender bridges of their fume,
    And o'er the breach in unctuous vapors fly.

CCXLVII

Part stays for passage, till a gust of wind   985
    Ships o'er their forces in a shining sheet;
Part, creeping under ground, their journey blind,
    And, climbing from below, their fellows meet.

CCXLVIII

Thus to some desert plain, or old wood-side,
    Dire night-hags come from far to dance their round,   990
And o'er broad rivers on their fiends they ride,
    Or sweep in clouds above the blasted ground.

CCXLIX

No help avails: for, *Hydra*°-like, the fire
    Lifts up his hundred heads to aim his way,
And scarce the wealthy can one half retire,   995
    Before he rushes in to share the prey.

CCL

The rich grow suppliant, and the poor grow proud;
    Those offer mighty gain, and these ask more;

---

977 powder . . . fire houses were blown up to prevent the spread of
the fire   **993 Hydra** many-headed serpent

So void of pity is th' ignoble crowd
1000   When others' ruin may increase their store.

CCLI

As those who live by shores with joy behold
    Some wealthy vessel split or stranded nigh,
And from the rocks leap down for shipwracked gold,
    And seek the tempests which the others fly:

CCLII

1005 So these but wait the owners' last despair,
    And what's permitted to the flames invade;
Even from their jaws they hungry morsels tear,
    And on their backs the spoils of Vulcan lade.

CCLIII

The days were all in this lost labor spent,
1010   And when the weary King gave place to night,
His beams he to his royal brother° lent,
    And so shone still in his reflective light.

CCLIV

Night came, but without darkness or repose,
    A dismal picture of the general doom;
1015 Where souls distracted, when the trumpet blows,
    And half unready with their bodies come.

CCLV

Those who have homes, when home they do repair,
    To a last lodging call their wandering friends;
Their short uneasy sleeps are broke with care,
1020   To look how near their own destruction tends.

CCLVI

Those who have none, sit round where once it was,
    And with full eyes each wonted room require;°
Haunting the yet warm ashes of the place,
    As murdered men walk where they did expire.

1011 **beams ... brother** Charles being supported by the Duke of York
1022 **require** seek again

CCLVII

Some stir up coals and watch the vestal fire,°   *1025*
  Others in vain from sight of ruin run;
And, while through burning labyrinths they retire,
  With loathing eyes repeat what they would shun.

CCLVIII

The most in fields like herded beasts lie down,
  To dews obnoxious° on the grassy floor;   *1030*
And while their babes in sleep their sorrows drown,
  Sad parents watch the remnants of their store.

CCLIX

While by the motion of the flames they guess
  What streets are burning now, and what are near,
An infant, waking, to the paps would press,   *1035*
  And meets, instead of milk, a falling tear.

CCLX

No thought can ease them but their sovereign's care,
  Whose praise th' afflicted as their comfort sing.
Even those whom want might drive to just despair,
  Think life a blessing under such a King.   *1040*

CCLXI

Meantime he sadly suffers in their grief,
  Out-weeps an hermit, and out-prays a saint.
All the long night he studies their relief,
  How they may be supplied, and he may want.

CCLXII

"O God," said he,° "thou patron of my days,   *1045*
  Guide of my youth in exile and distress!
Who me, unfriended, brought'st by wondrous ways,
  The kingdom of my fathers to possess:

CCLXIII

"Be thou my judge, with what unwearied care

1025 **vestal fire** fire burned for the Goddess of the Hearth   1030 **ob-noxious** exposed to   1045 **said he** "King's prayer"

1050   I since have labored for my people's good;
        To bind the bruises of a civil war,
            And stop the issues of their wasting blood.

                        CCLXIV

        "Thou, who hast taught me to forgive the ill,
            And recompense, as friends, the good misled;
1055   If mercy be a precept of thy will,
            Return that mercy on thy servant's head.

                        CCLXV

        "Or, if my heedless youth has stepped astray,
            Too soon forgetful of thy gracious hand;
        On me alone thy just displeasure lay,
1060   But take thy judgments from this mourning land.

                        CCLXVI

        "We all have sinned, and thou hast laid us low,
            As humble earth from whence at first we came:
        Like flying shades before the clouds we show,
            And shrink like parchment in consuming flame.

                        CCLXVII

1065   "O let it be enough what thou hast done;
            When spotted deaths° ran armed through every
                street,
        With poisoned darts, which not the good could shun,
            The speedy could out-fly, or valiant meet.

                        CCLXVIII

        "The living few, and frequent funerals then,
1070   Proclaimed thy wrath on this forsaken place;
        And now those few who are returned again,
            Thy searching judgments to their dwellings trace.

                        CCLXIX

        "O pass not, Lord, an absolute decree,
            Or bind thy sentence unconditional,

1066 spotted deaths the plague of 1665

But in thy sentence our remorse foresee, *1075*
    And, in that foresight, this thy doom recall.

CCLXX

"Thy threatenings, Lord, as thine thou mayst revoke;
    But, if immutable and fixed they stand,
Continue still thyself to give the stroke,
    And let not foreign foes oppress thy land." *1080*

CCLXXI

Th' Eternal heard, and from the Heav'nly Choir
    Chose out the cherub with the flaming sword;
And bade him swiftly drive th' approaching fire
    From where our naval magazines were stored.

CCLXXII

The blessed minister his wings displayed, *1085*
    And like a shooting star he cleft the night;
He charged the flames, and those that disobeyed
    He lashed to duty with his sword of light.

CCLXXIII

The fugitive flames, chastised, went forth to prey,
    On pious structures, by our fathers reared; *1090*
By which to Heav'n they did affect the way,
    Ere faith in churchmen without works was heard.

CCLXXIV

The wanting orphans saw with watery eyes
    Their founders' charity in dust laid low;
And sent to God their ever-answered cries, *1095*
    (For he protects the poor, who made them so.)

CCLXXV

Nor could thy fabric, Paul's,° defend thee long,
    Though thou wert sacred to thy Maker's praise;
Though made immortal by a poet's song,
    And poets' songs the Theban walls could raise. *1100*

1097 **Paul's** St. Paul's Cathedral

CCLXXVI

The daring flames peeped in, and saw from far
    The awful beauties of the sacred choir;
But, since it was profaned by civil war,
    Heav'n thought it fit to have it purged by fire.

CCLXXVII

1105 Now down the narrow streets it swiftly came,
    And, widely opening, did on both sides prey:
This benefit we sadly owe the flame,
    If only ruin must enlarge our way.

CCLXXVIII

And now four days the sun had seen our woes;
1110   Four nights the moon beheld th' incessant fire;
It seemed as if the stars more sickly rose,
    And farther from the feverish north retire.

CCLXXIX

In th' empyrean Heav'n (the blest abode,)
    The Thrones and the Dominions prostrate lie,
1115 Not daring to behold their angry God,
    And an hushed silence damps the tuneful sky.

CCLXXX

At length th' Almighty cast a pitying eye,
    And mercy softly touched his melting breast.
He saw the town's one half in rubbish lie,
1120   And eager flames drive on to storm the rest.

CCLXXXI

An hollow crystal pyramid he takes,
    In firmamental waters dipped above;
Of it a broad extinguisher he makes
    And hoods the flames that to their quarry strove.

CCLXXXII

1125 The vanquished fires withdraw° from every place,

1125 **fires withdraw** the fire subsided after three days

Or, full with feeding, sink into a sleep:
Each household genius shows again his face,
    And from the hearths the little Lares° creep.

CCLXXXIII

Our King this more than natural change beholds;
    With sober joy his heart and eyes abound;   *1130*
To the All-good his lifted hands he folds,
    And thanks him low on his redeemèd ground.

CCLXXXIV

As when sharp frosts had long constrained the earth,
    A kindly thaw unlocks it with mild rain;
And first the tender blade peeps up to birth,   *1135*
    And straight the green fields laugh with promised
        grain:

CCLXXXV

By such degrees the spreading gladness grew
    In every heart which fear had froze before;
The standing streets with so much joy they view
    That with less grief the perished they deplore.   *1140*

CCLXXXVI

The Father of the people opened wide
    His stores, and all the poor with plenty fed:
Thus God's anointed God's own place supplied,
    And filled the empty with his daily bread.

CCLXXXVII

This royal bounty brought its own reward,   *1145*
    And in their minds so deep did print the sense,
That if their ruins sadly they regard,
    'T is but with fear the sight might drive him thence.

CCLXXXVIII

But so may he live long, that town to sway,
    Which by his auspice they will nobler make,   *1150*

1128 **Lares** gods of the household honored by the Romans

As he will hatch their ashes by his stay,°
And not their humble ruins now forsake.

CCLXXXIX

They have not lost their loyalty by fire,
Nor is their courage or their wealth so low
1155 That from his wars they poorly would retire,
Or beg the pity of a vanquished foe.

CCXC

Not with more constancy the Jews of old,
By Cyrus from rewarded exile sent,
Their royal city did in dust behold,
1160   Or with more vigor to rebuild it went.°

CCXCI

The utmost malice of their stars is past,
And two dire comets which have scourged the town
In their own plague and fire have breathed their last,
Or, dimly, in their sinking sockets frown.

CCXCII

1165 Now frequent trines° the happier lights among,
And high-raised Jove, from his dark prison freed,
(Those weights took off that on his planet hung,)
Will gloriously the new-laid works succeed.

CCXCIII

Methinks already, from this chymic° flame,
1170   I see a city of more precious mold,
Rich as the town which gives the Indies name,°
With silver paved, and all divine with gold.

CCXCIV

Already, laboring with a mighty fate,
She shakes the rubbish from her mounting brow,

1151 **his stay** "City's request to the King not to leave them"
1159–60 **city . . . went** rebuilding Jerusalem in joy and in sorrow
1165 **trines** favorable astrological conjunctions   1169 **chymic** trans-
forming as through the power of alchemy   1171 **name** "Mexico"

And seems to have renewed her charter's date,   *1175*
  Which Heav'n will to the death of time allow.

CCXCV

More great than human, now, and more *august*°
  New-deified she from her fires does rise:
Her widening streets on new foundations trust,
  And, opening, into larger parts she flies.   *1180*

CCXCVI

Before, she like some shepherdess did show,
  Who sate to bathe her by a river's side;
Not answering to her fame, but rude and low,
  Nor taught the beauteous arts of modern pride.

CCXCVII

Now, like a maiden queen, she will behold,   *1185*
  From her high turrets, hourly suitors come.
The East with incense, and the West with gold,
  Will stand, like suppliants, to receive her doom.

CCXCVIII

The silver Thames, her own domestic flood,
  Shall bear her vessels like a sweeping train,   *1190*
And often wind (as of his mistress proud,)
  With longing eyes to meet her face again.

CCXCIX

The wealthy Tagus, and the wealthier Rhine,
  The glory of their towns no more shall boast;
And Seine, that would with Belgian rivers join,   *1195*
  Shall find her luster stained, and traffic lost.

CCC

The venturous merchant, who designed more far,
  And touches on our hospitable shore,
Charmed with the splendor of this northern star,
  Shall here unlade him, and depart no more.   *1200*

1177 august "Augusta, the old name of London"

CCCI

Our powerful navy shall no longer meet,
    The wealth of France or Holland to invade;
The beauty of this town, without a fleet,
    From all the world shall vindicate her trade.

CCCII

1205 And while this famed emporium we prepare,
    The British ocean shall such triumphs boast,
That those who now disdain our trade to share,
    Shall rob like pirates on our wealthy coast.

CCCIII

Already we have conquered half the war,
1210   And the less dangerous part is left behind;
Our trouble now is but to make them dare,
    And not so great to vanquish as to find.

CCCIV

Thus to the Eastern wealth through storms we go,
    But now, the Cape once doubled, fear no more;
1215 A constant trade-wind will securely blow,
    And gently lay us on the spicy shore.

Absalom and Achitophel°
Part I

°**Absalom and Achitophel** The poem satirizes certain
political involvements in 1681 that turned upon the succession to Charles II whose heir was his brother the Duke
of York. As a Roman Catholic the Duke was the center
of ancient as well as new controversies. In 1678 the
Popish Plot, associated with the name of Titus Oates, had
aroused fears that the Catholics were contemplating violent
revolution. More recently, a proposal in Parliament to
exclude the Duke of York from the succession had encouraged the Whigs, led by the Earl of Shaftesbury and the
Duke of Buckingham, to propose as successor to the
throne the Duke of Monmouth, an illegitimate son of
Charles II. In 1681 Shaftesbury was charged with treason
but the case was thrown out of court.

Entering this bramble of controversy Dryden—as he
himself said, "The design, I am sure, is honest"—used as
the structure of his satire an elaborate analogy from the
Old Testament. The central circumstance in the comparison is the rivalry of Absalom with his father, David. Israel
represents England, the Jews the English. Jerusalem is
London, Hebron Scotland, Egypt France, Tyrus Holland.
The Nile is the Seine. Gath is Brussels, where Charles had
been in exile. Solyma as a name for Jerusalem gave its
name to the London mob, the Jebusites are the Catholics,
the rabbins are the Church of England clergy, the Levites
are the Presbyterians, and "Aaron's race" is the priesthood
in general.

As for the chief persons, David is Charles, Bathsheba
is Charles's current mistress the Duchess of Portsmouth,
Absalom is Monmouth, Achitophel is Shaftesbury, Zimri
is the Duke of Buckingham, Shimei is the Whig Sheriff of
London, Barzillai is the Duke of Ormond, and Corah is
Titus Oates.

In pious times, ere priestcraft did begin,
Before polygamy was made a sin;
When man on many multiplied his kind,
Ere one to one was cursedly confined;
5   When nature prompted, and no law denied
Promiscuous use of concubine and bride;
Then Israel's monarch, after Heaven's own heart,
His vigorous warmth did variously impart
To wives and slaves; and, wide as his command,
10 Scattered his Maker's image through the land.
Michal,° of royal blood, the crown did wear,
A soil ungrateful to the tiller's care:
Not so the rest; for several mothers bore
To godlike David several sons before.
15 But since like slaves his bed they did ascend,
No true succession could their seed attend.
Of all this numerous progeny was none
So beautiful, so brave, as Absalom:
Whether, inspired by some diviner lust,
20 His father got him with a greater gust;
Or that his conscious destiny made way,
By manly beauty, to imperial sway.
Early in foreign fields he won renown,
With kings and states allied to Israel's crown:
25 In peace the thoughts of war he could remove,
And seemed as he were only born for love.
Whate'er he did, was done with so much ease,
In him alone 't was natural to please.
His motions all accompanied with grace;
30 And paradise was opened in his face.
With secret joy indulgent David viewed
His youthful image in his son renewed:
To all his wishes nothing he denied;
And made the charming Annabel° his bride.
35 What faults he had (for who from faults is free?)
His father could not, or he would not see.
Some warm excesses which the law forbore,
Were construed youth that purged by boiling o'er,

11 **Michal** Queen Catherine of Portugal, wife of Charles II 34
Annabel Anne, Duchess of Buccleuch and Monmouth

And Amnon's murther,° by a specious name,
Was called a just revenge for injured fame.   40
Thus praised and loved the noble youth remained,
While David, undisturbed, in Sion° reigned.
But life can never be sincerely blest;
Heav'n punishes the bad, and proves the best.
The Jews, a headstrong, moody, murmuring race,   45
As ever tried th' extent and stretch of grace;
God's pampered people, whom, debauched with ease,
No King could govern, nor no God could please;
(Gods they had tried of every shape and size,
That god-smiths could produce, or priests devise:)   50
These Adam-wits, too fortunately free,
Began to dream they wanted liberty;
And when no rule, no precedent was found,
Of men by laws less circumscribed and bound;
They led their wild desires to woods and caves,   55
And thought that all but savages were slaves.
They who, when Saul° was dead, without a blow,
Made foolish Ishbosheth° the crown forego;
Who banished David did from Hebron bring,
And with a general shout proclaimed him King: 60
Those very Jews, who, at their very best,
Their humor more than loyalty expressed,
Now wondered why so long they had obeyed
An idol-monarch, which their hands had made;
Thought they might ruin him they could create,   65
Or melt him to that golden calf, a State.
But these were random bolts; no formed design,
Nor interest made the factious crowd to join:
The sober part of Israel, free from stain,
Well knew the value of a peaceful reign;   70
And, looking backward with a wise affright,
Saw seams of wounds, dishonest to the sight:
In contemplation of whose ugly scars
They cursed the memory of civil wars.
The moderate sort of men, thus qualified,   75

39 **Amnon's murther** a murder, or a maiming, in which the Duke of
Monmouth was allegedly a participant   42 **Sion** London   57 **Saul**
Oliver Cromwell   58 **Ishbosheth** Richard Cromwell

Inclined the balance to the better side;
And David's mildness managed it so well,
The bad found no occasion to rebel.
But when to sin our biased nature leans,
80 The careful Devil is still at hand with means,
And providently pimps for ill desires.
The Good Old Cause° revived, a plot requires.
Plots, true or false, are necessary things,
To raise up commonwealths, and ruin Kings.
85   Th' inhabitants of old Jerusalem
Were Jebusites; the town so called from them;
And theirs the native right—
But when the chosen people° grew more strong,
The rightful cause at length became the wrong;
90 And every loss the men of Jebus bore,
They still were thought God's enemies the more.
Thus worn and weakened, well or ill content,
Submit they must to David's government:
Impoverished, and deprived of all command,
95 Their taxes doubled as they lost their land;
And, what was harder yet to flesh and blood,
Their gods disgraced, and burnt like common wood.
This set the heathen priesthood in a flame;
For priests of all religions are the same.
100 Of whatsoe'er descent their godhead be,
Stock, stone, or other homely pedigree,
In his defense his servants are as bold,
As if he had been born of beaten gold.
The Jewish rabbins, though their enemies,
105 In this conclude them honest men and wise:
For 't was their duty, all the learned think,
T' espouse his cause, by whom they eat and drink.
From hence began that Plot,° the nation's curse,
Bad in itself, but represented worse;
110 Raised in extremes, and in extremes decried;
With oaths affirmed, with dying vows denied;
Not weighed or winnowed by the multitude;

---

82 **Good . . . Cause** the Commonwealth   88 **chosen people** Protestants   108 **that Plot** according to Oates the plan was to murder Charles, make James King, and suppress the Protestants

But swallowed in the mass, unchewed and crude.
Some truth there was, but dashed and brewed with
    lies,
To please the fools, and puzzle all the wise.   *115*
Succeeding times did equal folly call,
Believing nothing, or believing all.
Th' Egyptian rites the Jebusites embraced,
Where gods were recommended by their taste.
Such savory deities must needs be good,   *120*
As served at once for worship and for food.
By force they could not introduce these gods,
For ten to one in former days was odds.
So fraud was used (the sacrificer's trade):
Fools are more hard to conquer than persuade.   *125*
Their busy teachers mingled with the Jews,
And raked for converts even the court and stews:
Which Hebrew priests the more unkindly took,
Because the fleece accompanies the flock.
Some thought they God's anointed meant to slay   *130*
By guns, invented since full many a day:
Our author swears it not; but who can know
How far the Devil and Jebusites may go?
This Plot, which failed for want of common sense,
Had yet a deep and dangerous consequence: *135*
For, as when raging fevers boil the blood,
The standing lake soon floats into a flood,
And every hostile humor, which before
Slept quiet in its channels, bubbles o'er;
So several factions from this first ferment   *140*
Work up to foam, and threat the government.
Some by their friends, more by themselves thought
    wise,
Opposed the power to which they could not rise.
Some had in courts been great, and thrown from
    thence,
Like fiends were hardened in impenitence.   *145*
Some, by their monarch's fatal mercy, grown
From pardoned rebels kinsmen to the throne,
Were raised in power and public office high;
Strong bands, if bands ungrateful men could tie.

150   Of these the false Achitophel was first,
    A name to all succeeding ages curst:
    For close designs and crooked counsels fit;
    Sagacious, bold, and turbulent of wit;
    Restless, unfixed in principles and place;
155   In power unpleased, impatient of disgrace:
    A fiery soul, which, working out its way,
    Fretted the pigmy body to decay,
    And o'er-informed the tenement of clay.
    A daring pilot in extremity,
160   Pleased with the danger, when the waves went high,
    He sought the storms, but, for a calm unfit,
    Would steer too nigh the sands, to boast his wit.
    Great wits are sure to madness near allied,
    And thin partitions do their bounds divide;
165   Else why should he, with wealth and honor blest,
    Refuse his age the needful hours of rest?
    Punish a body which he could not please;
    Bankrupt of life, yet prodigal of ease?
    And all to leave what with his toil he won,
170   To that unfeathered two-legged thing, a son;
    Got, while his soul did huddled notions try;
    And born a shapeless lump, like anarchy.
    In friendship false, implacable in hate;
    Resolved to ruin or to rule the State.
175   To compass this the triple bond he broke;°
    The pillars of the public safety shook;
    And fitted Israel for a foreign yoke.
    Then seized with fear, yet still affecting fame,
    Usurped a patriot's all-atoning name.
180   So easy still it proves in factious times
    With public zeal to cancel private crimes.
    How safe is treason, and how sacred ill,
    Where none can sin against the people's will!
    Where crowds can wink, and no offense be known,
185   Since in another's guilt they find their own!
    Yet fame deserved no enemy can grudge;
    The statesman we abhor, but praise the judge.

175 **triple . . . broke** Shaftesbury was influential in disrupting the alliance between England, Sweden, and Holland

In Israel's courts ne'er sat an Abbethdin°
With more discerning eyes, or hands more clean;
Unbribed, unsought, the wretched to redress;   190
Swift of dispatch, and easy of access.
O, had he been content to serve the crown,
With virtues only proper to the gown;
Or had the rankness of the soil been freed
From cockle, that oppressed the noble seed;   195
David for him his tuneful harp had strung,
And Heav'n had wanted one immortal song.
But wild Ambition loves to slide, not stand,
And Fortune's ice prefers to Virtue's land.
Achitophel, grown weary to possess   200
A lawful fame, and lazy happiness,
Disdained the golden fruit to gather free,
And lent the crowd his arm to shake the tree.
Now, manifest° of crimes contrived long since,
He stood at bold defiance with his Prince;   205
Held up the buckler of the people's cause
Against the crown, and skulked behind the laws.
The wished occasion of the Plot he takes;
Some circumstances finds, but more he makes.
By buzzing emissaries fills the ears   210
Of listening crowds with jealousies and fears
Of arbitrary counsels brought to light,
And proves the King himself a Jebusite.
Weak arguments! which yet he knew full well
Were strong with people easy to rebel.   215
For, governed by the moon, the giddy Jews
Tread the same track when she the prime° renews;
And once in twenty years, their scribes record,
By natural instinct they change their lord.
Achitophel still wants a chief, and none   220
Was found so fit as warlike Absalon
Not that he wished his greatness to create
(For politicians neither love nor hate,)
But, for he knew his title not allowed,

188 **Abbethdin** a high magistrate among the Jews, here applied to
Shaftesbury as Lord Chancellor   204 **manifest** evidently guilty   217
prime the beginning of a cycle

225 Would keep him still depending on the crowd:
That kingly power, thus ebbing out, might be
Drawn to the dregs of a Democracy.
Him he attempts with studied arts to please,
And sheds his venom in such words as these:

230   "Auspicious Prince! at whose nativity
Some royal planet ruled the southern sky;
Thy longing country's darling and desire;
Their cloudy pillar and their guardian fire;
Their second Moses, whose extended wand

235 Divides the seas, and shows the promised land;
Whose dawning day in every distant age
Has exercised the sacred prophets' rage:
The people's prayer, the glad diviners' theme,
The young men's vision, and the old men's dream!

240 Thee, Savior, thee, the nation's vows confess,
And, never satisfied with seeing, bless.
Swift unbespoken pomps thy steps proclaim,
And stammering babes are taught to lisp thy name.
How long wilt thou the general joy detain,

245 Starve and defraud the people of thy reign?
Content ingloriously to pass thy days
Like one of Virtue's fools that feeds on praise,
Till thy fresh glories, which now shine so bright,
Grow stale and tarnish with our daily sight.

250 Believe me, royal youth, thy fruit must be
Or gathered ripe, or rot upon the tree.
Heav'n has to all allotted, soon or late,
Some lucky revolution of their fate;
Whose motions if we watch and guide with skill,

255 (For human good depends on human will,)
Our Fortune rolls as from a smooth descent,
And from the first impression takes the bent:
But, if unseized, she glides away like wind,
And leaves repenting Folly far behind.

260 Now, now she meets you with a glorious prize,
And spreads her locks before her as she flies.
Had thus old David, from whose loins you spring,
Not dared, when Fortune called him, to be King,
At Gath an exile he might still remain,

And Heaven's anointing oil had been in vain.   265
Let his successful youth your hopes engage,
But shun th' example of declining age:
Behold him setting in his western skies,
The shadows lengthening as the vapors rise.
He is not now, as when on Jordan's sand°   270
The joyful people thronged to see him land,
Covering the beach, and blackening all the strand;
But, like the Prince of Angels, from his height
Comes tumbling downward with diminished light;
Betrayed by one poor plot to public scorn   275
(Our only blessing since his curst return;)
Those heaps of people which one sheaf did bind,
Blown off and scattered by a puff of wind.
What strength can he to your designs oppose,
Naked of friends, and round beset with foes?   280
If Pharaoh's° doubtful succor he should use,
A foreign aid would more incense the Jews;
Proud Egypt would dissembled friendship bring;
Foment the war, but not support the King;
Nor would the royal party e'er unite   285
With Pharaoh's arms t' assist the Jebusite;
Or if they should, their interest soon would break,
And with such odious aid make David weak.
All sorts of men by my successful arts,
Abhorring kings, estrange their altered hearts   290
From David's rule: and 't is the general cry,
'Religion, commonwealth, and liberty.'
If you, as champion of the public good,
Add to their arms a chief of royal blood,
What may not Israel hope, and what applause   295
Might such a general gain by such a cause?
Not barren praise alone, that gaudy flower
Fair only to the sight, but solid power;
And nobler is a limited command,
Given by the love of all your native land,   300
Than a successive title, long and dark,
Drawn from the moldy rolls of Noah's ark."
    What cannot praise effect in mighty minds,

270 **Jordan's sand** Dover   281 **Pharaoh's** Louis XIV's

When flattery soothes, and when ambition blinds!
305 Desire of power, on earth a vicious weed,
Yet sprung from high, is of celestial seed;
In God 't is glory; and when men aspire,
'T is but a spark too much of heavenly fire.
Th' ambitious youth, too covetous of fame,
310 Too full of angels' metal in his frame,
Unwarily was led from virtue's ways,
Made drunk with honor, and debauched with praise.
Half loath, and half consenting to the ill
(For loyal blood within him struggled still,)
315 He thus replied: "And what pretense have I
To take up arms for public liberty?
My father governs with unquestioned right,
The faith's defender, and mankind's delight;
Good, gracious, just, observant of the laws;
320 And Heav'n by wonders has espoused his cause.
Whom has he wronged in all his peaceful reign?
Who sues for justice to his throne in vain?
What millions has he pardoned of his foes,
Whom just revenge did to his wrath expose?
325 Mild, easy, humble, studious of our good,
Inclined to mercy, and averse from blood.
If mildness ill with stubborn Israel suit,
His crime is God's beloved attribute.
What could he gain, his people to betray,
330 Or change his right for arbitrary sway?
Let haughty Pharaoh curse with such a reign
His fruitful Nile, and yoke a servile train.
If David's rule Jerusalem displease,
The Dog-star heats their brains to this disease.
335 Why then should I, encouraging the bad,
Turn rebel and run popularly mad?
Were he a tyrant, who, by lawless might
Oppressed the Jews, and raised the Jebusite,
Well might I mourn, but nature's holy bands
340 Would curb my spirits and restrain my hands.
The people might assert their liberty,
But what was right in them were crime in me.
His favor leaves me nothing to require,

Prevents my wishes, and outruns desire.
What more can I expect while David lives?   345
All but his kingly diadem he gives:
And that"—But there he paused; then sighing, said—
"Is justly destined for a worthier head.
For when my father from his toils shall rest,
And late augment the number of the blest,   350
His lawful issue shall the throne ascend,
Or the *collateral* line, where that shall end.
His brother, though oppressed with vulgar spite,
Yet dauntless, and secure of native right,
Of every royal virtue stands possessed;   355
Still dear to all the bravest, and the best.
His courage foes, his friends his truth proclaim;
His loyalty the King, the world his fame.
His mercy even the offending crowd will find,
For sure he comes of a forgiving kind.   360
Why should I then repine at Heaven's decree,
Which gives me no pretense to royalty?
Yet O that fate, propitiously inclined,
Had raised my birth, or had debased my mind;
To my large soul not all her treasure lent,   365
And then betrayed it to a mean descent!
I find, I find my mounting spirits bold,
And David's part disdains my mother's mold.
Why am I scanted by a niggard birth?
My soul disclaims the kindred of her earth,   370
And, made for empire, whispers me within,
'Desire of greatness is a godlike sin.' "
  Him staggering so when hell's dire agent found,
While fainting Virtue scarce maintained her ground,
He pours fresh forces in, and thus replies: 375
  "The eternal God, supremely good and wise,
Imparts not these prodigious gifts in vain:
What wonders are reserved to bless your reign?
Against your will, your arguments have shown,
Such virtue's only given to guide a throne.   380
Not that your father's mildness I contemn,
But manly force becomes the diadem.
'T is true he grants the people all they crave,

And more, perhaps, than subjects ought to have:
385 For lavish grants suppose a monarch tame,
And more his goodness than his wit proclaim.
But when should people strive their bonds to break,
If not when Kings are negligent or weak?
Let him give on till he can give no more,
390 The thrifty Sanhedrin° shall keep him poor;
And every shekel which he can receive,
Shall cost a limb of his prerogative.
To ply him with new plots shall be my care;
Or plunge him deep in some expensive war;
395 Which when his treasure can no more supply,
He must, with the remains of kingship, buy.
His faithful friends, our jealousies and fears,
Call Jebusites, and Pharaoh's pensioners;
Whom when our fury from his aid has torn,
400 He shall be naked left to public scorn.
The next successor, whom I fear and hate,
My arts have made obnoxious to the State,
Turned all his virtues to his overthrow,
And gained our elders to pronounce a foe.
405 His right, for sums of necessary gold,
Shall first be pawned, and afterwards be sold;
Till time shall ever-wanting David draw,
To pass your doubtful title into law:
If not, the people have a right supreme
410 To make their Kings; for Kings are made for them.
All empire is no more than power in trust,
Which, when resumed, can be no longer just.
Succession, for the general good designed,
In its own wrong a nation cannot bind;
415 If altering that the people can relieve,
Better one suffer than a nation grieve.
The Jews well know their power: ere Saul they chose,
God was their King, and God they durst depose.
Urge now your piety, your filial name,
420 A father's right, and fear of future fame;
The public good, that universal call,
To which even Heav'n submitted, answers all.

390 **Sanhedrin** Parliament

Nor let his love enchant your generous mind;
'T is Nature's trick to propagate her kind.
Our fond begetters, who would never die, 425
Love but themselves in their posterity.
Or let his kindness by th' effects be tried,
Or let him lay his vain pretense aside.
God said he loved your father; could he bring
A better proof, than to anoint him King? 430
It surely showed he loved the shepherd well,
Who gave so fair a flock as Israel.
Would David have you thought his darling son?
What means he then, to alienate the crown?
The name of godly he may blush to bear: 435
'T is after God's own heart to cheat his heir.
He to his brother gives supreme command,
To you a legacy of barren land;
Perhaps th' old harp, on which he thrums his lays,
Or some dull Hebrew ballad in your praise. 440
Then the next heir, a Prince severe and wise,
Already looks on you with jealous eyes;
Sees through the thin disguises of your arts,
And marks your progress in the people's hearts.
Though now his mighty soul its grief contains, 445
He meditates revenge who least complains;
And, like a lion, slumbering in the way,
Or sleep dissembling, while he waits his prey,
His fearless foes within his distance draws,
Constrains his roaring, and contracts his paws; 450
Till at the last, his time for fury found,
He shoots with sudden vengeance from the ground;
The prostrate vulgar passes o'er and spares,
But with a lordly rage his hunters tears.
Your case no tame expedients will afford: 455
Resolve on death, or conquest by the sword,
Which for no less a stake than life you draw;
And self-defense is nature's eldest law.
Leave the warm people no considering time,
For then rebellion may be thought a crime. 460
Prevail yourself of what occasion gives,
But try your title while your father lives.

And that your arms may have a fair pretense,
Proclaim you take them in the King's defense,
465 Whose sacred life each minute would expose
To plots, from seeming friends, and secret foes.
And who can sound the depth of David's soul?
Perhaps his fear his kindness may control.
He fears his brother, though he loves his son,
470 For plighted vows too late to be undone.
If so, by force he wishes to be gained,
Like women's lechery, to seem constrained.
Doubt not, but, when he most affects the frown,
Commit a pleasing rape upon the crown.
475 Secure his person to secure your cause:
They who possess the Prince, possess the laws."

He said, and this advice above the rest,
With Absalom's mild nature suited best:
Unblamed of life (ambition set aside,)
480 Not stained with cruelty, nor puffed with pride;
How happy had he been, if destiny
Had higher placed his birth, or not so high!
His kingly virtues might have claimed a throne,
And blest all other countries but his own,
485 But charming greatness since so few refuse,
'T is juster to lament him than accuse.
Strong were his hopes a rival to remove,
With blandishments to gain the public love;
To head the faction while their zeal was hot,
490 And popularly prosecute the Plot.
To farther this, Achitophel unites
The malcontents of all the Israelites;
Whose differing parties he could wisely join,
For several ends, to serve the same design.
495 The best (and of the Princes some were such,)
Who thought the power of monarchy too much;
Mistaken men, and patriots in their hearts,
Not wicked, but seduced by impious arts.
By these the springs of property were bent,
500 And wound so high, they cracked the government.
The next for interest sought t' embroil the State,
To sell their duty at a dearer rate;

And make their Jewish markets of the throne,
Pretending public good, to serve their own.
Others thought Kings an useless heavy load,   505
Who cost too much, and did too little good.
These were for laying honest David by,
On principles of pure good husbandry.
With them joined all th' haranguers of the throng,
That thought to get preferment by the tongue.   510
Who follow next, a double danger bring,
Not only hating David, but the King.
The Solymæan rout, well-versed of old
In godly faction, and in treason bold;
Cowering and quaking at a conqueror's sword;   515
But lofty to a lawful Prince restored;
Saw with disdain an Ethnic plot° begun,
And scorned by Jebusites to be outdone.
Hot Levites headed these; who, pulled before
From th' ark,° which in the Judges' days they bore,   520
Resumed their cant, and with a zealous cry
Pursued their old beloved Theocracy:
Where Sanhedrin and priest enslaved the nation,
And justified their spoils by inspiration.
For who so fit for reign as Aaron's race,   525
If once dominion they could found in grace.
These led the pack, though not of surest scent,
Yet deepest mouthed against the government.
A numerous host of dreaming saints succeed,
Of the true old enthusiastic breed.   530
'Gainst form and order they their power employ,
Nothing to build, and all things to destroy.
But far more numerous was the herd of such
Who think too little, and who talk too much.
These, out of mere instinct, they knew not why,   535
Adored their fathers' God and property;
And, by the same blind benefit of fate,
The Devil and the Jebusite did hate:
Born to be saved, even in their own despite,

517 **Ethnic plot** Popish plot (as by the Gentiles)   519–20 **Levites ...
ark** the dissenting ministers deprived of their benefices by the Act of
Uniformity, 1662

540 Because they could not help believing right.
    Such were the tools; but a whole Hydra more
    Remains, of sprouting heads too long to score.
    Some of their chiefs were Princes of the land:
    In the first rank of these did Zimri stand,
545 A man so various, that he seemed to be
    Not one, but all mankind's epitome:
    Stiff in opinions, always in the wrong;
    Was everything by starts, and nothing long;
    But, in the course of one revolving moon,
550 Was chymist, fiddler, statesman, and buffoon:
    Then all for women, painting, rhyming, drinking,
    Besides ten thousand freaks that died in thinking.
    Blest madman, who could every hour employ,
    With something new to wish, or to enjoy!
555 Railing and praising were his usual themes;
    And both (to show his judgment) in extremes:
    So over-violent, or over-civil,
    That every man, with him, was God or Devil.
    In squandering wealth was his peculiar art:
560 Nothing went unrewarded but desert.
    Beggared by fools, whom still he found too late,
    He had his jest, and they had his estate.
    He laughed himself from court, then sought relief
    By forming parties, but could ne'er be chief;
565 For, spite of him, the weight of business fell
    On Absalom and wise Achitophel:
    Thus, wicked but in will, of means bereft,
    He left not faction, but of that was left.
      Titles and names 't were tedious to rehearse
570 Of lords, below the dignity of verse.
    Wits, warriors, Commonwealth's-men, were the best;
    Kind husbands, and mere nobles, all the rest.
    And therefore, in the name of dulness, be
    The well-hung Balaam° and cold Caleb° free;
575 And canting Nadab° let oblivion damn,
    Who made new porridge for the paschal lamb.
    Let friendship's holy band some names assure;

574 **Balaam** Theophilus Hastings, Earl of Huntingdon   574 **Caleb**
Lord Grey   575 **Nadab** William, Lord Howard of Esdrick

Some their own worth, and some let scorn secure.
Nor shall the rascal rabble here have place,
Whom Kings no titles gave, and God no grace;   580
Not bull-faced Jonas,° who could statutes draw
To mean rebellion, and make treason law.
But he, though bad, is followed by a worse,
The wretch who Heav'n's anointed dared to curse.
Shimei,° whose youth did early promise bring   585
Of zeal to God, and hatred to his King,
Did wisely from expensive sins refrain,
And never broke the Sabbath, but for gain;
Nor ever was he known an oath to vent,
Or curse, unless against the government.   590
Thus heaping wealth, by the most ready way
Among the Jews, which was to cheat and pray,
The city, to reward his pious hate
Against his master, chose him magistrate.
His hand a vare° of justice did uphold;   595
His neck was loaded with a chain of gold.
During his office treason was no crime.
The sons of Belial° had a glorious time,
For Shimei, though not prodigal of pelf,
Yet loved his wicked neighbor as himself.   600
When two or three were gathered to declaim ⎫
Against the Monarch of Jerusalem,   ⎬
Shimei was always in the midst of them;   ⎭
And if they cursed the King when he was by,
Would rather curse than break good company.   605
If any durst his factious friends accuse,
He packed a jury of dissenting Jews;
Whose fellow-feeling in the godly cause
Would free the suffering saint from human laws.
For laws are only made to punish those   610
Who serve the King, and to protect his foes.
If any leisure time he had from power
(Because 't is sin to misemploy an hour,)
His business was, by writing, to persuade

581 **Jonas** Sir William Jones, who conducted the prosecution of those
concerned in the Popish Plot   585 **Shimei** Whig sheriff of London
595 **vare** staff of authority   598 **Belial** the Devil

615 That Kings were useless, and a clog to trade;
And, that his noble style he might refine,
No Rechabite° more shunned the fumes of wine.
Chaste were his cellars, and his shrieval° board
The grossness of a city feast abhorred.

620 His cooks, with long disuse, their trade forgot;
Cool was his kitchen, though his brains were hot.
Such frugal virtue malice may accuse,
But sure 't was necessary to the Jews;
For towns once burnt such magistrates require

625 As dare not tempt God's providence by fire.
With spiritual food he fed his servants well,
But free from flesh that made the Jews rebel;
And Moses' laws he held in more account,
For forty days of fasting in the mount.

630   To speak the rest, who better are forgot,
Would tire a well-breathed witness of the Plot.
Yet, Corah,° thou shalt from oblivion pass:
Erect thyself thou monumental brass,
High as the serpent of thy metal made,

635 While nations stand secure beneath thy shade.
What though his birth were base, yet comets rise
From earthy vapors ere they shine in skies.
Prodigious actions may as well be done
By weaver's issue, as by Prince's son.

640 This arch-attestor for the public good
By that one deed ennobles all his blood.
Who ever asked the witnesses' high race,
Whose oath with martyrdom did Stephen grace?
Ours was a Levite, and as times went then,

645 His tribe were God Almighty's gentlemen.
Sunk were his eyes, his voice was harsh and loud,
Sure signs he neither choleric was nor proud.
His long chin proved his wit; his saintlike grace
A church vermilion, and a Moses' face;

650 His memory, miraculously great,
Could plots, exceeding man's belief, repeat;

617 **Rechabites** sons of Rechab, faithful observers of the Lord's law
618 **shrieval** pertaining to the sheriff   632 **Corah** Titus Oates, the
instigator of the Popish Plot

Which therefore cannot be accounted lies,
For human wit could never such devise.
Some future truths are mingled in his book;
But where the witness failed, the prophet spoke: *655*
Some things like visionary flights appear;
The spirit caught him up, the Lord knows where,
And gave him his rabbinical degree,
Unknown to foreign university.
His judgment yet his memory did excel,   *660*
Which pieced his wondrous evidence so well,
And suited to the temper of the times,
Then groaning under Jebusitic crimes.
Let Israel's foes suspect his heav'nly call,
And rashly judge his writ apocryphal;   *665*
Our laws for such affronts have forfeits made:
He takes his life, who takes away his trade.
Were I myself in witness Corah's place,
The wretch who did me such a dire disgrace,
Should whet my memory, though once forgot,   *670*
To make him an appendix of my plot.
His zeal to Heav'n made him his Prince despise,
And load his person with indignities;
But zeal peculiar privilege affords,
Indulging latitude to deeds and words.   *675*
And Corah might for Agag's murther° call,
In terms as coarse as Samuel used to Saul.°
What others in his evidence did join
(The best that could be had for love or coin,)
In Corah's own predicament will fall;   *680*
For *witness* is a common name to all.

Surrounded thus with friends of every sort,
Deluded Absalom forsakes the court;
Impatient of high hopes, urged with renown,
And fired with near possession of a crown.   *685*
Th' admiring crowd are dazzled with surprise,
And on his goodly person feed their eyes.

---

676 **Agag's murther** Sir Edmundbury Godfrey, before whom as magistrate Oates had made his deposition, was found murdered. In I SAMUEL, 15, God rejected Agag for the Kingship of Israel   677 **Samuel . . . Saul** Samuel denounced Saul for not killing Agag

His joy concealed, he sets himself to show,
On each side bowing popularly low;
690 His looks, his gestures, and his words he frames,
And with familiar ease repeats their names.
Thus formed by nature, furnished out with arts,
He glides unfelt into their secret hearts.
Then, with a kind compassionating look,
695 And sighs, bespeaking pity ere he spoke,
Few words he said, but easy those and fit,
More slow than Hybla-drops,° and far more sweet.
    "I mourn, my countrymen, your lost estate,
Though far unable to prevent your fate:
700 Behold a banished man, for your dear cause
Exposed a prey to arbitrary laws!
Yet O! that I alone could be undone,
Cut off from empire, and no more a son!
Now all your liberties a spoil are made; ⎫
705 Egypt and Tyrus intercept your trade, ⎬
And Jebusites your sacred rites invade. ⎭
My father, whom with reverence yet I name,
Charmed into ease, is careless of his fame;
And, bribed with petty sums of foreign gold,
710 Is grown in Bathsheba's embraces old;
Exalts his enemies, his friends destroys,
And all his power against himself employs.
He gives, and let him give, my right away;
But why should he his own and yours betray?
715 He, only he, can make the nation bleed,
And he alone from my revenge is freed.
Take then my tears, (with that he wiped his eyes,)
'T is all the aid my present power supplies:
No court-informer can these arms accuse;
720 These arms may sons against their fathers use:
And 't is my wish, the next successor's reign
May make no other Israelite complain."
    Youth, beauty, graceful action seldom fail
But common interest always will prevail;
725 And pity never ceases to be shown
To him who makes the people's wrongs his own.

697 **Hybla-drops** honey from Hybla in Sicily

The crowd, that still believe their Kings oppress,
With lifted hands their young Messiah bless,
Who now begins his progress to ordain
With chariots, horsemen, and a numerous train;   730
From east to west his glories he displays,
And, like the sun, the promised land surveys.
Fame runs before him as the morning star,
And shouts of joy salute him from afar;
Each house receives him as a guardian god,   735
And consecrates the place of his abode,
But hospitable treats did most commend
Wise Issachar,° his wealthy western friend.
This moving court, that caught the people's eyes,
And seemed but pomp, did other ends disguise: 740
Achitophel had formed it, with intent
To sound the depths, and fathom, where it went,
The people's hearts; distinguish friends from foes,
And try their strength, before they came to blows.
Yet all was colored with a smooth pretense   745
Of specious love, and duty to their Prince.
Religion, and redress of grievances,
Two names that always cheat and always please,
Are often urged; and good King David's life
Endangered by a brother and a wife.°   750
Thus in a pageant show a plot is made,
And peace itself is war in masquerade.
O foolish Israel! never warned by ill!
Still the same bait, and circumvented still!
Did ever men forsake their present ease,   755
In midst of health imagine a disease;
Take pains contingent mischiefs to foresee,
Make heirs for monarchs, and for God decree?
What shall we think! Can people give away,
Both for themselves and sons, their native sway?   760
Then they are left defenseless to the sword
Of each unbounded, arbitrary lord:
And laws are vain, by which we right enjoy,

---

738 Issachar Thomas Thynne, supporter of Monmouth   **750 brother
... wife** the Duke of York and the Queen were both accused of par-
ticipating in the Popish Plot

If Kings unquestioned can those laws destroy.
765 Yet if the crowd be judge of fit and just,
And Kings are only officers in trust,
Then this resuming covenant was declared
When Kings were made, or is for ever barred.
If those who gave the scepter could not tie
770 By their own deed their own posterity,
How then could Adam bind his future race?
How could his forfeit on mankind take place?
Or how could Heavenly justice damn us all,
Who ne'er consented to our father's fall?
775 Then Kings are slaves to those whom they command,
And tenants to their people's pleasure stand.
Add, that the power for property allowed
Is mischievously seated in the crowd;
For who can be secure of private right,
780 If sovereign sway may be dissolved by might?
Nor is the people's judgment always true:
The most may err as grossly as the few;
And faultless Kings run down, by common cry,
For vice, oppression, and for tyranny.
785 What standard is there in a fickle rout,
Which, flowing to the mark, runs faster out?°
Nor only crowds, but Sanhedrins may be
Infected with this public lunacy,
And share the madness of rebellious times,
790 To murther monarchs for imagined crimes.
If they may give and take whene'er they please,
Not Kings alone (the Godhead's images,)
But government itself at length must fall
To nature's state, where all have right to all.
795 Yet, grant our lords the people Kings can make,
What prudent men a settled throne would shake?
For whatsoe'er their sufferings were before,
That change they covet makes them suffer more.
All other errors but disturb a state,
800 But innovation° is the blow of fate.
If ancient fabrics nod, and threat to fall,

786 **flowing . . . out** the higher the tide, the faster the ebb   800 **innovation** revolution

To patch the flaws, and buttress up the wall,
Thus far 't is duty; but here fix the mark:
For all beyond it is to touch our ark.
To change foundations, cast the frame anew,   *805*
Is work for rebels, who base ends pursue,
At once divine and human laws control,
And mend the parts by ruin of the whole.
The tampering world is subject to this curse,
To physic their disease into a worse.   *810*
   Now what relief can righteous David bring?
How fatal 't is to be too good a King!
Friends he has few, so high the madness grows,
Who dare be such, must be the people's foes.
Yet some there were, even in the worst of days;   *815*
Some let me name, and naming is to praise.
   In this short file Barzillai° first appears,
Barzillai, crowned with honor and with years.
Long since, the rising rebels he withstood
In regions waste, beyond the Jordan's flood: *820*
Unfortunately brave to buoy the State;
But sinking underneath his master's fate:
In exile with his godlike Prince he mourned;
For him he suffered, and with him returned.
The court he practiced, not the courtier's art;   *825*
Large was his wealth, but larger was his heart,
Which well the noblest objects knew to choose,
The fighting warrior, and recording Muse.
His bed could once a fruitful issue boast;
Now more than half a father's name is lost.   *830*
His eldest hope,° with every grace adorned,
By me (so Heav'n will have it) always mourned,
And always honored, snatched in manhood's prime
By unequal° fates, and Providence's crime;
Yet not before the goal of honor won,   ⎫   *835*
All parts fulfilled of subject and of son;   ⎬
Swift was the race, but short the time to run. ⎭
O narrow circle, but of power divine,
Scanted in space, but perfect in thy line!

817 **Barzillai** the Duke of Ormond   831 **eldest hope** Thomas, Earl of
Ossory   834 **unequal** unjust

840 By sea, by land, thy matchless worth was known,
Arms thy delight, and war was all thy own.
Thy force, infused, the fainting Tyrians propped;
And haughty Pharaoh found his fortune stopped.
O ancient honor! O unconquered hand,
845 Whom foes unpunished never could withstand!
But Israel was unworthy of thy name;
Short is the date of all immoderate fame.
It looks as Heav'n our ruin had designed,
And durst not trust thy fortune and thy mind.
850 Now, free from earth, thy disencumbered soul
Mounts up, and leaves behind the clouds and starry
       pole:
From thence thy kindred legions mayst thou bring,
To aid the guardian angel of thy King.
Here stop, my Muse, here cease thy painful flight;
855 No pinions can pursue immortal height:
Tell good Barzillai thou canst sing no more,
And tell thy soul she should have fled before.
Or fled she with his life, and left this verse
To hang on her departed patron's hearse?
860 Now take thy steepy flight from Heav'n, and see
If thou canst find on earth another *He:*
Another *He* would be too hard to find;
See then whom thou canst see not far behind.
Zadoc° the priest, whom, shunning power and place,
865 His lowly mind advanced to David's grace.
With him the Sagan of Jerusalem,°
Of hospitable soul, and noble stem;
Him of the western dome,° whose weighty sense
Flows in fit words and heavenly eloquence.
870 The prophets' sons,° by such example led,
To learning and to loyalty were bred:
For colleges on bounteous Kings depend,
And never rebel was to arts a friend.
To these succeed the pillars of the laws;

864 **Zadoc** William Sancroft, Archbishop of Canterbury   866 **Sagan
of Jerusalem** Henry Compton, Bishop of London (the *sagan* being a
priest of high rank)   868 **Him . . . dome** John Dolben, Dean of
Westminster   870 **prophets' sons** the pupils of Westminster School

Who best could plead, and best can judge a cause.   875
Next them a train of loyal peers ascend:
Sharp-judging Adriel,° the Muses' friend;
Himself a Muse—in Sanhedrin's debate
True to his Prince, but not a slave of state:
Whom David's love with honors did adorn   880
That from his disobedient son were torn.
Jotham° of piercing wit, and pregnant thought;
Endued by nature, and by learning taught
To move assemblies, who but only tried
The worse a while, then chose the better side: 885
Nor chose alone, but turned the balance too;
So much the weight of one brave man can do.
Hushai,° the friend of David in distress;
In public storms, of manly steadfastness:
By foreign treaties he informed his youth,   890
And joined experience to his native truth.
His frugal care supplied the wanting throne;
Frugal for that, but bounteous of his own:
'T is easy conduct when exchequers flow,
But hard the task to manage well the low;   895
For sovereign power is too depressed or high,
When Kings are forced to sell, or crowds to buy.
Indulge one labor more, my weary Muse,
For Amiel:° who can Amiel's praise refuse?
Of ancient race by birth, but nobler yet   900
In his own worth, and without title great:
The Sanhedrin long time as chief he ruled,
Their reason guided, and their passion cooled.
So dexterous was he in the crown's defense,
So formed to speak a loyal nation's sense,   905
That, as their band was Israel's tribes in small,
So fit was he to represent them all.
Now rasher charioteers the seat ascend,
Whose loose careers his steady skill commend;
They, like th' unequal ruler of the day,°   910

877 **Adriel** John Sheffield, Earl of Mulgrave   882 **Jotham** George
Savile, Viscount Halifax   888 **Hushai** Laurence Hyde, son of the
Earl of Clarendon   899 **Amiel** Edward Seymour   910 **unequal . . .
day** Phaethon, son of Apollo, who mismanaged the chariot of the sun

Misguide the seasons, and mistake the way;
While he withdrawn at their mad labor smiles,
And safe enjoys the sabbath of his toils.
    These were the chief, a small but faithful band ⎞
915 Of worthies, in the breach who dared to stand, ⎬
And tempt th' united fury of the land. ⎠
With grief they viewed such powerful engines bent,
To batter down the lawful government.
A numerous faction, with pretended frights,
920 In Sanhedrins to plume° the regal rights.
The true successor from the court removed;
The Plot, by hireling witnesses, improved.
These ills they saw, and, as their duty bound,
They showed the King the danger of the wound;
925 That no concessions from the throne would please,
But lenitives° fomented the disease;
That Absalom, ambitious of the crown,
Was made the lure to draw the people down;
That false Achitophel's pernicious hate
930 Had turned the Plot to ruin Church and State;
The council violent, the rabble worse;
That Shimei taught Jerusalem to curse.
    With all these loads of injuries oppressed,
And long revolving in his careful breast
935 Th' event of things, at last, his patience tired,
Thus from his royal throne, by Heav'n inspired,
The godlike David spoke: with awful fear
His train their Maker in their master hear:
    "Thus long have I, by native mercy swayed,
940 My wrongs dissembled, my revenge delayed:
So willing to forgive th' offending age;
So much the father did the king assuage.
But now so far my clemency they slight,
Th' offenders question my forgiving right.
945 That one was made for many, they contend;
But 't is to rule, for that's a monarch's end.
They call my tenderness of blood, my fear;
Though manly tempers can the longest bear.
Yet, since they will divert my native course,

920 **plume** pluck, despoil   926 **lenitives** soothing drugs

'T is time to show I am not good by force.   *950*
Those heaped affronts that haughty subjects bring,
Are burthens for a camel, not a King.
Kings are the public pillars of the State,
Born to sustain and prop the nation's weight;
If my young Samson will pretend a call   *955*
To shake the column, let him share the fall:
But O that yet he would repent and live!
How easy 't is for parents to forgive!
With how few tears a pardon might be won
From nature, pleading for a darling son!   *960*
Poor pitied youth, by my paternal care
Raised up to all the height his frame could bear!
Had God ordained his fate for empire born,
He would have given his soul another turn:
Gulled with a patriot's name, whose modern sense   *965*
Is one that would by law supplant his Prince;
The people's brave, the politician's tool;
Never was patriot yet, but was a fool.
Whence comes it that religion and the laws
Should more be Absalom's than David's cause?   *970*
His old instructor, ere he lost his place,
Was never thought endued with so much grace.
Good heav'ns, how faction can a patriot paint!
My rebel ever proves my people's saint.
Would *they* impose an heir upon the throne?   *975*
Let Sanhedrins be taught to give their own.
A King's at least a part of government,
And mine as requisite as their consent.
Without my leave a future King to choose,
Infers a right the present to depose.   *980*
True, they petition me t' approve their choice;
But Esau's hands suit ill with Jacob's voice.
My pious subjects for my safety pray,
Which to secure, they take my power away.
From plots and treasons Heav'n preserve my years,   *985*
But save me most from my petitioners!
Unsatiate as the barren womb or grave;
God cannot grant so much as they can crave.
What then is left, but with a jealous eye

990   To guard the small remains of royalty?
     The law shall still direct my peaceful sway,
     And the same law teach rebels to obey:
     Votes shall no more established power control—
     Such votes as make a part exceed the whole:
995   No groundless clamors shall my friends remove,
     Nor crowds have power to punish ere they prove;
     For gods and godlike Kings their care express,
     Still to defend their servants in distress.
     O that my power to saving were confined!
1000 Why am I forced, like Heav'n, against my mind, ⎫
     To make examples of another kind?   ⎬
     Must I at length the sword of justice draw? ⎭
     O curst effects of necessary law!
     How ill my fear they by my mercy scan!
1005 Beware the fury of a patient man.
     Law they require, let Law then show her face;
     They could not be content to look on Grace,
     Her hinder parts,° but with a daring eye
     To tempt the terror of her front, and die.
1010 By their own arts, 't is righteously decreed,
     Those dire artificers of death shall bleed.
     Against themselves their witnesses will swear,
     Till viper-like their mother Plot they tear;
     And suck for nutriment that bloody gore,
1015 Which was their principle of life before.
     Their Belial with their Belzebub will fight;
     Thus on my foes, my foes shall do me right.
     Nor doubt th' event, for factious crowds engage,
     In their first onset, all their brutal rage.
1020 Then let 'em take an unresisted course;
     Retire, and traverse, and delude their force;
     But, when they stand all breathless, urge the fight,
     And rise upon 'em with redoubled might;
     For lawful power is still superior found;
     When long driven back, at length it stands the
1025   ground."
       He said. Th' Almighty, nodding, gave consent;

1007–8 **Grace . . . parts** God (Grace) permitted Moses to look only on
his hinder parts

And peals of thunder shook the firmament.
Henceforth a series of new time began,
The mighty years in long procession ran:
Once more the godlike David was restored,   *1030*
And willing nations knew their lawful lord.

From the second part of
Absalom and Achitophel°

Next these, a troop of busy spirits press,
Of little fortunes, and of conscience less;
With them the tribe, whose luxury had drained
Their banks, in former sequestrations gained;
5 Who rich and great by past rebellions grew,
And long to fish the troubled streams anew.
Some future hopes, some present payment draws,
To sell their conscience and espouse the cause.
Such stipends those vile hirelings best befit,
10 Priests without grace, and poets without wit.
Shall that false Hebronite° escape our curse,
Judas, that keeps the rebels' pension-purse;
Judas, that pays the treason-writer's fee,
Judas, that well deserves his namesake's tree;
15 Who at Jerusalem's own gates erects
His college° for a nursery of sects;
Young prophets with an early care secures,
And with the dung of his own arts manures!
What have the men of Hebron here to do?
20 What part in Israel's promised land have you?

° The success of Dryden's application of the story of David, Absolom, and Achitophel to current politics led to the almost immediate continuance of the fable. This second poem was largely the work of Nahum Tate, but Dryden had a part in it and the most famous lines, given here, are his.   11 **false Hebronite** Robert Ferguson, a Scot, known as the arch-plotter of rebellion and assassination; an Independent preacher and a Whig   16 **His college** Ferguson kept a boys' school

Here Phaleg,° the lay Hebronite, is come,
'Cause like the rest he could not live at home;
Who from his own possessions could not drain
An omer° even of Hebronitish grain,
Here struts it like a patriot, and talks high   25
Of injured subjects, altered property;
An emblem of that buzzing insect just,
That mounts the wheel, and thinks she raises dust.
Can dry bones live?° or skeletons produce
The vital warmth of cuckoldizing juice?   30
Slim Phaleg could, and at the table fed,
Returned the grateful product to the bed.
A waiting-man to traveling nobles chose,
He his own laws would saucily impose,
Till bastinadoed back again he went,   35
To learn those manners he to teach was sent.
Chastised, he ought to have retreated home,
But he reads politics to Absalom;
For never Hebronite, tho' kicked and scorned,
To his own country willingly returned.   40
—But leaving famished Phaleg to be fed,
And to talk treason for his daily bread,
Let Hebron, nay, let hell produce a man
So made for mischief as Ben-Jochanan.°
A Jew of humble parentage was he,   45
By trade a Levite, tho' of low degree:
His pride no higher than the desk aspired,
But for the drudgery of priests was hired
To read and pray in linen ephod brave,
And pick up single shekels from the grave.   50
Married at last, and finding charge come faster,
He could not live by God, but changed his master;
Inspired by want, was made a factious tool,
They got a villain, and we lost a fool:
Still violent, whatever cause he took,   55

---

21 **Phaleg** James Forbes, a Scottish dissenting clergyman   24 **omer**
sheaf (Hebrew measure)   29 **Can . . . live** EZEKIEL xxxvii.3.   44 **Ben-
Jochanan** Samuel Johnson, chaplain, and writer upon Julian the
Apostate, arguing against the power of the state in religious matters

But most against the party he forsook;
For renegadoes, who ne'er turn by halves,
Are bound in conscience to be double knaves.
So this prose-prophet took most monstrous pains
60 To let his masters see he earned his gains.
But as the Devil owes all his imps a shame,
He chose th' Apostate° for his proper theme;
With little pains he made the picture true,
And from reflection took the rogue he drew:
65 A wondrous work, to prove the Jewish nation
In every age a murmuring generation;
To trace 'em from their infancy of sinning,
And show 'em factious from their first beginning;
To prove they could rebel, and rail, and mock,
70 Much to the credit of the chosen flock;
A strong authority, which must convince,
That saints own no allegiance to their prince;
As 't is a leading card to make a whore,
To prove her mother had turned up before.
75 But, tell me, did the drunken patriarch° bless
The son° that showed his father's nakedness?
Such thanks the present Church thy pen will give,
Which proves rebellion was so primitive.
Must ancient failings be examples made?
80 Then murtherers from Cain may learn their trade.
As thou the heathen and the saint hast drawn,
Methinks th' Apostate was the better man;
And thy hot father,° (waiving my respect,)
Not of a mother church, but of a sect.
85 And such he needs must be of thy inditing;
This comes of drinking asses' milk and writing.
If Balak° should be called to leave his place,
(As profit is the loudest call of grace,)
His temple dispossessed of one, would be
90 Replenished with seven devils more by thee.
    Levi, thou art a load, I'll lay thee down,

---

62 **th' Apostate** Julian, the Roman Emperor who abjured Christianity
75 **drunken patriarch** Noah   76 **son** Ham discovered his father Noah
drunk and naked   83 **hot father** St. Gregory Nazianzen condemned
Julian, neither to Johnson's satisfaction nor Dryden's   87 **Balak**
Gilbert Burnet, a famous Whig clergyman

And show rebellion bare, without a gown;
Poor slaves in meter, dull and addle-pated,
Who rhyme below even David's psalms translated;
Some in my speedy pace I must outrun,⁣ 95
As lame Mephibosheth the wizard's son;°
To make quick way I'll leap o'er heavy blocks,
Shun rotten Uzza,° as I would the pox;
And hasten Og° and Doeg° to rehearse,
Two fools that crutch their feeble sense on verse; 100
Who, by my Muse, to all succeeding times
Shall live, in spite of their own doggerel rhymes.

   Doeg, though without knowing how or why,
Made still a blundering kind of melody;
Spurred boldly on, and dashed thro' thick and thin, 105
Thro' sense and nonsense, never out nor in;
Free from all meaning, whether good or bad,
And, in one word, heroically mad:
He was too warm on picking-work to dwell ⎫
But fagoted° his notions as they fell,   ⎬ 110
And if they rhymed and rattled, all was well. ⎭
Spiteful he is not, tho' he wrote a satire,
For still there goes some *thinking* to ill-nature:
He needs no more than birds and beasts to think;
All his occasions are to eat and drink. 115
If he call rogue and rascal from a garret,
He means you no more mischief than a parrot;
The words for friend and foe alike were made,
To fetter 'em in verse is all his trade.
For almonds he'll cry whore° to his own mother; 120
And call young Absalom King David's brother.
Let him be gallows-free by my consent,
And nothing suffer, since he nothing meant;
Hanging supposes human soul and reason,
This animal's below committing treason. 125
Shall he be hanged who never could rebel?

96 **Mephibosheth . . . son** Samuel Pordage, son of an astrologer   98
Uzza an uncertain allusion   99 **Og** Thomas Shadwell, the butt of
Mac Flecknoe   99 **Doeg** Elkanah Settle, playwright   110 **fagoted**
wrapped loosely, as with pieces of kindling-wood   120 **almonds . . .
whore** to escape a duel with Otway Settle is said to have confessed
himself the son of a whore

That's a preferment for Achitophel.
The woman that committed buggary.
Was rightly sentenced by the law to die;
130 But 't was hard fate that to the gallows led
The dog that never heard the statute read.
Railing in other men may be a crime,
But ought to pass for mere instinct in him:
Instinct he follows, and no farther knows,
135 For to write verse with him is to *transpose.*°
'T were pity treason at his door to lay,
Who *makes Heaven's gate a lock to its own key:*°
Let him rail on, let his invective Muse
Have four and twenty letters to abuse,
140 Which if he jumbles to one line of sense,
Indict him of a capital offense.
In fireworks give him leave to vent his spite,°
Those are the only serpents he can write;
The height of his ambition is, we know,
145 But to be master of a puppet show:
On that one stage his works may yet appear,
And a month's harvest keeps him all the year.
   Now stop your noses, readers, all and some;)
For here's a tun of midnight work to come,   }
150 Og, from a treason-tavern rolling home.   )
Round as a globe, and liquored every chink,
Goodly and great he sails behind his link.°
With all this bulk there's nothing lost in Og,
For every inch that is not fool is rogue:
155 A monstrous mass of foul corrupted matter,
As all the devils had spewed to make the batter.
When wine has given him courage to blaspheme,
He curses God, but God before cursed him;
And if man could have reason, none has more,
160 That made his paunch so rich, and him so poor.
With wealth he was not trusted, for Heav'n knew
What 't was of old to pamper up a Jew;

135 **transpose** Settle's poem was called *Achitophel Transprosed*   137
Heaven's . . . key quoting Settle's poem   142 **fireworks . . . spite**
Settle had arranged for burning the effigy of the Pope amid fireworks
152 **link** torch

To what would he on quail and pheasant swell,
That even on tripe and carrion could rebel?
But tho' Heav'n made him poor, (with reverence
　　　speaking,)   *165*
He never was a poet of God's making.
The midwife laid her hand on his thick skull,
With this prophetic blessing: *Be thou dull;*
Drink, swear, and roar, forbear no lewd delight
Fit for thy bulk, do anything but write: *170*
Thou art of lasting make, like thoughtless men,
A strong nativity—but for the pen;
Eat opium,° mingle arsenic in thy drink,
Still thou mayst live, avoiding pen and ink.
I see, I see, 't is counsel given in vain,   *175*
For treason botched in rhyme will be thy bane;
Rhyme is the rock on which thou art to wreck,
'T is fatal to thy fame and to thy neck:
Why should thy meter good King David blast?
A psalm of his will surely be thy last.   *180*
Dar'st thou presume in verse to meet thy foes,
Thou whom the penny pamphlet foiled in prose?
Doeg, whom God for mankind's mirth has made,
O'ertops thy talent in thy very trade;
Doeg to thee, thy paintings are so coarse,   *185*
A poet is, tho' he 's the poets' horse.
A double noose thou on thy neck dost pull,
For writing treason, and for writing dull;
To die for faction is a common evil,
But to be hanged for nonsense is the devil.   *190*
Hadst thou the glories of thy king expressed,
Thy praises had been satire at the best;
But thou in clumsy verse, unlicked, unpointed,
Hast shamefully defied the Lord's anointed:
I will not rake the dunghill of thy crimes,   *195*
For who would read thy life that reads thy rhymes?
But of King David's foes, be this the doom,
May all be like the young man Absalom;
And for my foes may this their blessing be,
To talk like Doeg, and to write like thee.   *200*

173 **Eat opium** Shadwell was addicted to the drug

Mac Flecknoe

or, A Satire upon the True-Blue
Protestant Poet, T.S.°

All human things are subject to decay,
And when fate summons, monarchs must obey.
This Flecknoe found, who, like Augustus, young
Was called to empire, and had governed long;
5 In prose and verse, was owned, without dispute,
Through all the realms of *Nonsense,* absolute.
This aged Prince, now flourishing in peace,
And blest with issue of a large increase,
Worn out with business, did at length debate
10 To settle the succession of the State;
And, pondering which of all his sons was fit
To reign, and wage immortal war with wit,
Cried: " 'T is resolved; for nature pleads, that he
Should only rule, who most resembles me.
15 Sh—— alone my perfect image bears,
Mature in dulness from his tender years.
Sh—— alone, of all my sons, is he
Who stands confirmed in full stupidity.
The rest to some faint meaning make pretense,
20 But Sh—— never deviates into sense.
Some beams of wit on other souls may fall,
Strike through, and make a lucid interval;
But Sh——'s genuine night admits no ray,
His rising fogs prevail upon the day.
25 Besides, his goodly fabric fills the eye,

° In mocking the pretensions of two contemporary poets Dryden
exploits as the central device the idea of monarchical succession in
the Kingdom of Dullness. The King who is dying, Richard Flecknoe,
an Irish priest, was in fact no kin to the one Dryden presents as his
son, Thomas Shadwell the playwright. Shadwell was to supersede
Dryden as Poet Laureate.

And seems designed for thoughtless majesty;
Thoughtless as monarch oaks that shade the plain,
And, spread in solemn state, supinely reign.
Heywood° and Shirley° were but types of thee,
Thou last great prophet of tautology.   *30*
Even I, a dunce of more renown than they,
Was sent before but to prepare thy way;
And, coarsely clad in Norwich drugget,° came
To teach the nations in thy greater name.
My warbling lute, the lute I whilom° strung,   *35*
When to King John of Portugal° I sung,
Was but the prelude to that glorious day,
When thou on silver Thames didst cut thy way,
With well-timed oars before the royal barge,
Swelled with the pride of thy celestial charge;   *40*
And big with hymn, commander of a host,
The like was ne'er in Epsom blankets tossed.°
Methinks I see the new Arion° sail,
The lute still trembling underneath thy nail.
At thy well-sharpened thumb from shore to shore   *45*
The treble squeaks for fear, the basses roar;
Echoes from Pissing Alley° Sh—— call,
And Sh—— they resound from Aston Hall.°
About thy boat the little fishes throng,
As at the morning toast that floats along.   *50*
Sometimes, as Prince of thy harmonious band,
Thou wieldest thy papers in thy threshing hand.
St. André's° feet ne'er kept more equal time,
Not even the feet of thy own *Psyche's* rhyme;°
Though they in number as in sense excel: *55*
So just, so like tautology, they fell,

29 **Heywood** Thomas Heywood, voluminous Elizabethan playwright
29 **Shirley** James Shirley, Jacobean playwright   33 **Norwich drugget**
coarse woolen fabric   35 **whilom** formerly   36 **King . . . Portugal**
Flecknoe claimed to have been patronized by the King of Portugal
42 **Epsom . . . tossed** punishment of a character in Shadwell's *Virtuoso*
43 **Arion** ancient Greek musician   47 **Pissing Alley** street near The
Strand   48 **Aston Hall** the meaning of this reference has not been
explained   53 **St. André's** famous dancing master   54 **Psyche's
rhyme** Shadwell's *Psyche* is imitated from Molière's play of the same
name   57 **Singleton** well-known operatic performer who sang the
part of Villerius in Davenant's *Siege of Rhodes*

That, pale with envy, Singleton° forswore
　The lute and sword, which he in triumph bore,
And vowed he ne'er would act Villerius more."
60 Here stopped the good old sire, and wept for joy
In silent raptures of the hopeful boy.
All arguments, but most his plays, persuade,
That for anointed dulness he was made.
　Close to the walls which fair Augusta° bind
65 (The fair Augusta much to fears inclined,)
An ancient fabric raised t' inform the sight,
There stood of yore, and Barbican it hight:
A watchtower once; but now, so fate ordains,
Of all the pile an empty name remains.
70 From its old ruins brothel-houses rise,
Scenes of lewd loves, and of polluted joys;
Where their vast courts the mother-strumpets keep,
And, undisturbed by watch, in silence sleep.
Near these a Nursery° erects its head,
75 Where queens are formed, and future heroes bred;
Where unfledged actors learn to laugh and cry,
Where infant punks their tender voices try,
And little Maximins° the gods defy.
Great Fletcher° never treads in buskins° here,
80 Nor greater Jonson° dares in socks° appear;
But gentle Simkin° just reception finds
Amidst this monument of vanished minds.
Pure clinches° the suburbian Muse affords,
And Panton° waging harmless war with words.
85 Here Flecknoe, as a place to fame well known,
Ambitiously designed his Sh——'s throne;
For ancient Dekker° prophesied long since,
That in this pile° should reign a mighty Prince,
Born for a scourge of wit, and flail of sense;

---

64 **Augusta** London　74 **Nursery** theater sponsored by Charles II for
training of child actors　78 **Maximins** types of ranting hero　79
Fletcher John Fletcher, playwright collaborating with Francis Beaumont　79 **buskins** boots worn by tragic actors　80 **Jonson** Ben
Jonson, comic playwright　80 **socks** comic actor's light shoes　81
Simkin farcical character　83 **clinches** quibbles　84 **Panton** celebrated punster　87 **Dekker** Thomas Dekker, Elizabethan playwright
and pamphlet writer　88 **pile** lofty building

To whom true dulness should some *Psyches* owe,   *90*
But worlds of *Misers*° from his pen should flow;
Humorists and *Hypocrites* it should produce,
Whole *Raymond* families, and tribes of *Bruce*.
   Now Empress Fame had published the renown
Of Sh——'s coronation through the town.   *95*
Roused by report of Fame, the nations meet,
From near Bunhill, and distant Watling Street.
No Persian carpets spread th' imperial way,
But scattered limbs of mangled poets lay;
From dusty shops neglected authors come,   *100*
Martyrs of pies and relics of the bum.°
Much Heywood, Shirley, Ogleby° there lay,
But loads of Sh—— almost choked the way.
Bilked stationers for yeomen stood prepared,
And Herringman° was captain of the guard.   *105*
The hoary Prince in majesty appeared,
High on a throne of his own labors reared.
At his right hand our young Ascanius° sate,
Rome's other hope, and pillar of the State.
His brows thick fogs, instead of glories, grace,   *110*
And lambent dulness played around his face.
As Hannibal° did to the altars come,
Sworn by his sire a mortal foe to Rome;
So Sh—— swore, nor should his vow be vain,
That he till death true dulness would maintain;   *115*
And, in his father's right, and realm's defense,
Ne'er to have peace with wit, nor truce with sense.
The King himself the sacred unction made,
As King by office, and as priest by trade.
In his sinister hand, instead of ball,   *120*
He placed a mighty mug of potent ale;
Love's Kingdom° to his right he did convey,
At once his scepter, and his rule of sway;
Whose righteous lore the Prince had practiced young,
And from whose loins recorded *Psyche* sprung.   *125*

91 **Misers** Shadwell adapted Molière's *L'Avare* as *The Miser*   101
bum backside   102 **Ogleby** John Ogleby, translator and epic poet
105 **Herringman** London publisher   108 **Ascanius** son to Aeneas
112 **Hannibal** Carthaginian general who as a child vowed enmity to
Rome   122 **Love's Kingdom** comedy by Flecknoe

His temples, last, with poppies° were o'er-spread,
That nodding seemed to consecrate his head.
Just at that point of time, if fame not lie,
On his left hand twelve reverend owls did fly.
130 So Romulus, 't is sung, by Tiber's brook,
Presage of sway from twice six vultures took.
Th' admiring throng loud acclamations make,
And omens of his future empire take.
The sire then shook the honors° of his head,
135 And from his brows damps of oblivion shed
Full on the filial dulness: long he stood,
Repelling from his breast the raging god;° ⎫
At length burst out in this prophetic mood: ⎭
    "Heavens bless my son, from Ireland let him reign
140 To far Barbadoes on the western main;
Of his dominion may no end be known,
And greater than his father's be his throne.
Beyond *Love's Kingdom* let him stretch his pen!"
He paused, and all the people cried, "Amen!"
145 Then thus continued he: "My son, advance
Still in new impudence, new ignorance.
Success let others teach, learn thou from me
Pangs without birth, and fruitless industry.
Let *Virtuosos*° in five years be writ;
150 Yet not one thought accuse thy toil of wit.
Let gentle George° in triumph tread the stage,
Make Dorimant betray, and Loveit° rage;
Let Cully,° Cockwood,° Fopling,° charm the pit,
And in their folly show the writer's wit.
155 Yet still thy fools shall stand in thy defense,
And justify their author's want of sense.
Let 'em be all by thy own model made
Of dulness, and desire no foreign aid;
That they to future ages may be known,

126 **poppies** Shadwell used opium   134 **honors** locks   137 **raging god** divine inspiration   149 **Virtuosos** Shadwell's comedy satirizing the Royal Society   151 **gentle George** Sir George Etherege, Restoration comic dramatist   152 **Dorimant . . . Loveit** characters in Etherege's *The Man of Mode*   153 **Cully** character in *The Comical Revenge*   153 **Cockwood** character in *She Would if She Could*   153 **Fopling** titular character of *The Man of Mode*

Not copies drawn, but issue of thy own.   160
Nay, let thy men of wit too be the same,
All full of thee, and differing but in name.
But let no alien S—dl—y° interpose,
To lard with wit thy hungry *Epsom* prose.
And when false flowers of rhetoric thou wouldst cull,   165
Trust nature, do not labor to be dull;
But write thy best, and top; and in each line,
Sir Formal's oratory° will be thine:
Sir Formal, though unsought, attends thy quill,
And does thy northern dedications° fill.   170
Nor let false friends seduce thy mind to fame,
By arrogating Jonson's hostile name.°
Let father Flecknoe fire thy mind with praise,
And uncle Ogleby thy envy raise.
Thou art my blood, where Jonson has no part: 175
What share have we in nature, or in art?
Where did his wit on learning fix a brand,
And rail at arts he did not understand?
Where made he love in Prince Nicander's° vein,
Or swept the dust in *Psyche's* humble strain?   180
Where sold he bargains,° 'whip-stitch, kiss my arse,'
Promised a play and dwindled to a farce?
When did his Muse from Fletcher scenes purloin,
As thou whole Etherege dost transfuse to thine?
But so transfused, as oil on water's flow,   185
His always floats above, thine sinks below.
This is thy province, this thy wondrous way,
New humors to invent for each new play:
This is that boasted bias of thy mind,
By which one way, to dulness, 't is inclined;   190
Which makes thy writings lean on one side still,
And, in all changes, that way bends thy will.
Nor let thy mountain-belly make pretense

163 S—dl—y Sir Charles Sedley, comic playwright charged with con-
tributing to Shadwell's comedy, *Epsom Wells*   168 Sir . . . oratory
inflated speech of a character in *The Virtuoso*   170 northern dedica-
tions Shadwell dedicated several works to the Duke of Newcastle
172 Jonson's . . . name in claiming himself a follower of Jonson,
Shadwell set himself up as an enemy to Dryden   179 Prince Nicander's refers to a character in Shadwell's *Psyche*   181 bargains coarse
answers to simple questions

Of likeness; thine 's a tympany of sense.
195 A tun of man in thy large bulk is writ,
But sure thou 'rt but a kilderkin° of wit.
Like mine, thy gentle numbers feebly creep;
Thy tragic Muse gives smiles, thy comic sleep.
With whate'er gall thou settest thyself to write,
200 Thy inoffensive satires never bite.
In thy felonious heart though venom lies,
It does but touch thy Irish pen,° and dies.
Thy genius calls thee not to purchase fame
In keen iambics, but mild anagram.
205 Leave writing plays and choose for thy command
Some peaceful province in acrostic land.
There thou mayest wings display and altars raise,°
And torture one poor word ten thousand ways.
Or, if thou wouldst thy different talents suit,
210 Set thy own songs, and sing them to thy lute."
    He said: but his last words were scarcely heard;
For Bruce and Longvil° had a trap prepared,
And down they sent the yet declaiming bard.
Sinking he left his drugget° robe behind,
215 Borne upwards by a subterranean wind.
The mantle° fell to the young prophet's part,
With double portion of his father's art.

---

196 **kilderkin** a small cask   202 **Irish pen** Shadwell denied Dryden's
allegation of his Irishness   207 **wings . . . raise** alluding to custom of
arranging lines of verse to represent likenesses, of altars, wings, etc.
212 **Bruce . . . Longvil** characters in *The Virtuoso* who disposed of
another character through a trap door   214 **drugget** see note on line
33   216 **mantle** cloak symbolizing inheritance

Religio Laici
or, A Layman's Faith

Dim as the borrowed beams of moon and stars
To lonely, weary, wandering travelers,
Is Reason to the Soul; and as on high
Those rolling fires discover but the sky,
Not light us here, so Reason's glimmering ray)   5
Was lent, not to assure our doubtful way,
But guide us upward to a better day.
And as those nightly tapers disappear,
When day's bright lord ascends our hemisphere;
So pale grows Reason at Religion's sight;   10
So dies, and so dissolves in supernatural light.
Some few, whose lamp shone brighter, have been led
From cause to cause, to Nature's secret head;
And found that one first principle must be:
But what, or who, that UNIVERSAL HE;   15
Whether some Soul encompassing this ball,
Unmade, unmoved; yet making, moving all;
Or various atoms' interfering dance
Leapt into form (the noble work of chance;)
Or this great all was from eternity;   20
Not even the Stagirite° himself could see,
And Epicurus° guessed as well as he:
As blindly groped they for a future state;
As rashly judged of Providence and fate:
But least of all could their endeavors find   25
What most concerned the good of humankind;
For happiness was never to be found,
But vanished from 'em like enchanted ground.
One thought Content the good to be enjoyed;
This every little accident destroyed: 30

21 **Stagirite** Aristotle   22 **Epicurus** philosopher for whom pleasure
was the highest good

The wiser madmen did for Virtue toil,
A thorny, or at best a barren soil;
In Pleasure some their glutton souls would steep, ⎫
But found their line too short, the well too deep, ⎬
35 And leaky vessels which no bliss could keep. ⎭
Thus, anxious thoughts in endless circles roll,
Without a center where to fix the Soul;
In this wild maze their vain endeavors end:
How can the less the greater comprehend?
40 Or finite Reason reach Infinity?
For what could fathom GOD were more than He.
    The Deist thinks he stands on firmer ground;
Cries: "Εὕρεκα, the mighty secret's found:
God is that spring of good; supreme and best;
45 We, made to serve, and in that service blest."
If so, some rules of worship must be given,
Distributed alike to all by Heaven:
Else God were partial, and to some denied
The means his justice should for all provide.
50 This general worship is to PRAISE and PRAY,
One part to borrow blessings, one to pay;
And when frail Nature slides into offense,
The sacrifice for crimes is penitence.
Yet, since th' effects of Providence, we find,
55 Are variously dispensed to humankind;
That vice triumphs, and virtue suffers here,
(A brand that Sovereign Justice cannot bear;)
Our reason prompts us to a future state,
The last appeal from fortune and from fate:
60 Where God's all-righteous ways will be declared,
The bad meet punishment, the good, reward.
    Thus man by his own strength to Heaven would
        soar,
And would not be obliged to God for more.
Vain, wretched creature, how art thou misled
65 To think thy wit these godlike notions bred!
These truths are not the product of thy mind,
But dropped from Heaven, and of a nobler kind.
Revealed Religion first informed thy sight,
And Reason saw not, till Faith sprung the light.

Hence all thy natural worship takes the source: *70*
'T is Revelation what thou think'st Discourse.
Else, how comest thou to see these truths so clear,
Which so obscure to heathens did appear?
Not Plato these, nor Aristotle found;
Nor he whose wisdom oracles renowned.°   *75*
Hast thou a wit so deep, or so sublime,
Or canst thou lower dive, or higher climb?
Canst thou, by Reason, more of Godhead know
Than Plutarch, Seneca, or Cicero?
Those giant wits, in happier ages born   *80*
(When arms and arts did Greece and Rome adorn,)
Knew no such system; no such piles could raise
Of natural worship, built on prayer and praise,
To One sole GOD:
Nor did remorse to expiate sin prescribe,   *85*
But slew their fellow creatures for a bribe.
The guiltless victim groaned for their offense,
And cruelty and blood was penitence.
If sheep and oxen could atone for men,
Ah! at how cheap a rate the rich might sin!   *90*
And great oppressors might Heaven's wrath beguile,
By offering his own creatures for a spoil!
    Darest thou, poor worm, offend Infinity?
And must the terms of peace be given by thee?
Then thou art Justice in the last appeal: *95*
Thy easy God instructs thee to rebel,
And, like a King remote, and weak, must take
What satisfaction thou art pleased to make.
    But if there be a Power too just and strong
To wink at crimes, and bear unpunished wrong,   *100*
Look humbly upward, see his will disclose
The forfeit first, and then the fine impose:
A mulct thy poverty could never pay,
Had not eternal wisdom found the way,
And with celestial wealth supplied thy store,   *105*
His justice makes the fine, his Mercy quits the score.
See God descending in thy human frame;
Th' offended suffering in th' offender's name;

75 he . . . renowned Socrates

All thy misdeeds to him imputed see,
110 And all his righteousness devolved on thee.
     For granting we have sinned, and that th' offense
Of man is made against Omnipotence,
Some price that bears proportion must be paid,
And infinite with infinite be weighed.
115 See then the Deist lost: remorse for vice,
Not paid; or paid, inadequate in price:
What farther means can Reason now direct,
Or what relief from human wit expect?
That shows us sick; and sadly are we sure
120 Still to be sick, till Heav'n reveal the cure.
If then Heav'n's will must needs be understood
(Which must, if we want cure, and Heaven be good,)
Let all records of will revealed be shown;
With scripture all in equal balance thrown, }
125 And our one Sacred Book will be that one.)
     Proof needs not here, for whether we compare
That impious, idle, superstitious ware
Of rites, lustrations, offerings (which before,
In various ages, various countries bore,)
130 With Christian faith and virtues, we shall find
None answering the great ends of humankind,
But this one rule of life, that shows us best
How God may be appeased, and mortals blest.
Whether from length of time its worth we draw,
135 The world is scarce more ancient than the Law,
Heav'n's early care prescribed for every age;
First, in the soul, and after, in the page.
Or, whether more abstractedly we look,
Or on the writers, or the written book,
140 Whence, but from Heav'n, could men unskilled in arts,
In several ages born, in several parts,
Weave such agreeing truths? or how, or why,
Should *all* conspire to cheat us with a lie?
Unasked their pains, ungrateful their advice,
145 Starving their gain, and martydom their price.
     If on the Book itself we cast our view,
Concurrent heathens prove the story true;
The doctrine, miracles; which must convince,

For Heav'n in them appeals to human sense:
And though they prove not, they confirm the cause, 150
When what is taught agrees with Nature's Laws.
    Then for the style: majestic and divine,
It speaks no less than God in every line:
Commanding words; whose force is still the same
As the first fiat that produced our frame. 155
All faiths beside or did by arms ascend,
Or sense indulged has made mankind their friend:
This only doctrine does our lusts oppose,
Unfed by Nature's soil, in which it grows;
Cross to our interests, curbing sense and sin; 160
Oppressed without, and undermined within,
It thrives through pain; its own tormentors tires;
And with a stubborn patience still aspires.
To what can Reason such effects assign,
Transcending Nature, but to laws divine? 165
Which in that Sacred Volume are contained;
Sufficient, clear, and for that use ordained.
    But stay: the Deist here will urge anew,
No supernatural worship can be true
Because a general law is that alone 170
Which must to all, and everywhere, be known:
A style so large as not this Book can claim,
Nor aught that bears revealed Religion's name.
'T is said the sound of a Messiah's birth
Is gone through all the habitable earth; 175
But still that text must be confined alone
To what was then inhabited, and known:
And what provision could from thence accrue
To Indian souls, and worlds discovered new?
In other parts it helps, that, ages past, 180
The Scriptures there were known, and were embraced,
Till Sin spread once again the shades of night:
What's that to these who never saw the light?
    Of all objections this indeed is chief
To startle Reason, stagger frail Belief. 185
We grant, 't is true, that Heav'n from human sense
Has hid the secret paths of Providence;
But boundless wisdom, boundless mercy, may

Find even for those bewildered souls a way:
190 If from his Nature foes may pity claim,
    Much more may strangers who ne'er heard his Name.
    And though no name be for salvation known,
    But that of his eternal Son's alone,
    Who knows how far transcending goodness can
195 Extend the merits of that Son to man?
    Who knows what reasons may his mercy lead,
    Or ignorance invincible may plead?
    Not only charity bids hope the best,
    But more the great apostle has expressed:
200 That if the Gentiles (whom no Law inspired)
    By Nature did what was by Law required;
    They, who the written rule had never known,
    Were to themselves both rule and law alone;
    To Nature's plain indictment they shall plead,
205 And by their conscience be condemned or freed.
    Most righteous doom! because a rule revealed
    Is none to those from whom it was concealed.
    Then those who followed Reason's dictates right,
    Lived up, and lifted high their natural light;
210 With Socrates may see their Maker's face,
    While thousand rubric-martyrs° want a place.
        Nor does it balk my charity, to find
    Th' Egyptian bishop° of another mind:
    For though his creed eternal truth contains,
215 'T is hard for man to doom to endless pains
    All who believed not all his zeal required,
    Unless he first could prove he was inspired.
    Then let us either think he meant to say
    This Faith, where published, was the only way;
220 Or else conclude that, Arius° to confute,
    The good old man, too eager in dispute,
    Flew high; and, as his Christian fury rose,
    Damned all for heretics who durst oppose.

---

211 **rubric-martyrs** saints listed in the calendar   213 **Egyptian bishop**
Athanasius of Alexandria, orthodox interpreter of the doctrine of
the Trinity   220 **Arius** founder of an heretical doctrine concerning
the Trinity

Thus far my Charity this path° has tried,
(A much unskilful, but well-meaning guide:)   225
Yet what they are, even these crude thoughts were
    bred
By reading that, which better thou hast read:
Thy matchless author's work: which thou,° my friend,
By well translating better dost commend.
Those youthful hours which of thy equals most   230
In toys have squandered, or in vice have lost,
Those hours hast thou to nobler use employed;
And the severe delights of Truth enjoyed.
Witness this weighty book, in which appears
The crabbed toil of many thoughtful years,   235
Spent by thy author in the sifting care
Of Rabbins' old sophisticated ware
From gold divine; which he who well can sort
May afterwards make algebra a sport:
A treasure, which if country curates buy,   240
They Junius and Tremellius° may defy;
Save pains in various readings and translations,
And without Hebrew make most learned quotations:
A work so full with various learning fraught,
So nicely pondered, yet so strongly wrought,   245
As Nature's height and Art's last hand required;
As much as man could compass, uninspired.
Where we may see what errors have been made
Both in the copier's and translator's trade;
How Jewish, Popish interests have prevailed,   250
And where infallibility has failed.
    For some, who have his secret meaning guessed,
Have found our author not too much a priest:
For fashion's sake he seems to have recourse
To Pope, and councils, and tradition's force;   255
But he that old traditions could subdue,
Could not but find the weakness of the new:
If Scripture, though derived from heav'nly birth,

---

224 **this path** "Digression to the translation of Father Simon's Critical
History of the Old Testament"   228 **thou** Henry Dickinson, the
translator of Simon's work   241 **Junius . . . Tremellius** sixteenth-
century Calvinist translators of Scripture

Has been but carelessly preserved on earth;
260 If God's own people, who of God before
Knew what we know, and had been promised more,
In fuller terms, of Heav'n's assisting care,
And who did neither time nor study spare
To keep this Book untainted, unperplexed,
265 Let in gross errors to corrupt the text,
Omitted paragraphs, embroiled the sense,
With vain traditions stopped the gaping fence,
Which every common hand pulled up with ease;
What safety from such brushwood-helps as these?
270 If written words from time are not secured,
How can we think have oral sounds endured?
Which thus transmitted, if one mouth has failed,
Immortal lies on ages are entailed;
And that some such have been, is proved too plain;
275 If we consider interest, Church, and gain.
    "O, but," says one, "tradition set aside,
Where can we hope for an unerring guide?
For since th' original Scripture has been lost,
All copies disagreeing, maimed the most,
280 Or Christian faith can have no certain ground,
Or truth in Church tradition must be found."
    Such an omniscient Church we wish indeed;
'T were worth both Testaments; and cast in the Creed:
But if this mother be a guide so sure,
285 As can all doubts resolve, all truth secure,
Then her infallibility as well
Where copies are corrupt or lame can tell;
Restore lost canon with as little pains,
As truly explicate what still remains;
290 Which yet no council dare pretend to do, ⎫
Unless like Esdras° they could write it new: ⎬
Strange confidence, still to interpret true, ⎭
Yet not be sure that all they have explained,
Is in the blest original contained.
295 More safe, and much more modest 't is, to say
God would not leave mankind without a way;

291 **Esdras** God commanded Ezra to make public what had been
revealed to him (II ESDRAS, 14)

And that the Scriptures though not everywhere
Free from corruption, or entire, or clear,
Are uncorrupt, sufficient, clear, entire,
In all things which our needful faith require.   *300*
If others in the same glass better see,
'T is for themselves they look, but not for me:
For MY salvation must its doom receive,
Not from what OTHERS but what *I* believe.

    Must all tradition then be set aside?°   *305*
This to affirm were ignorance or pride.
Are there not many points, some needful sure
To saving faith, that Scripture leaves obscure?
Which every sect will wrest a several way
(For what one sect interprets, all sects may):   *310*
We hold, and say we prove from Scripture plain, ⎫
That Christ is GOD; the bold Socinian°   ⎬
From the same Scripture urges he 's but MAN. ⎭
Now what appeal can end th' important suit;
Both parts talk loudly, but the Rule is mute?   *315*

    Shall I speak plain, and in a nation free
Assume an honest layman's liberty?
I think (according to my little skill,
To my own Mother Church submitting still)
That many have been saved and many may,   *320*
Who never heard this question brought in play.
Th' unlettered Christian, who believes in gross,°
Plods on to Heaven, and ne'er is at a loss;
For the strait gate would be made straiter yet,
Were none admitted there but men of wit.   *325*
The few by Nature formed, with learning fraught,
Born to instruct, as others to be taught,
Must study well the sacred page, and see
Which doctrine, this, or that, does best agree
With the whole tenor of the work divine,   *330*
And plainliest points to Heav'n's revealed design;
Which exposition flows from genuine sense,
And which is forced by wit and eloquence.

---

305 **tradition . . . aside** "Objection in behalf of tradition urged by
Father Simon" (Dryden's note)   312 **Socinian** follower of a sect denying the doctrine of the Trinity   322 **in gross** in general

Not that tradition's parts are useless here,
335 When general, old, disinteress'd and clear:
That ancient Fathers thus expound the page
Gives truth the reverend majesty of age;
Confirms its force, by biding every test;
For best authority's, next rules, are best.
340 And still the nearer to the spring we go,
More limpid, more unsoiled the waters flow.
Thus, first traditions were a proof alone,
Could we be certain such they were, so known;
But since some flaws in long descent may be,
345 They make not truth, but probability.
Even Arius° and Pelagius° durst provoke
To what the centuries preceding spoke.
Such difference is there in an oft-told tale;
But truth by its own sinews will prevail.
350 Tradition written therefore more commends
Authority, than what from voice descends;
And this, as perfect as its kind can be,
Rolls down to us the sacred history,
Which, from the Universal Church received,
355 Is tried, and after for itself believed.
      The partial Papists would infer from hence
Their Church, in last resort, should judge the sense;
But first they would assume, with wondrous art,
Themselves to be the whole, who are but part
360 Of that vast frame, the Church; yet grant they were
The handers down, can they from thence infer
A right t' interpret? or would they alone
Who brought the present, claim it for their own?
The Book's a common largess to mankind,
365 Not more for them than every man designed;
The welcome news is in the letter found;
The carrier's not commissioned to expound.
It speaks itself, and what it does contain,
In all things needful to be known, is plain.
370   In times o'ergrown with rust and ignorance,
A gainful trade their clergy did advance;

346 **Arius** heretic with regard to the Trinity   346 **Pelagius** heretic
with regard to the doctrine of Original Sin

When want of learning kept the laymen low,
And none but priests were authorized to know;
When what small knowledge was, in them did dwell,
And he a god who could but read or spell.   375
Then Mother Church did mightily prevail;
She parcelled out the Bible by retail;
But still expounded what she sold or gave,
To keep it in her power to damn and save.
Scripture was scarce, and, as the market went,   380
Poor laymen took salvation on content;
As needy men take money, good or bad:
God's word they had not, but the priest's they had.
Yet, whate'er false conveyances they made,
The lawyer still was certain to be paid.   385
In those dark times they learned their knack so well,
That by long use they grew infallible.
At last, a knowing age began t' inquire
If they the Book, or that did them inspire;
And, making narrower search, they found, though late, 390
That what they thought the priest's was their estate,
Taught by the Will produced (the written Word,)
How long they had been cheated on record.
Then every man who saw the title fair
Claimed a child's part, and put in for a share;   395
Consulted soberly his private good,
And saved himself as cheap as e'er he could.
  'T is true, my friend, (and far be flattery hence,)
This good Book had full as bad a consequence:
The Book thus put in every vulgar hand,   400
Which each presumed he best could understand,
The common rule was made the common prey,
And at the mercy of the rabble lay.
The tender page with horny fists was galled,
And he was gifted most that loudest bawled.   405
The spirit gave the doctoral degree;   ⎫
And every member of a company   ⎬
Was of his trade and of the Bible free.   ⎭
Plain truths enough for needful use they found,
But men would still be itching to expound: 410
Each was ambitious of th' obscurest place,

No measure ta'en from knowledge, all from GRACE.
Study and pains were now no more their care;
Texts were explained by fasting and by prayer:
415 This was the fruit the private spirit brought,
Occasioned by great zeal and little thought.
While crowds unlearned, with rude devotion warm,
About the sacred viands buzz and swarm,
The fly-blown text creates a crawling brood,
420 And turns to maggots what was meant for food.
A thousand daily sects rise up and die;
A thousand more the perished race supply:
So all we make of Heav'n's discovered will
Is, not to have it, or to use it ill.
425 The danger's much the same; on several shelves
If others wreck us, or we wreck ourselves.
     What then remains, but, waiving each extreme,
The tides of ignorance and pride to stem?
Neither so rich a treasure to forego;
430 Nor proudly seek beyond our power to know:
Faith is not built on disquisitions vain;
The things we must believe are few and plain:
But since men will believe more than they need,
And every man will make himself a creed,
435 In doubtful questions 't is the safest way
To learn what unsuspected ancients say;
For 't is not likely we should higher soar
In search of Heav'n, than all the Church before;
Nor can we be deceived, unless we see
440 The Scripture and the Fathers disagree.
If, after all, they stand suspected still
(For no man's faith depends upon his will;)
'T is some relief that points not clearly known
Without much hazard may be let alone:
445 And after hearing what our Church can say,
If still our Reason runs another way,
That private Reason 't is more just to curb,
Than by disputes the public peace disturb.
For points obscure are of small use to learn:
450 But common quiet is mankind's concern.
     Thus have I made my own opinions clear;

Yet neither praise expect, nor censure fear:
And this unpolished, rugged verse, I chose,
As fittest for discourse, and nearest prose;
For while from Sacred Truth I do not swerve,   *455*
Tom Sternhold's,° or Tom Sha——ll's° rhymes will
    serve.

456 **Tom Sternhold** early translator of the PSALMS   456 **Tom Sha—ll**
Shadwell, the butt of *Mac Flecknoe*

The Hind and the Panther°
The First Part

A milk-white Hind, immortal and unchanged,
Fed on the lawns, and in the forest ranged;
Without unspotted, innocent within,
She feared no danger, for she knew no sin.
5 Yet had she oft been chased with horns and hounds
And Scythian shafts;° and many winged wounds
Aimed at her heart; was often forced to fly,
And doomed to death, though fated not to die.
    Not so her young; for their unequal line
10 Was hero's make, half human, half divine.
Their earthly mold obnoxious° was to fate,
Th' immortal part assumed immortal state.
Of these a slaughtered army lay in blood,
Extended o'er the Caledonian wood,
15 Their native walk; whose vocal blood arose,
And cried for pardon on their perjured foes.
Their fate was fruitful, and the sanguine seed,
Endued with souls, increased the sacred breed.
So captive Israel multiplied in chains
20 A numerous exile, and enjoyed her pains.
With grief and gladness mixed, their mother viewed
Her martyred offspring, and their race renewed;

° The poem (in three parts) proceeds allegorically through presenting
arguments for the primacy of the Roman Catholic Church in matters
of faith and in the state. Various animals represent institutions,
parties, and persons involved in the religious and political controversies of James II's reign. The Hind stands for the Roman Catholic
Church in its doctrines and its organization. The Panther is the
Church of England. James II is the Lion, England is Caledonia. The
Swallows are the English Catholics. The references to other denomi-
nations are explained at the appropriate places in the text.   6 **Scythian shafts** poisoned arrows   11 **obnoxious** exposed to

Their corps° to perish, but their kind to last,
So much the deathless plant the dying fruit surpassed.

　Panting and pensive now she ranged alone,　　　　　*25*
And wandered in the kingdoms, once her own.
The common hunt, though from their rage restrained
By sovereign power, her company disdained;
Grinned as they passed, and with a glaring eye
Gave gloomy signs of secret enmity.　　　　　　　　*30*
'T is true, she bounded by, and tripped so light,
They had not time to take a steady sight;
For Truth has such a face and such a mien,
As to be loved needs only to be seen.

　The bloody Bear, an *Independent* beast,°　　　　　*35*
Unlicked to form, in groans her hate expressed.
Among the timorous kind the *Quaking* Hare°
Professed neutrality, but would not swear.
Next her the *buffoon* Ape,° as atheists use,
Mimicked all sects, and had his own to choose:　　　*40*
Still when the Lion° looked, his knees he bent,
And paid at church a courtier's compliment.

　The bristled *Baptist* Boar,° impure as he
(But whitened with the foam of sanctity,)°
With fat pollutions filled the sacred place, ⎫　　　*45*
And mountains levelled in his furious race: ⎬
So first rebellion founded was in grace. ⎭
But since the mighty ravage which he made
In German forests had his guilt betrayed,
With broken tusks, and with a borrowed name,　　　　*50*
He shunned the vengeance, and concealed the shame;
So lurked in sects unseen. With greater guile
False Reynard° fed on consecrated spoil:
The graceless beast by Athanasius° first
Was chased from Nice; then, by Socinus° nursed,　　　*55*
His impious race their blasphemy renewed,

23 **corps** corpses　35 **Bear . . . beast** sect of Independents, rejecting
all ecclesiastical authority except the Congregation　37 **Quaking Hare**
Quakers　39 **buffoon Ape** mocking free-thinkers, as certain courtiers
41 **Lion** James II　43 **Baptist Boar** Baptists originating in Germany
44 **whitened . . . sanctity** made free from sin　53 **Reynard** Unitarians
54 **Athanasius** defender of orthodox doctrine of the Trinity as prom-
ulgated at Nicæa　55 **Socinus** Italian founder of a sect denying the
doctrine of the Trinity

And nature's King through nature's optics viewed.
Reversed, they viewed him lessened to their eye,
Nor in an Infant could a God descry:
60 New swarming sects to this obliquely tend,
Hence they began, and here they all will end.
  What weight of ancient witness can prevail,
If private reason hold the public scale?
But, gracious God, how well dost thou provide
65 For erring judgments an unerring guide!
Thy throne is darkness in th' abyss of light,
A blaze of glory that forbids the sight.
O teach me to believe Thee thus concealed,
And search no farther than Thyself revealed;
70 But her alone for my director take,
Whom Thou hast promised never to forsake!
My thoughtless youth was winged with vain desires,
My manhood, long misled by wandering fires,
Followed false lights; and, when their glimpse was
        gone,
75 My pride struck out new sparkles of her own.
Such was I, such by nature still I am;
Be thine the glory, and be mine the shame.
Good life be now my task: my doubts are done
(What more could fright my Faith, than Three in
        One?)
80 Can I believe eternal God could lie   ⎫
Disguised in mortal mold and infancy?   ⎬
That the great Maker of the world could die? ⎭
And after that trust my imperfect sense,
Which calls in question his omnipotence?
85 Can I my reason to my faith compel,
And shall my sight, and touch, and taste rebel?
Superior faculties are set aside;
Shall their subservient organs be my guide?
Then let the moon usurp the rule of day,
90 And winking tapers show the sun his way;
For what my senses can themselves perceive
I need no revelation to believe.
Can they who say the Host should be descried
By sense, define a body glorified?

Impassible, and penetrating parts?   95
Let them declare by what mysterious arts
He shot that body through th' opposing might
Of bolts and bars impervious to the light,
And stood before his train confessed in open sight.

    For since thus wondrously he passed, 't is plain,   100
One single place two bodies did contain.
And sure the same Omnipotence as well
Can make one body in more places dwell.
Let Reason then at her own quarry fly,
But how can finite grasp infinity?   105
    'T is urged again that faith did first commence
By miracles, which are appeals to sense,
And thence concluded that our sense must be
The motive still of credibility.
For latter ages must on former wait,   110
And what began belief, must propagate.
    But winnow well this thought, and you shall find
'T is light as chaff that flies before the wind.
Were all those wonders wrought by power divine,
As means or ends of some more deep design?   115
Most sure as means, whose end was this alone,
To prove the Godhead of th' eternal Son.
God thus asserted: man is to believe
Beyond what sense and reason can conceive,
And for mysterious things of faith rely   120
On the proponent, Heav'n's authority.
If then our faith we for our guide admit,
Vain is the farther search of human wit;
As, when the building gains a surer stay,
We take th' unuseful scaffolding away.   125
Reason by sense no more can understand;
The game is played into another hand.
Why choose we then like *bilanders*° to creep
Along the coast, and land in view to keep,
When safely we may launch into the deep?   130
In the same vessel which our Savior bore,
Himself the pilot, let us leave the shore,
And with a better guide a better world explore.

128 **bilanders** coasting vessels

Could He his Godhead veil with flesh and blood,
135 And not veil these again to be our food?
His grace in both is equal in extent,
The first affords us life, the second nourishment.
And if he can, why all this frantic pain
To construe what his clearest words contain, }
140 And make a riddle what He made so plain?)
To take up half on trust, and half to try,
Name it not faith, but bungling bigotry.
Both knave and fool the merchant we may call,
To pay great sums, and to compound the small: }
For who would break with Heav'n, and would not }
145   break for all?)
Rest then, my soul, from endless anguish freed:
Nor sciences thy guide, nor sense thy creed.
Faith is the best insurer of thy bliss;
The bank above must fail before the venture miss.
150 But heav'n and heav'n-born faith are far from thee,
Thou first apostate to divinity.
Unkenneled range in thy Polonian plains;°
A fiercer foe th' insatiate Wolf° remains.
    Too boastful Britain, please thyself no more,
155 That beasts of prey are banished from thy shore:
The Bear, the Boar, and every savage name,
Wild in effect, though in appearance tame,
Lay waste thy woods, destroy thy blissful bower,
And, muzzled though they seem, the mutes devour.
160 More haughty than the rest, the *wolfish* race)
Appear with belly gaunt, and famished face: }
Never was so deformed a beast of grace.)
His ragged tail° betwixt his legs he wears,
Close clapped for shame; but his rough crest he rears, }
165 And pricks up his predestinating ears.)
His wild disordered walk, his haggard eyes,
Did all the bestial citizens surprise.
Though feared and hated, yet he ruled a while,

---

152 **Polonian plains** the Socinian doctrine had spread widely in
Poland   153 **Wolf** Presbyterians   163 **ragged tail** the Genevan habit
gave a rough appearance

As captain or companion° of the spoil.
Full many a year his hateful head had been   170
For tribute paid, nor since in Cambria° seen:
The last of all the litter scaped by chance,
And from Geneva first infested France.
Some authors thus his pedigree will trace,
But others write him of an upstart race;   175
Because of Wycliffe's brood no mark he brings,
But his innate antipathy to Kings,
These last deduce him from th' Helvetian kind,
Who near the Leman lake his consort lined.
That fiery Zuinglius° first th' affection bred,   180
And meager Calvin blessed the nuptial bed.
In Israel some believe him whelped long since,
When the proud Sanhedrim° oppressed the Prince,
Or, since he will be Jew, derive him higher,
When Corah with his brethren did conspire   185
From Moses' hand the sovereign sway to wrest,
And Aaron of his ephod° to divest:
Till opening earth made way for all to pass,
And could not bear the burden of a *class*.
The Fox and he came shuffled in the dark,   190
If ever they were stowed in Noah's ark:
Perhaps not made; for all their barking train
The Dog (a common species) will contain.
And some wild curs, who from their masters ran, ⎫
Abhorring the supremacy of man,   ⎬   195
In woods and caves the rebel-race began.   ⎭
   O happy pair, how well have you increased!
What ills in Church and State have you redressed!
With teeth untried, and rudiments of claws,
Your first essay was on your native laws: 200
Those having torn with ease, and trampled down, ⎫
Your fangs you fastened on the mitered crown,   ⎬
And freed from God and monarchy your town.   ⎭

---

169 **captain . . . companion** the Presbyterians were temporarily in
power   171 **Cambria** Wales   180 **Zuinglius** Swiss Reformer   183
Sanhedrim Old Testament assembly of elders, here applied to governing assembly of Presbyterians   187 **ephod** Corah led a rebellion to
take away the ephod (mantle of authority) of Moses and Aaron

What though your native kennel° still be small,
205 Bounded betwixt a puddle and a wall;
Yet your victorious colonies are sent
Where the north ocean girds the continent.
Quickened with fire below, your monsters breed
In fenny Holland, and in fruitful Tweed:°
210 And, like the first, the last affects to be
Drawn to the dregs of a democracy.
As, where in fields the fairy rounds are seen,
A rank sour herbage rises on the green;
So, springing where these midnight elves advance,
215 Rebellion prints the footsteps of the dance.
Such are their doctrines, such contempt they show ⎱
To Heav'n above, and to their prince below, ⎰
As none but traitors and blasphemers know. ⎰
God, like the tyrant of the skies, is placed,
220 And Kings, like slaves, beneath the crowd debased.
So fulsome is their food that flocks refuse
To bite, and only dogs for physic use.
As, where the lightning runs along the ground,
No husbandry can heal the blasting wound;
225 Nor bladed grass, nor bearded corn succeeds,
But scales of scurf and putrefaction breeds:
Such wars, such waste, such fiery tracks of dearth
Their zeal has left, and such a teemless earth.
But, as the poisons of the deadliest kind
230 Are to their own unhappy coasts confined;
As only Indian shades of sight deprive,
And magic plants will but in Colchos° thrive;
So Presbytery and pestilential zeal
Can only flourish in a commonweal.
235   From Celtic woods° is chased the *wolfish* crew;
But ah! some pity e'en to brutes is due.
Their native walks, methinks, they might enjoy,
Curbed of their native malice to destroy.
Of all the tyrannies on humankind,
240 The worst is that which persecutes the mind.

204 **native kennel** Geneva   209 **Tweed** Scotland   232 **Colchos** Black
Sea region famous for magic herbs   235 **Celtic woods** Scotland,
where James II made some overtures of toleration

Let us but weigh at what offense we strike;
'T is but because we cannot think alike.
In punishing of this, we overthrow
The laws of nations and of nature too.
Beasts are the subjects of tyrannic sway,   245
Where still the stronger on the weaker prey;
Man only of a softer mold is made,
Not for his fellows' ruin, but their aid:
Created kind, beneficent, and free,
The noble image of the Deity.   250
    One portion of informing fire was given
To brutes, th' inferior family of Heav'n:
The smith divine, as with a careless beat,
Struck out the mute creation at a heat;
But, when arrived at last to human race,   255
The Godhead took a deep considering space;
And, to distinguish man from all the rest,
Unlocked the sacred treasures of his breast;
And mercy mixed with reason did impart,
One to his head, the other to his heart: 260
Reason to rule, but mercy to forgive:
The first is law, the last prerogative.
And like his mind his outward form appeared,
When, issuing naked to the wondering herd,
He charmed their eyes; and, for they loved, they
    feared.   265
Not armed with horns of arbitrary might,
Or claws to seize their furry spoils in fight,
Or with increase of feet t' o'ertake 'em in their flight;
Of easy shape, and pliant every way;
Confessing still the softness of his clay,   270
And kind as Kings upon their coronation day;
With open hands, and with extended space
Of arms, to satisfy a large embrace.
Thus kneaded up with milk, the new-made man
His kingdom o'er his kindred world began;   275
Till knowledge misapplied, misunderstood,
And pride of empire soured his balmy blood.
Then, first rebelling, his own stamp he coins;
The murtherer Cain was latent in his loins:

280 And blood began its first and loudest cry
   For differing worship of the Deity.
   Thus persecution rose, and farther space
   Produced the mighty hunter° of his race.
   Not so the blessed Pan° his flock increased,
285 Content to fold 'em from the famished beast:
   Mild were his laws; the Sheep and harmless Hind
   Were never of the persecuting kind.
   Such pity now the pious Pastor shows,
   Such mercy from the British Lion° flows,   }
290 That both provide protection for their foes.   }
      O happy regions, Italy and Spain,
   Which never did those monsters entertain!
   The Wolf, the Bear, the Boar, can there advance
   No native claim of just inheritance.
295 And self-preserving laws, severe in show,
   May guard their fences from th' invading foe.
   Where birth has placed 'em, let 'em safely share
   The common benefit of vital air.
   Themselves unharmful, let them live unharmed;
300 Their jaws disabled, and their claws disarmed:
   Here, only in nocturnal howlings bold,
   They dare not seize the Hind, nor leap the fold.
   More powerful, and as vigilant as they,
   The Lion awfully forbids the prey.
   Their rage repressed, though pinched with famine }
305   sore,   }
   They stand aloof, and tremble at his roar: }
   Much is their hunger, but their fear is more.
      These are the chief; to number o'er the rest,
   And stand, like Adam, naming every beast,
310 Were weary work: nor will the Muse describe
   A slimy-born and sun-begotten tribe;
   Who, far from steeples and their sacred sound,
   In fields their sullen conventicles found.
   These gross, half-animated lumps I leave;
315 Nor can I think what thoughts they can conceive.
   But if they think at all, 't is sure no higher

283 **mighty hunter** Nimrod   284 **blessed Pan** Christ   289 **British Lion** James II

Than matter, put in motion, may aspire:
Souls that can scarce ferment their mass of clay: ⎫
So drossy, so divisible are they,   ⎬
As would but serve pure bodies for allay: ⎭   *320*
Such souls as shards° produce, such beetle things
As only buzz to heav'n with evening wings;
Strike in the dark, offending but by chance,
Such are the blindfold blows of ignorance.
They know not beings, and but hate a name;   *325*
To them the Hind and Panther are the same.

    The Panther, sure the noblest, next the Hind,
And fairest creature of the spotted kind;
O, could her inborn stains be washed away,
She were too good to be a beast of prey!   *330*
How can I praise, or blame, and not offend,
Or how divide the frailty from the friend!
Her faults and virtues lie so mixed that she
Nor wholly stands condemned, nor wholly free.
Then, like her injured Lion, let me speak;   *335*
He cannot bend her, and he would not break.°
Unkind already, and estranged in part,
The Wolf begins to share her wandering heart.
Though unpolluted yet with actual ill,
She half commits, who sins but in her will.   *340*
If, as our dreaming Platonists report,
There could be spirits of a middle sort,
Too black for heav'n, and yet too white for hell,
Who just dropped halfway down, nor lower fell;
So poised, so gently she descends from high,   *345*
It seems a soft dismission from the sky.
Her house not ancient, whatsoe'er pretense
Her clergy heralds make in her defense;
A second century not halfway run,
Since the new honors of her blood begun.   *350*
A Lion,° old, obscene, and furious made
By lust, compressed her mother in a shade;
Then, by a left-hand marriage, weds the dame,

---

321 **shards** dung   336 **bend . . . break** James II was unable to persuade the Church of England to tolerate Catholics   351 **Lion** Henry
VIII

Covering adultery with a specious name:
355 So schism begot; and sacrilege and she,
A well-matched pair, got graceless heresy.
God's and Kings' rebels have the same good cause,
To trample down divine and human laws;
Both would be called reformers, and their hate
360 Alike destructive both to Church and State:
The fruit proclaims the plant; a lawless Prince ⎫
By luxury reformed incontinence;   ⎬
By ruins, charity; by riots, abstinence. ⎭
Confessions, fasts, and penance set aside; ⎫
365 O, with what ease we follow such a guide, ⎬
Where souls are starved, and senses gratified; ⎭
Where marriage pleasures midnight prayer supply, ⎫
And matin bells (a melancholy cry) ⎬
Are tuned to merrier notes, *increase* and *multiply!* ⎭
370 Religion shows a rosy-colored face; ⎫
Not hattered° out with drudging works of grace: ⎬
A downhill reformation rolls apace. ⎭
What flesh and blood would crowd the narrow gate, ⎫
Or, till they waste their pampered paunches, wait? ⎬
375 All would be happy at the cheapest rate. ⎭
    Though our lean faith these rigid laws has given,
The full-fed Mussulman goes fat to Heav'n;
For his Arabian prophet with delights
Of sense allured his Eastern proselytes.
380 The jolly Luther, reading him, began
T' interpret Scriptures by his Alcoran;
To grub the thorns beneath our tender feet,
And make the paths of Paradise more sweet:
Bethought him of a wife ere halfway gone
385 (For 't was uneasy travailing alone;)
And, in this masquerade of mirth and love,
Mistook the bliss of Heav'n for Bacchanals above.
Sure he presumed of praise, who came to stock
Th' ethereal pastures with so fair a flock,
390 Burnished, and battening on their food, to show
The diligence of careful herds below.

371 **hattered** beaten, bruised

Our Panther, though like these she changed her
    head,
Yet, as the mistress of a monarch's bed,°
Her front erect with majesty she bore,
The crosier wielded, and the miter wore.   *395*
Her upper part of decent discipline
Showed affectation of an ancient line;
And Fathers, councils, Church and Church's head,
Were on her reverend phylacteries° read.
But what disgraced and disavowed the rest,   *400*
Was Calvin's brand, that stigmatized the beast.
Thus, like a creature of a double kind,
In her own labyrinth she lives confined;
To foreign lands no sound of her is come,
Humbly content to be despised at home.   *405*
Such is her faith, where good cannot be had,
At least she leaves the refuse of the bad.
Nice in her choice of ill, though not of best,
And least deformed, because reformed the least.
In doubtful points betwixt her differing friends,   *410*
Where one for substance, one for sign° contends,
Their contradicting terms she strives to join;
Sign shall be substance, substance shall be sign.
A real presence all her sons allow,
And yet 't is flat idolatry to bow,   *415*
Because the Godhead's there they know not how.
Her novices are taught that bread and wine
Are but the visible and outward sign,
Received by those who in communion join;
But th' inward grace, or the thing signified,   *420*
His blood and body, who to save us died:
The faithful this thing signified receive.
What is 't those faithful then partake or leave?
For what is signified and understood,
Is, by her own confession, flesh and blood.   *425*
Then, by the same acknowledgment, we know

---

393 **monarch's bed** the Church of England acknowledged the King
as its head   399 **phylacteries** boxes containing texts of Scripture
worn by Jews   411 **substance . . . sign** referring to different doctrines
of the nature of the bread and wine of the Eucharist

They take the sign, and take the substance too.
The literal sense is hard to flesh and blood,
But nonsense never can be understood.
430   Her wild belief on every wave is tossed,
But sure no Church can better morals boast:
True to her king her principles are found;
O that her practice were but half so sound!
Steadfast in various turns of state she stood,
435 And sealed her vowed affection with her blood.°
Nor will I meanly tax her constancy,
That interest or obligement made the tie   }
(Bound to the fate of murdered monarchy.)   }
Before the sounding ax so falls the vine,
440 Whose tender branches round the poplar twine.
She chose her ruin, and resigned her life,
In death undaunted as an Indian wife.
A rare example! but some souls we see
Grow hard, and stiffen with adversity,
445 Yet these by fortune's favors are undone;   }
Resolved, into a baser form they run,   }
And bore the wind, but cannot bear the sun. }
Let this be Nature's frailty, or her fate,
Or Isgrim's° counsel, her new-chosen mate;
450 Still she's the fairest of the fallen crew,
No mother more indulgent, but the true.
    Fierce to her foes, yet fears her force to try,
Because she wants innate auctority;°
For how can she constrain them to obey,
455 Who has herself cast off the lawful sway?
Rebellion equals all, and those who toil
In common theft will share the common spoil.
Let her produce the title and the right
Against her old superiors first to fight;
460 If she reform by text, ev'n that's as plain
For her own rebels to reform again.
As long as words a different sense will bear,
And each may be his own interpreter,
Our airy faith will no foundation find;

435 **sealed . . . blood** the Church of England fell with the monarchy
449 **Isgrim's** name of wolf in old fable   453 **auctority** authority

The word's a weathercock for every wind: 465
The Bear, the Fox, the Wolf, by turns prevail;
The most in power supplies the present gale.
The wretched Panther cries aloud for aid
To Church and councils, whom she first betrayed;
No help from Fathers or tradition's train: 470
Those ancient guides she taught us to disdain,
And by that Scripture which she once abused
To Reformation stands herself accused.
What bills for breach of laws can she prefer,
Expounding which she owns herself may err?   475
And, after all her winding ways are tried,   ⎫
If doubts arise, she slips herself aside,   ⎬
And leaves the private conscience for the guide. ⎭
If then that conscience set th' offender free,
It bars her claim to church auctority.   480
How can she censure, or what crime pretend,
But Scripture may be construed to defend?
Even those whom for rebellion she transmits
To civil power, her doctrine first acquits;
Because no disobedience can ensue,   485
Where no submission to a judge is due;
Each judging for himself, by her consent,
Whom thus absolved she sends to punishment.
Suppose the magistrate revenge her cause,
'T is only for transgressing human laws.   490
How answering to its end a church is made,
Whose power is but to counsel and persuade?
O solid rock, on which secure she stands!
Eternal house, not built with mortal hands!
O sure defense against th' infernal gate,   495
A patent during pleasure of the State!
   Thus is the Panther neither loved nor feared,
A mere mock queen of a divided herd,
Whom soon by lawful power she might control,
Herself a part submitted to the whole.   500
Then, as the moon who first receives the light
By which she makes our nether regions bright,
So might she shine, reflecting from afar
The rays she borrowed from a better star;

505 Big with the beams which from her mother flow,
   And reigning o'er the rising tides below:
   Now, mixing with a savage crowd, she goes,
   And meanly flatters her inveterate foes;
   Ruled while she rules, and losing every hour
510 Her wretched remnants of precarious power.
      One evening, while the cooler shade she sought,
   Revolving many a melancholy thought,
   Alone she walked, and looked around in vain,
   With rueful visage, for her vanished train:
515 None of her sylvan subjects made their court;
   Levées and couchées° passed without resort.
   So hardly can usurpers manage well
   Those whom they first instructed to rebel:
   More liberty begets desire of more;
520 The hunger still increases with the store.
   Without respect they brushed along the wood,   )
   Each in his clan, and, filled with loathsome food, }
   Asked no permission to the neighboring flood.   )
   The Panther, full of inward discontent,
525 Since they would go, before 'em wisely went;
   Supplying want of power by drinking first,
   As if she gave 'em leave to quench their thirst.
   Among the rest, the Hind, with fearful face,
   Beheld from far the common watering place,
530 Nor durst approach; till with an awful roar
   The sovereign Lion bade her fear no more.
   Encouraged thus she brought her younglings nigh,
   Watching the motions of her patron's eye,
   And drank a sober draught; the rest amazed
535 Stood mutely still, and on the stranger gazed;
   Surveyed her part by part, and sought to find   )
   The ten-horned monster° in the harmless Hind, }
   Such as the Wolf and Panther had designed.   )
   They thought at first they dreamed, for 't was offense
540 With them to question certitude of sense,

516 **Levées . . . couchées** royal receptions, referring to the Dissenters'
abandonment of Church of England morning and evening services
537 **tend-horned monster** figure of REVELATIONS taken by Reformers
to signify the Church of Rome

Their guide in faith; but nearer when they drew, ⎫
And had the faultless object full in view,   ⎬
Lord, how they all admired her heav'nly hue!   ⎭
Some, who before her fellowship disdained,   ⎫
Scarce, and but scarce, from inborn rage restrained, ⎬ *545*
Now frisked about her, and old kindred feigned.   ⎭
Whether for love or interest, every sect
Of all the savage nation showed respect:
The viceroy Panther could not awe the herd;
The more the company, the less they feared.   *550*
The surly Wolf with secret envy burst,   ⎫
Yet could not howl, the Hind had seen him first:° ⎬
But what he durst not speak, the Panther durst.   ⎭
  For when the herd, sufficed, did late repair
To ferny heaths, and to their forest lair,   *555*
She made a mannerly excuse to stay,
Proffering the Hind to wait her half the way;
That, since the sky was clear, an hour of talk
Might help her to beguile the tedious walk.
With much good will the motion was embraced,   *560*
To chat a while on their adventures passed;
Nor had the grateful Hind so soon forgot
Her friend and fellow-sufferer in the Plot.
Yet wondering how of late she grew estranged,
Her forehead cloudy, and her countenance changed,   *565*
She thought this hour th' occasion would present
To learn her secret cause of discontent,
Which well she hoped might be with ease redressed,
Considering her a well-bred civil beast,
And more a gentlewoman than the rest.   *570*
After some common talk what rumors ran,
The lady of the spotted muff began.

---

552 **Hind . . . first** referring to ancient superstition that a man loses
his speech if a wolf sees him before he sees the wolf

PROLOGUES AND EPILOGUES

Prologue to *The Tempest*
or, *The Enchanted Island*

As, when a tree 's cut down, the secret root
Lives under ground, and thence new branches shoot;
So from old Shakespeare's honored dust, this day
Springs up and buds a new reviving play.
5 Shakespeare, who (taught by none) did first impart
To Fletcher wit, to laboring Jonson art.
He, monarch-like, gave those his subjects law,
And is that Nature which they paint and draw.
Fletcher reached that which on his heights did grow,
10 Whilst Jonson crept, and gathered all below.
This did his love, and this his mirth digest:
One imitates him most, the other best.
If they have since outwrit all other men,
'T is with the drops which fell from Shakespeare's
       pen.
15 The storm which vanished on the neighboring shore,
Was taught by Shakespeare's *Tempest* first to roar.
That innocence and beauty which did smile
In Fletcher, grew on this *Enchanted Isle*.
But Shakespeare's magic could not copied be;
20 Within that circle none durst walk but he.
I must confess 't was bold, nor would you now
That liberty to vulgar wits allow,
Which works by magic supernatural things;
But Shakespeare's power is sacred as a King's.
25 Those legends from old priesthood were received,
And he then writ, as people then believed.
But if for Shakespeare we your grace implore,
We for our theater shall want it more:

Who by our dearth of youths are forced t' employ
One of our women to present a boy; 30
And that's a transformation you will say
Exceeding all the magic in the play.
Let none expect in the last act to find
Her sex transformed from man to woman-kind.
Whate'er she was before the play began, 35
All you shall see of her is perfect man.
Or if your fancy will be farther led
To find her woman, it must be abed.

Epilogue to *Tyrannic Love*

Spoken by Mrs. Ellen,° when she was to
be carried off dead by the Bearers

[*To the Bearer*.] Hold, are you mad? you damned
    confounded dog,
I am to rise, and speak the epilogue.
   [*To the Audience*.] I come, kind gentlemen, strange
    news to tell ye,
I am the ghost of poor departed Nelly.
5 Sweet ladies, be not frighted, I'll be civil,
I'm what I was, a little harmless Devil.
For after death, we sprites have just such natures
We had for all the world, when human creatures;
And therefore I that was an actress here,
10 Play all my tricks in Hell, a goblin there.
Gallants, look to 't, you say there are no sprites;
But I'll come dance about your beds at nights.
And faith you'll be in a sweet kind of taking,
When I surprise you between sleep and waking.
15 To tell you true, I walk because I die
Out of my calling in a tragedy.
O poet, damned dull poet, who could prove
So senseless! to make Nelly die for love!
Nay, what 's yet worse, to kill me in the prime
20 Of Easter term, in tart and cheese-cake time!°
I'll fit the fop, for I'll not one word say
T' excuse his godly out-of-fashion play:
A play, which if you dare but twice sit out,
You'll all be slandered, and be thought devout.

° **Mrs. Ellen** the actress Nell Gwyn, one-time mistress of Charles II,
"the indiscreetest and wildest creature that ever was in a Court"
20 **tart . . . time** (From *Sir Martin Mar-All:* "I came up, madam, as
we country gentlewomen use, at an Easter-time, to the destruction of
tarts and cheese-cakes, to see a new play, buy a new gown, take a
turn in the park, and so down again to sleep with my forefathers."

But farewell, gentlemen, make haste to me;   25
I'm sure ere long to have your company.
As for my epitaph, when I am gone,
I'll trust no poet, but will write my own.

Here Nelly lies, who though she lived a slattern,
Yet died a princess, acting in St. Cathar'n.   30

Prologue to *Julius Cæsar*

In country beauties as we often see
Something that takes in their simplicity;
Yet while they charm, they know not they are fair,
And take without their spreading of the snare:
5 Such artless beauty lies in Shakespeare's wit;
'T was well in spite of him whate'er he writ.
His excellencies came and were not sought;
His words like casual atoms made a thought,
Drew up themselves in rank and file and writ,
10 He wondering how the devil it was such wit.
Thus, like the drunken tinker in his play,
He grew a prince and never knew which way.
He did not know what trope or figure meant,
But to persuade is to be eloquent;
15 So in this *Cæsar* which today you see,
Tully ne'er spoke as he makes Anthony.
Those then that tax his learning are to blame;
He knew the thing, but did not know the name.
Great Jonson did that ignorance adore,
20 And, though he envied much, admired him more.
The faultless Jonson equally writ well;
Shakespeare made faults, but then did more excel.
One close at guard like some old fencer lay;
T'other more open, but he showed more play.
25 In imitation Jonson's wit was shown;
Heav'n made his men, but Shakespeare made his own.
Wise Jonson's talent in observing lay,
But others' follies still made up his play.
He drew the like in each elaborate line,
30 But Shakespeare like a master did design.
Jonson with skill dissected humankind,
And showed their faults that they their faults might
    find;

But then, as all anatomists must do,
He to the meanest of mankind did go,
And took from gibbets such as he would show.   *35*
Both are so great that he must boldly dare
Who both of 'em does judge and both compare.
If amongst poets one more bold there be,
The man that dare attempt in either way, is he.

Prologue to *Aureng-Zebe*

Our author by experience finds it true,
'T is much more hard to please himself than you;
And out of no feigned modesty, this day
Damns his laborious trifle of a play:
5 Not that it 's worse than what before he writ,
But he has now another taste of wit;
And, to confess a truth (though out of time,)
Grows weary of his long-loved mistress, Rhyme.
Passion 's too fierce to be in fetters bound,
10 And nature flies him like enchanted ground.
What verse can do, he has performed in this,
Which he presumes the most correct of his;
But spite of all his pride a secret shame
Invades his breast at Shakespeare's sacred name:
15 Awed when he hears his godlike Romans rage,
He, in a just despair, would quit the stage;
And to an age less polished, more unskilled,
Does, with disdain, the foremost honors yield.
As with the greater dead he dares not strive,
20 He would not match his verse with those who live:
Let him retire, betwixt two ages cast,
The first of this, and hindmost of the last.
A losing gamester, let him sneak away;
He bears no ready money from the play.
25 The fate which governs poets thought it fit
He should not raise his fortunes by his wit.
The clergy thrive, and the litigious bar;
Dull heroes fatten with the spoils of war:
All southern vices, Heav'n be praised, are here;
30 But wit 's a luxury you think too dear.
When you to cultivate the plant are loth,
'T is a shrewd sign 't was never of your growth;
And wit in northern climates will not blow,
Except, like orange trees, 't is housed from snow.
35 There needs no care to put a playhouse down,

'T is the most desert place of all the town.
We and our neighbors, to speak proudly, are,
Like monarchs, ruined with expensive war;
While, like wise English, unconcerned you sit,
And see us play the tragedy of wit.   *40*

Prologue to *Oedipus*

When Athens all the Grecian state did guide,
And Greece gave laws to all the world beside,
Then Sophocles with Socrates did sit,
Supreme in wisdom one, and one in wit:
5 And wit from wisdom differed not in those,
But as 't was sung in verse, or said in prose.
Then, Œdipus, on crowded theaters,
Drew all admiring eyes and listening ears:
The pleased spectator shouted every line,
10 The noblest, manliest, and the best design!
And every critic of each learned age,
By this just model has reformed the stage.
Now, should it fail (as Heav'n avert our fear!)
Damn it in silence, lest the world should hear.
15 For were it known this poem did not please,
You might set up for perfect savages:
Your neighbors would not look on you as men,
But think the nation all turned Picts again.
Faith, as you manage matters, 't is not fit
20 You should suspect yourselves of too much wit.
Drive not the jest too far, but spare this piece;
And, for this once, be not more wise than Greece.
See twice! do not pellmell to damning fall,
Like true-born Britons, who ne'er think at all:
25 Pray be advised; and though at Mons° you won,
On pointed cannon do not always run.
With some respect to ancient wit proceed;
You take the four first councils° for your creed.
But, when you lay tradition wholly by,   ⎫
30 And on the private spirit alone rely,   ⎬
You turn fanatics in your poetry.   ⎭

---

25 **Mons** battle in which the Prince of Orange defeated a French
army   28 **first councils** the doctrines of the Church Councils of
Nicæa, Constantinople, Ephesus, and Chalcedon were accepted in the
Act of Supremacy (1559) as equal in authority to those of Scripture

If, notwithstanding all that we can say,
You needs will have your pen'worths of the play, }
And come resolved to damn, because you pay,   }
Record it, in memorial of the fact,   *35*
The first play buried since the Woolen Act.°

Epilogue to *The Duke of Guise*

Spoken by Mrs. Cooke

Much time and trouble this poor play has cost;
And, faith, I doubted once the cause was lost.
Yet no one man was meant, nor great nor small;
Our poets, like frank gamesters, threw at all.
They took no single aim——   *5*
But, like bold boys, true to their Prince and hearty,
Huzza'd, and fired broadsides at the whole party.
Duels are crimes; but, when the cause is right,
In battle every man is bound to fight.
For what should hinder me to sell my skin   }   *10*
Dear as I could, if once my hand were in?   }
Se defendendo never was a sin.   }
'T is a fine world, my masters; right or wrong,
The Whigs must talk, and Tories hold their tongue.
They must do all they can——   *15*
But we, forsooth, must bear a Christian mind,
And fight, like boys, with one hand tied behind;
Nay, and when one boy 's down, 't were wondrous wise
To cry: "Box fair, and give him time to rise."
When fortune favors, none but fools will dally: }   *20*
Would any of you sparks, if Nan or Mally   }
Tipped you th' inviting wink, stand shall I, shall I? }
A Trimmer° cried, that heard me tell this story:

36 **Woolen Act** Act of 1678 requiring persons to be buried in wool
23 **Trimmer** one who keeps a cautious middle course

"Fie, Mistress Cooke! faith you're too rank a Tory!
25 Wish not Whigs hanged, but pity their hard cases;
You women love to see men make wry faces."
"Pray, sir," said I, "don't think me such a Jew;
I say no more, but give the Devil his due."
"Lenitives," says he, "suit best with our condition."
30 "Jack Ketch," says I, " 's an excellent physician."
"I love no blood."—"Nor I, sir, as I breathe;
But hanging is a fine dry kind of death."
"We Trimmers are for holding all things even."
"Yes—just like him that hung 'twixt hell and heaven."
35 "Have we not had men's lives enow already?"
"Yes, sure,—but you're for holding all things steady.
Now since the weight hangs all on one side, brother,
You Trimmers should, to poise it, hang on t'other."
Damned neuters, in their middle way of steering,
40 Are neither fish, nor flesh, nor good red herring:
Not Whigs, nor Tories they; nor this, nor that;
Not birds, nor beasts; but just a kind of bat:
A twilight animal, true to neither cause,
With Tory wings, but Whiggish teeth and claws.

Epilogue to the University of Oxford,

Spoken at the acting of *The Silent Woman*

No poor Dutch peasant, winged with all his fear,
Flies with more haste, when the French arms draw
        near,
Than we with our poetic train come down
For refuge hither from th' infected town:
5 Heav'n for our sins this summer has thought fit
To visit us with all the plagues of wit.
   A French troop first swept all things in its way;
But those hot Monsieurs were too quick to stay:

Yet, to our cost, in that short time, we find
They left their itch of novelty behind.   10
    Th' Italian merry-andrews took their place,
And quite debauched the stage with lewd grimace;
Instead of wit and humors, your delight
Was there to see two hobby-horses fight;
Stout Scaramoucha with rush lance rode in,   15
And ran a tilt at centaur Arlequin.
For love you heard how amorous asses brayed,
And cats in gutters gave their serenade.
Nature was out of countenance, and each day
Some new-born monster shown you for a play.   20
    But when all failed, to strike the stage quite dumb,
Those wicked engines called machines are come.
Thunder and lightning now for wit are played,
And shortly scenes in Lapland will be laid:
Art magic is for poetry professed;   25
And cats and dogs, and each obscener beast,
To which Egyptian dotards once did bow,
Upon our English stage are worshipped now.
Witchcraft reigns there, and raises to renown
Macbeth, the Simon Magus° of the town,   30
Fletcher's despised, your Jonson out of fashion,
And wit the only drug in all the nation.
In this low ebb our wares to you are shown;   ⎫
By you those staple authors' worth is known; ⎬
For wit 's a manufacture of your own.   ⎭   35
When you, who only can, their scenes have praised,
We'll boldly back, and say their price is raised.

30 **Simon Magus** a Samarian sorcerer

Prologue to *Arviragus and Philicia,* Revived

With sickly actors and an old house too,
We're matched with glorious theaters and new,
And with our alehouse scenes, and clothes bare worn,
Can neither raise old plays, nor new adorn.
5 If all these ills could not undo us quite,
A brisk French troop is grown your dear delight,
Who with broad bloody bills° call you each day,
To laugh and break your buttons at their play;
Or see some serious piece, which we presume
10 Is fallen from some incomparable plume;
And therefore, Messieurs, if you'll do us grace,
Send lackeys early to preserve your place.
We dare not on your privilege intrench,
Or ask you why you like 'em.—They are French.
15 Therefore some go with courtesy exceeding,
Neither to hear nor see, but show their breeding;
Each lady striving to out-laugh the rest,
To make it seem they understood the jest.
Their countrymen come in and nothing pay,
20 To teach us English where to clap the play:
Civil, egad! our hospitable land
Bears all the charge, for them to understand:
Meantime we languish, and neglected lie,
Like wives, while you keep better company;
25 And wish for our own sakes, without a satire,
You'd less good breeding, or had more good nature.

---

7 bloody bills the playbills of the French actors, printed in red

Epilogue to *Albion and Albanius*

After our Æsop's fable shown today,
I come to give the moral of the play.
Feigned Zeal, you saw, set out the speedier pace;
But, the last heat, Plain Dealing won the race.
Plain Dealing for a jewel has been known,   5
But ne'er till now the jewel of a crown.
When Heav'n made man, to show the work divine,
Truth was his image stamped upon the coin:
And, when a King is to a God refined,
On all he says and does he stamps his mind: 10
This proves a soul without allay, and pure;
Kings, like their gold, should every touch endure.
To dare in fields is valor; but how few
Dare be so throughly valiant to be true!
The name of great let other Kings affect: 15
He's great indeed, the Prince that is direct.
His subjects know him now, and trust him more
Than all their Kings, and all their Laws before.
What safety could their public acts afford?
Those he can break, but cannot break his word.   20
So great a trust to him alone was due;
Well have they trusted whom so well they knew.
The saint, who walked on waves, securely trod,
While he believed the beck'ning of his God;
But, when his faith no longer bore him out,   25
Began to sink, as he began to doubt.
Let us our native character maintain;
'T is of our growth, to be sincerely plain.
T' excel in truth we loyally may strive,
Set privilege against prerogative: 30
He plights his faith, and we believe him just;
His honor is to promise, ours to trust.
Thus Britain's basis on a word is laid,
As by a Word the world itself was made.

SONGS

Song from *Tyrannic Love*

Ah how sweet it is to love,
Ah how gay is young desire!
And what pleasing pains we prove
When we first approach love's fire!
    Pains of love be sweeter far
    Than all other pleasures are.

Sighs which are from lovers blown,
Do but gently heave the heart:
Ev'n the tears they shed alone
Cure, like trickling balm, their smart.
    Lovers when they lose their breath,
    Bleed away in easy death.

Love and time with reverence use,
Treat 'em like a parting friend:
Nor the golden gifts refuse
Which in youth sincere they send:
    For each year their price is more,
    And they less simple than before.

Love, like spring-tides full and high,
Swells in every youthful vein,
But each tide does less supply,
Till they quite shrink in again:
    If a flow in age appear,
    'T is but rain, and runs not clear.

Songs from *Sir Martin Mar-All*

I

Make ready, fair lady, to-night
  And stand at the door below,
For I will be there
To receive you with care,
  And to your true love you shall go.   5

THE LADY'S ANSWER

And when the stars twinkle so bright,
  Then down to the door will I creep,
To my love will I fly,
Ere the jealous can spy,
  And leave my old daddy asleep.   10

II

  Blind Love to this hour
Had never, like me, a slave under his power.
    Then blest be the dart
    That he threw at my heart,
      For nothing can prove   5
A joy so great as to be wounded with love.

  My days and my nights
Are filled to the purpose with sorrows and frights;
    From my heart still I sigh,
    And my eyes are ne'er dry,   10
      So that, Cupid be praised,
I am to the top of love's happiness raised.

  My soul's all on fire,
So that I have the pleasure to dote and desire,
    Such a pretty soft pain   15
    That it tickles each vein;

183

'T is the dream of a smart,
Which makes me breathe short when it beats at my
        heart.

        Sometimes in a pet,
20 When I am despised, I my freedom would get;
        But straight a sweet smile
        Does my anger beguile,
            And my heart does recall,
Then the more I do struggle, the lower I fall.

25   Heaven does not impart
Such a grace as to love unto every one's heart;
        For many may wish
        To be wounded and miss:
            Then blest be love's fire,
30 And more blest her eyes that first taught me desire.

Songs from *An Evening's Love*

I

You charmed me not with that fair face
    Though it was all divine:
To be another's is the grace
    That makes me wish you mine.

5 The gods and Fortune take their part
    Who like young Monarchs fight,
And boldly dare invade that heart
    Which is another's right.

First, mad with hope, we undertake
10   To pull up every bar;
But, once possessed, we faintly make
    A dull defensive war.

Now, every friend is turned a foe,
  In hope to get our store;
And passion makes us cowards grow,   *15*
  Which made us brave before.

II

After the pangs of a desperate lover,
  When day and night I have sighed all in vain,
Ah what a pleasure it is to discover,
  In her eyes pity, who causes my pain!

When with unkindness our love at a stand is,   *5*
  And both have punished ourselves with the pain,
Ah what a pleasure the touch of her hand is,
  Ah what a pleasure to press it again!

When the denial comes fainter and fainter,
  And her eyes give what her tongue does deny,   *10*
Ah what a trembling I feel when I venture,
  Ah what a trembling does usher my joy!

When, with a sigh, she accords me the blessing,
  And her eyes twinkle 'twixt pleasure and pain,
Ah what a joy 't is, beyond all expressing,   *15*
  Ah what a joy to hear: "Shall we again?"

III

Calm was the even, and clear was the sky,
  And the new-budding flowers did spring,
When all alone went Amyntas and I
  To hear the sweet nightingale sing.
I sate, and he laid him down by me,   *5*
  But scarcely his breath he could draw;
For when with a fear, he began to draw near,
  He was dashed with: "A ha ha ha ha!"

He blushed to himself, and lay still for a while,
  And his modesty curbed his desire;   *10*
But straight I convinced all his fear with a smile,

Which added new flames to his fire.
"O Sylvia," said he, "you are cruel,
    To keep your poor lover in awe;"
Then once more he pressed with his hand to my
15   breast,
    But was dash'd with: "A ha ha ha ha!"

I knew 't was his passion that caused all his fear,
    And therefore I pitied his case;
I whispered him softly: "There's nobody near,"
20   And laid my cheek close to his face:
But as he grew bolder and bolder,
    A shepherd came by us and saw,
And just as our bliss we began with a kiss,
    He laughed out with: "A ha ha ha ha!"

IV

Damon.   Celimena, of my heart,
        None shall e'er bereave you:
        If with your good leave I may
        Quarrel with you once a day,
5   I will never leave you.

Celimena. Passion 's but an empty name
        Where respect is wanting:
        Damon, you mistake your aim;
        Hang your heart, and burn your flame,
10   If you must be ranting.

Damon.   Love as dull and muddy is
        As decaying liquor:
        Anger sets it on the lees,
        And refines it by degrees,
15   Till it works it quicker.

Celimena. Love by quarrels to beget
        Wisely you endeavor;
        With a grave physician's wit

        Who, to cure an ague fit,
        Put me in a fever.   *20*

Damon.   Anger rouses love to fight,
        And his only bait is:
        'T is the spur to dull delight,
        And is but an eager bite,
        When desire at height is.   *25*

Celimena. If such drops of heat can fall
        In our wooing weather,
        If such drops of heat can fall,
        We shall have the Devil and all
        When we come together.   *30*

Songs from *The Conquest of Granada*

I

THE ZAMBRA DANCE

Beneath a myrtle shade
Which love for none but happy lovers made,
I slept, and straight my love before me brought
Phyllis, the object of my waking thought.
Undressed she came my flames to meet,   *5*
While love strowed flowers beneath her feet;
Flowers which, so pressed by her, became more
    sweet.

From the bright vision's head
A careless veil of lawn was loosely spread:
From her white temples fell her shaded hair,   *10*
Like cloudy sunshine, not too brown nor fair;
Her hands, her lips, did love inspire;

Her every grace my heart did fire:
But most her eyes, which languished with desire.

15 "Ah, charming fair," said I,
"How long can you my bliss and yours deny?
By nature and by love this lonely shade
Was for revenge of suffering lovers made.
Silence and shades with love agree;
20 Both shelter you and favor me:
You cannot blush, because I cannot see."

"No, let me die," she said,
"Rather than lose the spotless name of maid!"
Faintly, methought, she spoke, for all the while
25 She bid me not believe her, with a smile.
"Then die," said I; she still denied;
"And is it thus, thus, thus," she cried,
"You use a harmless maid?"—and so she died!

I waked, and straight I knew,
30 I loved so well it made my dream prove true:
Fancy, the kinder mistress of the two,
Fancy had done what Phyllis would not do!
Ah, cruel nymph, cease your disdain,
While I can dream, you scorn in vain—
35 Asleep or waking, you must ease my pain.

II

Wherever I am, and whatever I do,
    My Phyllis is still in my mind;
When angry, I mean not to Phyllis to go,
    My feet of themselves the way find:
5 Unknown to myself I am just at her door,
    And, when I would rail I can bring out no more
        Than: "Phyllis too fair and unkind!"

When Phyllis I see, my heart bounds in my breast,
    And the love I would stifle is shown;
10 But asleep or awake I am never at rest

 When from my eyes Phyllis is gone
Sometimes a sad dream does delude my sad mind,
 But, alas! when I wake and no Phyllis I find,
  How I sigh to myself all alone!

Should a King be my rival in her I adore   *15*
 He should offer his treasure in vain:
O let me alone to be happy and poor,
 And give me my Phyllis again!
Let Phyllis be mine, and but ever be kind
 I could to a desert with her be confined,   *20*
  And envy no monarch his reign.

Alas! I discover too much of my love,
 And she too well knows her own power!
She makes me each day a new martyrdom prove,
 And makes me grow jealous each hour.   *25*
But let her each minute torment my poor mind,
 I had rather love Phyllis, both false and unkind,
  Than ever be freed from her power.

III

He. How unhappy a lover am I,
   While I sigh for my Phyllis in vain;
  All my hopes of delight
  Are another man's right,
   Who is happy while I am in pain!   *5*

She. Since her honor allows no relief,
   But to pity the pains which you bear,
  'T is the best of your fate,
  (In a hopeless estate,)
   To give o'er, and betimes to despair.   *10*

He. I have tried the false medicine in vain;
   For I wish what I hope not to win:
  From without, my desire
  Has no food to its fire,
   But it burns and consumes me within.   *15*

She. Yet at least 't is a pleasure to know
    That you are not unhappy alone:
  For the nymph you adore
  Is as wretched and more;
20   And accounts all your sufferings her own.

He. O ye gods, let me suffer for both;
    At the feet of my Phyllis I 'll lie:
  I 'll resign up my breath,
  And take pleasure in death,
25   To be pitied by her when I die.

She. What her honor denied you in life,
    In her death she will give to your love.
  Such a flame as is true
  After fate will renew,
30   For the souls to meet closer above.

Songs from *Marriage-à-la-Mode*

I

Why should a foolish marriage vow
  Which long ago was made,
Oblige us to each other now
  When passion is decayed?
5 We loved, and we loved, as long as we could,
  Till our love was loved out in us both;
But our marriage is dead, when the pleasure is fled:
  'T was pleasure first made it an oath.

If I have pleasures for a friend,
10 And farther love in store,
What wrong has he whose joys did end,
  And who could give no more?

'T is a madness that he should be jealous of me,
  Or that I should bar him of another:
For all we can gain is to give ourselves pain,   15
  When neither can hinder the other.

II

Whilst Alexis lay pressed
In her arms he loved best,
With his hands round her neck, and his head on her
    breast,
He found the fierce pleasure too hasty to stay,
And his soul in the tempest just flying away.   5

When Celia saw this,
With a sigh and a kiss,
She cried: "O my dear, I am robbed of my bliss!
'T is unkind to your love, and unfaithfully done,
To leave me behind you, and die all alone."   10

The youth, though in haste,
And breathing his last,
In pity died slowly, while she died more fast;
Till at length she cried: "Now, my dear, now let us
    go;
Now die, my Alexis, and I will die too!"   15

Thus entranced they did lie,
Till Alexis did try
To recover new breath, that again he might die:
Then often they died; but the more they did so,
The nymph died more quick, and the shepherd more
    slow.   20

Song from *Troilus and Cressida*

Can life be a blessing,
Or worth the possessing,
Can life be a blessing if love were away?
Ah, no! though our love all night keep us waking,
5   And though he torment us with cares all the day,
Yet he sweetens, he sweetens our pains in the taking,
There 's an hour at the last, there 's an hour to repay.

In every possessing,
The ravishing blessing,
10   In every possessing the fruit of our pain,
Poor lovers forget long ages of anguish,
Whate'er they have suffered and done to obtain;
'T is a pleasure, a pleasure to sigh and to languish,
When we hope, when we hope to be happy again.

Song from *The Spanish Friar*

1

Farewell, ungrateful traitor,
    Farewell, my perjured swain!
Let never injured creature
    Believe a man again.
5   The pleasure of possessing
Surpasses all expressing,
But 't is too short a blessing,
    And love too long a pain.

2

'T is easy to deceive us
   In pity of your pain;
But when we love, you leave us   10
   To rail at you in vain.
Before we have descried it,
There is no bliss beside it,
But she that once has tried it   15
   Will never love again.

3

The passion you pretended,
   Was only to obtain,
But when the charm is ended,
   The charmer you disdain.
Your love by ours we measure   20
Till we have lost our treasure,
But dying is a pleasure,
   When living is a pain.

Song from *The Secular Masque*

Momus.   All, all of a piece throughout:
       (*Pointing to* DIANA.)
     Thy chase had a beast in view;
       (*To* MARS.)
     Thy wars brought nothing about;
       (*To* VENUS.)
     Thy lovers were all untrue.
Janus.   'T is well an old age is out: 5
Chronos. And time to begin a new.

Chorus of All.

> All, all of a piece throughout:
> Thy chase had a beast in view;
> Thy wars brought nothing about;
> Thy lovers were all untrue.
> 'T is well an old age is out,
> And time to begin a new.

10

Sylvia the Fair

1

Sylvia the fair, in the bloom of fifteen,
Felt an innocent warmth as she lay on the green;
She had heard of a pleasure, and something she guessed
By the towzing and tumbling and touching her breast.
She saw the men eager, but was at a loss,   *5*
What they meant by their sighing, and kissing so close;
    By their praying and whining
    And clasping and twining,
    And panting and wishing,
    And sighing and kissing   *10*
And sighing and kissing so close.

2

"Ah!" she cried, "ah! for a languishing maid,
In a country of Christians to die without aid!
Not a Whig, or a Tory, or Trimmer at least,
Or a Protestant parson, or Catholic priest,   *15*
To instruct a young virgin, that is at a loss
What they meant by their sighing, and kissing so close!
    By their praying and whining
    And clasping and twining,
    And panting and wishing,   *20*
    And sighing and kissing
And sighing and kissing so close."

3

Cupid, in shape of a swain, did appear,
He saw the sad wound, and in pity drew near,
Then showed her his arrow, and bid her not fear,   *25*
For the pain was no more than a maiden may bear.

When the balm was infused she was not at a loss,
What they meant by their sighing, and kissing so close;
   By their praying and whining,
30   And clasping and twining,
    And panting and wishing,
    And sighing and kissing
And sighing and kissing so close.

To the Memory of Mr. Oldham

Farewell, too little, and too lately known,
Whom I began to think and call my own;
For sure our souls were near allied, and thine
Cast in the same poetic mold with mine.
One common note on either lyre did strike, 5
And knaves and fools we both abhorred alike.
To the same goal did both our studies drive;
The last set out the soonest did arrive.
Thus Nisus° fell upon the slippery place,
While his young friend performed and won the race. 10
O early ripe! to thy abundant store
What could advancing age have added more?
It might (what nature never gives the young)
Have taught the numbers of thy native tongue.
But satire needs not those, and wit will shine 15
Through the harsh cadence of a rugged line.
A noble error, and but seldom made,
When poets are by too much force betrayed.
Thy generous fruits, though gathered ere their prime,
Still showed a quickness; and maturing time 20
But mellows what we write to the dull sweets of
rhyme.
Once more, hail and farewell; farewell, thou young,
But ah too short, Marcellus° of our tongue;
Thy brows with ivy, and with laurels bound;
But fate and gloomy night encompass thee around. 25

9 Nisus friend of Aeneas 23 Marcellus nephew of Augustus, who
died young

To the Pious Memory of the Accomplished Young Lady, Mrs. Anne Killigrew,
excellent in the two Sister-Arts of Poesy and Painting,
An Ode

I

Thou youngest virgin-daughter of the skies,
   Made in the last promotion of the blest;
Whose palms, new plucked from paradise,
In spreading branches more sublimely rise,
5   Rich with immortal green above the rest:
Whether, adopted to some neighboring star,
Thou rollest above us in thy wandering race,
   Or, in procession fixed and regular.
   Moved with the Heav'ns' majestic pace;
10   Or, called to more superior bliss,
Thou treadest, with seraphims, the vast abyss.
Whatever happy region is thy place,
Cease thy celestial song a little space;
(Thou wilt have time enough for hymns divine,
15   Since Heav'n's Eternal Year is thine.)
Hear then a mortal Muse thy praise rehearse,
          In no ignoble verse;
But such as thy own voice did practice here,
When thy first fruits of Poesy were given,
20 To make thyself a welcome inmate there,
        While yet a young probationer,
        And candidate of Heav'n.

II

If by traduction° came thy mind,
  Our wonder is the less to find
A soul so charming from a stock so good;   25
Thy father was transfused into thy blood:
So wert thou born into the tuneful strain
(An early, rich, and inexhausted vein.)
    But if thy pre-existing soul
    Was formed, at first, with myriads more,   30
It did through all the mighty poets roll,
    Who Greek or Latin laurels wore,
    If so, then cease thy flight, *O Heav'n-born Mind!*
Thou hast no dross to purge from thy rich ore;
And was that sappho last, which once it was before.   35
    Nor can thy soul a fairer mansion find
    Than was the beauteous frame she left behind:
Return, to fill or mend the quire° of thy celestial
    kind.

III

May we presume to say that at thy birth
New joy was sprung in Heav'n, as well as here on
    earth?   40
    For sure the milder planets did combine
    On thy auspicious horoscope to shine,
    And even the most malicious were in trine.°
Thy brother-angels at thy birth
    Strung each his lyre, and tuned it high,   45
    That all the people of the sky
Might know a poetess was born on earth.
    And then, if ever, mortal ears
    Had heard the music of the spheres!
    And if no clustering swarm of bees°   50
On thy sweet mouth distilled their golden dew,

---

23 **traduction** begotten by your like; her father, Henry, was chaplain
to Charles I   38 **quire** this spelling for choir puns on the idea of a
chorus and of a quire of paper used by the poet-painter   43 **trine** a
certain planetary aspect of benign influence   50 **swarm of bees**
legend of miracle prophesying of the infant Plato's future eloquence

'T was that such vulgar miracles
   Heav'n had not leisure to renew:
For all the blest fraternity of love
Solemnized there thy birth, and kept thy holyday
55   above.

IV

O gracious God! how far have we
Profaned thy Heav'nly Gift of Poesy!
Made prostitute and profligate the Muse,
Debased to each obscene and impious use,
60 Whose harmony was first ordained above
For tongues of angels, and for hymns of love!
O wretched we! why were we hurried down
   This lubric° and adulterate age,
  (Nay, added fat pollutions of our own,)
65   T' increase the steaming ordures of the stage?
What can we say t' excuse our *Second Fall?*
Let this thy *vestal,*° Heav'n, atone for all:
Her Arethusian stream° remains unsoiled,
Unmixed with foreign filth, and undefiled;
70 Her wit was more than man, her innocence a child!

V

Art she had none, yet wanted none,
   For Nature did that want supply:
So rich in treasures of her own
   She might our boasted stores defy:
75 Such noble vigor did her verse adorn
That it seemed borrowed, where 't was only born.
Her morals too were in her bosom bred,
   By great examples daily fed,
What in the best of books, her father's life, she read.
80   And to be read herself she need not fear;
   Each test, and every light, her Muse will bear,
   Though Epictetus° with his lamp were there.

63 **lubric** lascivious   67 **vestal** vowed to virginity   68 **Arethusian stream** fountain of a nymph, companion to Diana   82 **Epictetus** Dryden is here confusing Epictetus with Diogenes

Ev'n love (for love sometimes her Muse expressed)
Was but a *lambent flame*° which played about her
   breast,
 Light as the vapors of a morning dream,   *85*
So cold herself, whilst she such warmth expressed,
'T was Cupid bathing in Diana's stream.

VI

Born to the spacious empire of the Nine,
One would have thought she should have been
  content
To manage well that mighty government;   *90*
But what can young ambitious souls confine?
 To the next realm she stretched her sway, ⎫
 For *painture*° near adjoining lay,   ⎬
A plenteous province, and alluring prey.   ⎭
 A chamber of dependences° was framed,   *95*
(As conquerors will never want pretense,
 When armed, to justify th' offense,)
And the whole fief in right of poetry she claimed.
The country open lay without defense;
For poets frequent inroads there had made,   *100*
 And perfectly could represent
 The shape, the face, with every lineament;
And all the large domains which the *Dumb Sister*°
  swayed,
 All bowed beneath her government;
 Received in triumph wheresoe'er she went. *105*
Her pencil drew whate'er her soul designed,
And oft the happy draught surpassed the image in
  her mind.
 The sylvan scenes of herds and flocks,
 And fruitful plains and barren rocks,
 Of shallow brooks that flowed so clear   *110*
 The bottom did the top appear;
 Of deeper too and ampler floods,

---

84 **lambent flame** quickly darting desire, like a will-o'-the wisp   93
painture painting   95 **chamber of dependences** sphere of authority
103 **Dumb Sister** painting personified as the silent sister to poetry,
which is thought of as the "speaking picture"

Which, as in mirrors, showed the woods;
Of lofty trees, with sacred shades,
115   And perspectives of pleasant glades,
Where nymphs of brightest form appear, ⎫
And shaggy satyrs standing near,   ⎬
Which them at once admire and fear.   ⎭
The ruins too of some majestic piece,
120   Boasting the power of ancient Rome or Greece,
Whose statues, friezes, columns broken lie,
And, though defaced, the wonder of the eye:
What nature, art, bold fiction, e'er durst frame,
Her forming hand gave feature to the name.
125   So strange a concourse ne'er was seen before,
But when the peopled ark the whole creation bore.

VII

The scene then changed, with bold erected look
Our martial King the sight with reverence strook;
For, not content t' express his outward part,
130   Her hand called out the image of his heart;
His warlike mind, his soul devoid of fear, ⎫
His high-designing thoughts were figured there, ⎬
As when, by magic, ghosts are made appear.   ⎭
Our Phoenix queen° was portrayed too so bright,
135   Beauty alone could Beauty take so right:
Her dress, her shape, her matchless grace,
Were all observed, as well as heav'nly face.
With such a peerless majesty she stands
As in that day she took the crown from sacred hands;
140   Before a train of heroines was seen,
In Beauty foremost, as in rank the Queen.
Thus nothing to her *genius* was denied,
But like a ball of fire the further thrown,
Still with a greater blaze she shone,
145   And her bright soul broke out on every side.
What next she had designed, Heav'n only knows;
To such immoderate growth her conquest rose
That fate alone its progress could oppose.

134 **Phœnix queen** Queen to James II

VIII

Now all those charms, that blooming grace,
The well-proportioned shape, and beauteous face,   *150*
Shall never more be seen by mortal eyes:
In earth the much-lamented virgin lies!
  Not wit, nor piety could fate prevent;
  Nor was the cruel Destiny content
  To finish all the murder at a blow,   *155*
  To sweep at once her life, and beauty too;
But, like a hardened felon, took a pride
  To work more mischievously slow,
And plundered first, and then destroyed.
O double sacrilege on things divine,   *160*
To rob the relic, and deface the shrine!
    But thus Orinda° died:
Heav'n, by the same disease, did both translate;
As equal were their souls, so equal was their fate.

IX

Meantime her warlike brother on the seas   *165*
  His waving streamers to the winds displays,
And vows for his return, with vain devotion, pays.
  Ah, generous youth, that wish forbear,
  The winds too soon will waft thee here!
  Slack all thy sails, and fear to come,   *170*
Alas, thou knowest not, thou art wrecked at home!
No more shalt thou behold thy sister's face,
Thou hast already had her last embrace.
But look aloft, and if thou kennest from far
Among the Pleiads a new kindled star;   *175*
If any sparkles than the rest more bright,
'T is she that shines in that propitious light.

X

When in mid-air the golden trump shall sound,
  To raise the nations under ground;

162 **Orinda** Mrs. Katherine Philips, contemporary poetess

180   When in the Valley of Jehosaphat°
    The judging God shall close the book of fate,
        And there the last assizes° keep
        For those who wake and those who sleep;
        When rattling bones together fly
185   From the four corners of the sky;
    When sinews o'er the skeletons are spread,
    Those clothed with flesh, and life inspires the dead;
    The sacred poets first shall hear the sound,   ⎫
    And foremost from the tomb shall bound,   ⎬
190 For they are covered with the lightest ground;   ⎭
    And straight, with inborn vigor, on the wing,
    Like mounting larks, to the new morning sing.
    There thou, sweet saint, before the choir shalt go,
    As harbinger of Heav'n, the way to show,
195 The way which thou so well hast learned below.

A Song for St. Cecilia's Day,
November 22, 1687

I

From Harmony, from heav'nly Harmony
    This universal frame began.
  When Nature underneath a heap
    Of jarring atoms lay,
  And could not heave her head,   *5*
The tuneful voice was heard from high:
    "Arise, ye more than dead."
Then cold, and hot, and moist, and dry,
  In order to their stations leap,
    And Music's power obey.   *10*
From Harmony, from heav'nly Harmony
    This universal frame° began;
    From Harmony to Harmony
Through all the compass of the notes it ran,
The diapason closing full in Man.   *15*

II

What passion cannot Music raise and quell!
    When Jubal° struck the corded shell,
  His listening brethren stood around,
    And, wondering, on their faces fell
  To worship that celestial sound.   *20*
Less than a god they thought there could not dwell
    Within the hollow of that shell
    That spoke so sweetly and so well.
What passion cannot Music raise and quell!

12 frame machine, system   **17 Jubal** inventor of the harp

III

25 The Trumpet's loud clangor
  Excites us to arms
 With shrill notes of anger
  And mortal alarms.
 The double double double beat
30 Of the thundering Drum
  Cries: "Hark! the foes come;
Charge, charge, 't is too late to retreat."

IV

 The soft complaining Flute
 In dying notes discovers
35 The woes of hopeless lovers,
Whose dirge is whispered by the warbling Lute.

V

 Sharp Violins proclaim
Their jealous pangs, and desperation,
Fury, frantic indignation,
40 Depth of pains, and height of passion,
 For the fair, disdainful dame.

VI

 But O! what art can teach,
 What human voice can reach
The sacred Organ's praise?
45 Notes inspiring holy love,
Notes that wing their heav'nly ways
 To mend the choirs above.

VII

Orpheus could lead the savage race,
And trees unrooted left their place,
50 Sequacious° of the lyre;
But bright Cecilia raised the wonder higher:

50 **Sequacious** following

When to her Organ vocal breath was given,
An angel heard, and straight appeared,
  Mistaking earth for Heav'n.

GRAND CHORUS

As from the power of sacred lays   55
  The spheres began to move,
And sung the great Creator's praise
  To all the blest above;
So, when the last and dreadful hour
This crumbling pageant shall devour,   60
The Trumpet shall be heard on high,
The dead shall live, the living die,
And Music shall untune the sky.

Lines printed under the Engraved Portrait of Milton,
in Tonson's Folio Edition of the "Paradise Lost," 1688

Three poets, in three distant ages born,
Greece, Italy, and England, did adorn.
The first in loftiness of thought surpassed,
The next in majesty, in both the last:
5 The force of Nature could no farther go;
To make a third she joined the former two.

Veni, Creator Spiritus°
Translated in Paraphrase

Creator Spirit, by whose aid
The world's foundations first were laid,
Come visit every pious mind;
Come pour thy joys on humankind;
From sin and sorrow set us free,   5
And make thy temples worthy thee.
  O source of uncreated light,
The Father's promised Paraclite!°
Thrice holy fount, thrice holy fire,
Our hearts with Heav'nly love inspire;   10
Come, and thy sacred unction bring
To sanctify us, while we sing!
  Plenteous of grace, descend from high,
Rich in thy sevenfold energy!
Thou strength of his Almighty Hand,   15
Whose power does Heav'n and earth command!
Proceeding Spirit, our defense, ⎫
Who dost the gift of tongues dispense, ⎬
And crownest thy gift with eloquence! ⎭
  Refine and purge our earthy parts;   20
But, O, inflame and fire our hearts!
Our frailties help, our vice control,
Submit the senses to the soul;
And when rebellious they are grown,
Then lay thy hand, and hold 'em down.   25
  Chase from our minds th' infernal foe,
And peace, the fruit of love, bestow;
And lest our feet should step astray,
Protect, and guide us in the way.
  Make us eternal truths receive,   30

° An ancient Latin hymn for Pentecost when the Disciples were given
the gift of tongues   8 **Paraclite** Holy Ghost

And practice all that we believe:
Give us thyself, that we may see
The Father and the Son, by thee.
Immortal honor, endless fame,
35 Attend th' Almighty Father's name:
The Savior Son be glorified,
Who for lost man's redemption died,
And equal adoration be,
Eternal Paraclete, to thee.

To my Dear Friend, Mr. Congreve,
on his Comedy called *The Double-Dealer*

Well then, the promised hour is come at last;
The present age of wit obscures the past:
Strong were our sires, and as they fought they writ,
Conquering with force of arms, and dint of wit;
Theirs was the giant race, before the flood; *5*
And thus, when Charles returned, our Empire stood.
Like Janus° he the stubborn soil manured,
With rules of husbandry the rankness cured;
Tamed us to manners, when the stage was rude;
And boisterous English wit with art indued. *10*
Our age was cultivated thus at length,
But what we gained in skill we lost in strength.
Our builders were with want of genius curst;
The second temple° was not like the first:
Till you, the best Vitruvius,° come at length; *15*
Our beauties equal, but excel our strength.
Firm Doric pillars found your solid base;
The fair Corinthian crowns the higher space:
Thus all below is strength, and all above is grace.
In easy dialogue is Fletcher's praise; *20*
He moved the mind, but had not power to raise.
Great Jonson did by strength of judgment please,
Yet, doubling Fletcher's force, he wants his ease.
In differing talents both adorned their age;
One for the study, t'other for the stage. *25*
But both to Congreve justly shall submit,
One matched in judgment, both o'ermatched in wit.

---

7 **Janus** Roman god credited with bringing agriculture to Italy 14
second temple built after the Exile 15 **Vitruvius** Roman architect
of the Augustan Age

In him all beauties of this age we see,
Etherege his courtship,° Southern's purity, 〕
30 The satire, wit, and strength of Manly Wycherley. 〕
All this in blooming youth you have achieved,
Nor are your foiled contemporaries grieved.
So much the sweetness of your manners move,
We cannot envy you, because we love.
35 Fabius might joy in Scipio, when he saw
A beardless consul° made against the law;
And join his suffrage to the votes of Rome
Though he with Hannibal was overcome.
Thus old Romano° bowed to Raphael's fame,
40 And scholar to the youth he taught became.
    O that your brows my laurel had sustained;
Well had I been deposed,° if you had reigned!
The father had descended for the son;
For only you are lineal to the throne.
45 Thus, when the state one Edward did depose,
A greater Edward in his room arose.
But now, not I, but poetry is curst;
For Tom the Second reigns like Tom the First.°
But let 'em not mistake my patron's° part,
50 Nor call his charity their own desert.
Yet this I prophesy: thou shalt be seen
(Though with some short parenthesis between)
High on the throne of wit; and, seated there,
Not mine—that's little—but thy laurel wear.
55 Thy first attempt an early promise made;
That early promise this has more than paid.
So bold, yet so judiciously you dare,
That your least praise is to be regular.
Time, place, and action, may with pains be wrought,
60 But genius must be born, and never can be taught.

---

29 **courtship** courtliness   35–6 **Fabius . . . consul** Fabius had opposed the young Scipio's plans for the Carthaginian War   39 **Romano** Giulio Romano was Raphael's pupil, not his master   42 **Well . . . deposed** on his accession, William III removed Dryden from his laureateship   45–8 **Edward . . . Tom the First** Edward II was succeeded by a greater monarch, Edward III, but Thomas Shadwell was succeeded by Thomas Rymer, another dullard, as Historiographer-Royal   49 **patron's** the Earl of Dorset

This is your portion; this your native store;
Heav'n, that but once was prodigal before,
To Shakespeare gave as much; she could not give him
    more.
    Maintain your post: that's all the fame you need;
For 't is impossible you should proceed.   65
Already I am worn with cares and age,
And just abandoning th' ungrateful stage;
Unprofitably kept at Heav'n's expense,
I live a rent-charge on his Providence:
But you, whom every Muse and Grace adorn,   70
Whom I foresee to better fortune born,
Be kind to my remains; and O defend,
Against your judgment, your departed friend!
Let not th' insulting foe my fame pursue,
But shade those laurels which descend to you;   75
And take for tribute what these lines express:
You merit more; nor could my love do less.

Alexander's Feast;
or, The Power of Music; an Ode in Honor of St. Cecilia's Day: 1697.

I

'T was at the royal feast, for Persia won
     By Philip's warlike son:
     Aloft in awful state
     The godlike hero sate
5   On his imperial throne.
His valiant peers were placed around,
Their brows with roses and with myrtles bound.
(So should desert in arms be crowned.)
The lovely Thais by his side,
10 Sate like a blooming Eastern bride
In flower of youth and beauty's pride.
     Happy, happy, happy pair!
       None but the brave,
       None but the brave,
15 None but the brave deserves the fair.

CHORUS

Happy, happy, happy pair!
*   None but the brave,*
*   None but the brave,*
None but the brave deserves the fair.

II

20 Timotheus placed on high
     Amid the tuneful choir,
     With flying fingers touched the lyre:

The trembling notes ascend the sky,
  And heav'nly joys inspire.
The song began from Jove,   25
Who left his blissful seats above
(Such is the power of mighty love.)
A dragon's fiery form belied the god:
Sublime on radiant spires° he rode,
    When he to fair Olympia° pressed;   30
    And while he sought her snowy breast:
Then, round her slender waist he curled,
And stamped an image of himself, a sovereign of the
    world.
The listening crowd admire the lofty sound,
"A present deity," they shout around;   35
"A present deity," the vaulted roofs rebound:
      With ravished ears
      The monarch hears,
      Assumes the god,
      Affects to nod,   40
    And seems to shake the spheres.

CHORUS

      With ravished ears
      The monarch hears,
      Assumes the god,
      Affects to nod,   45
  And seems to shake the spheres.

III

The praise of Bacchus then the sweet musician sung,
  Of Bacchus ever fair, and ever young:
    The jolly god in triumph comes;
    Sound the trumpets; beat the drums;   50
      Flushed with a purple grace
      He shows his honest face:
Now give the hautboys breath; he comes, he comes.
    Bacchus, ever fair and young,

29 **spires** spirals   30 **Olympia** mother of Alexander

55   Drinking joys did first ordain;
      Bacchus' blessings are a treasure,
      Drinking is the soldier's pleasure:
        Rich the treasure,
        Sweet the pleasure,
60   Sweet is pleasure after pain.

CHORUS

Bacchus' blessings are a treasure,
Drinking is the soldier's pleasure:
  Rich the treasure,
  Sweet the pleasure,
65 *Sweet is pleasure after pain.*

IV

Soothed with the sound, the King grew vain;
    Fought all his battles o'er again;
And thrice he routed all his foes; and thrice he slew
    the slain.
The master saw the madness rise;
70   His glowing cheeks, his ardent eyes;
And, while he Heav'n and earth defied,
Changed his hand, and checked his pride.
    He chose a mournful Muse,
    Soft pity to infuse:
75 He sung Darius great and good,
    By too severe a fate,
  Fallen, fallen, fallen, fallen,
    Fallen from his high estate,
And weltering in his blood;
80 Deserted, at his utmost need,
By those his former bounty fed,
On the bare earth exposed he lies,
With not a friend to close his eyes.
With downcast looks the joyless victor sate,
85   Revolving in his altered soul
      The various turns of chance below;
    And, now and then, a sigh he stole;
      And tears began to flow.

CHORUS

Revolving in his altered soul
  The various turns of chance below;   90
And, now and then, a sigh he stole;
  And tears began to flow.

V

The mighty master smiled to see
That love was in the next degree:
'T was but a kindred sound to move,   95
For pity melts the mind to love.
  Softly sweet, in Lydian measures,
  Soon he soothed his soul to pleasures.
"War," he sung, "is toil and trouble;
Honor, but an empty bubble;   100
  Never ending, still beginning,
Fighting still, and still destroying:
  If the world be worth thy winning,
Think, O think it worth enjoying.
  Lovely Thais sits beside thee,   105
  Take the good the gods provide thee."
The many rend the skies with loud applause;
So Love was crowned, but Music won the cause.
  The Prince, unable to conceal his pain,
    Gazed on the fair   110
    Who caused his care,
And sighed and looked, sighed and looked,
Sighed and looked, and sighed again:
At length, with love and wine at once oppressed,
The vanquished victor sunk upon her breast.   115

CHORUS

The Prince, unable to conceal his pain,
  Gazed on the fair
  Who caused his care,
And sighed and looked, sighed and looked,
Sighed and looked, and sighed again: 120

At length, with love and wine at once oppressed,
The vanquished victor sunk upon her breast.

VI

Now strike the golden lyre again:
A louder yet, and yet a louder strain.
125 Break his bands of sleep asunder,
And rouse him, like a rattling peal of thunder.
    Hark, hark, the horrid sound
      Has raised up his head:
      As awaked from the dead,
130   And amazed, he stares around.
  "Revenge, revenge!" Timotheus cries,
    "See the Furies arise!
    See the snakes that they rear,
    How they hiss in their hair,
135 And the sparkles that flash from their eyes!
    Behold a ghastly band,
    Each a torch in his hand!
Those are Grecian ghosts, that in battle were slain,
    And unburied remain
140   Inglorious on the plain;
    Give the vengeance due
    To the valiant crew.
Behold how they toss their torches on high,
    How they point to the Persian abodes,
145 And glittering temples of their hostile gods!"
The Princes applaud, with a furious joy;
And the King seized a flambeau° with zeal to destroy;
    Thais led the way,
    To light him to his prey,
150 And, like another Helen, fired another Troy.

Chorus

And the King seized a flambeau with zeal to destroy;
    Thais led the way,
    To light him to his prey,
And, like another Helen, fired another Troy.

147 **flambeau** torch

VII

Thus, long ago   *155*
Ere heaving bellows learned to blow,
While organs yet were mute,
Timotheus, to his breathing flute,
And sounding lyre,
Could swell the soul to rage, or kindle soft desire.   *160*
At last, divine Cecilia came,
Inventress of the vocal frame;°
The sweet enthusiast, from her sacred store,
Enlarged the former narrow bounds,
And added length to solemn sounds,   *165*
With nature's mother-wit, and arts unknown before.
Let old Timotheus yield the prize,
Or both divide the crown;
He raised a mortal to the skies;
She drew an Angel down.   *170*

Grand Chorus

At last, divine Cecilia came,
Inventress of the vocal frame;
The sweet enthusiast, from her sacred store,
Enlarged the former narrow bounds,
And added length to solemn sounds,   *175*
With nature's mother-wit, and arts unknown before.
Let old Timotheus yield the prize,
Or both divide the crown;
He raised a mortal to the skies;
She drew an Angel down.   *180*

162 **vocal frame** organ

To my honored Kinsman,
JOHN DRIDEN,
of Chesterton, in the county of Huntingdon, Esquire

How blest is he, who leads a country life,
Unvexed with anxious cares, and void of strife!
Who, studying peace and shunning civil rage,
Enjoyed his youth, and now enjoys his age:
5 All who deserve his love, he makes his own;
And, to be loved himself, needs only to be known.
    Just, good, and wise, contending neighbors come,
From your award to wait their final doom;
And, foes before, return in friendship home.
10 Without their cost, you terminate the cause,
And save th' expense of long litigious laws:
Where suits are traversed,° and so little won,
That he who conquers is but last undone.
Such are not your decrees; but so designed,
15 The sanction leaves a lasting peace behind:
Like your own soul, serene; a pattern of your mind.
    Promoting concord, and composing strife,
Lord of yourself, uncumbered with a wife;
Where, for a year, a month, perhaps a night,
20 Long penitence succeeds a short delight:
Minds are so hardly matched, that ev'n the first,
Though paired by Heav'n, in Paradise were curst.
For man and woman, though in one they grow,
Yet, first or last, return again to two.
25 He to God's image, she to his was made;
So, farther from the fount, the stream at random
    strayed.
    How could he stand, when, put to double pain,

12 **traversed** opposed

He must a weaker than himself sustain!
Each might have stood perhaps, but each alone;
Two wrestlers help to pull each other down.   30
    Not that my verse would blemish all the fair;
But yet if *some* be bad, 't is wisdom to beware;
And better shun the bait than struggle in the snare.
Thus have you shunned, and shun, the married state,
Trusting as little as you can to fate.   35
    No porter guards the passage of your door,
T' admit the wealthy, and exclude the poor;
For God, who gave the riches, gave the heart,
To sanctify the whole, by giving part.
Heav'n, who foresaw the will, the means has wrought,   40
And to the second son a blessing brought;
The first-begotten had his father's share,
But you, like Jacob, are Rebecca's heir.
    So may your stores and fruitful fields increase;
And ever be you blest, who live to bless.   45
As Ceres sowed, where'er her chariot flew;
As Heav'n in deserts rained the bread of dew;
So free to many, to relations most,
You feed with manna your own Israel host.
    With crowds attended of your ancient race,   50
You seek the champian° sports or sylvan chase;
With well-breathed beagles you surround the wood,
Ev'n then industrous of the common good;
And often have you brought the wily fox
To suffer for the firstlings of the flocks;   55
Chased ev'n amid the folds, and made to bleed,
Like felons, where they did the murderous deed.
This fiery game your active youth maintained,
Not yet by years extinguished, though restrained:
You season still with sports your serious hours;   60
For age but tastes of pleasures, youth devours.
The hare in pastures or in plains is found,
Emblem of human life, who runs the round;
And after all his wandering ways are done, ⎫
His circle fills and ends where he begun, ⎬   65
Just as the setting meets the rising sun. ⎭

51 **champian** open country

Thus Princes ease their cares; but happier he
Who seeks not pleasure through necessity,
Than such as once on slippery thrones were placed;
70 And chasing, sigh to think themselves are chased.
So lived our sires, ere doctors learned to kill,
And multiplied with theirs the weekly bill.
The first physicians by debauch were made;
Excess began, and sloth sustains the trade.
75 Pity the generous kind their cares bestow
To search forbidden truths; (a sin to know:)
To which if human science could attain,
The doom of death, pronounced by God, were vain.
In vain the leech would interpose delay;
80 Fate fastens first, and vindicates the prey.
What help from art's endeavors can we have?
Gibbons° but guesses, nor is sure to save;
But Maurus° sweeps whole parishes, and peoples
      every grave;
And no more mercy to mankind will use,
85 Than when he robbed and murdered Maro's° Muse.
Wouldst thou be soon dispatched, and perish whole?
Trust Maurus with thy life, and M-lb–rne° with thy
      soul.
By chase our long-lived fathers earned their food;
Toil strung the nerves and purified the blood:
90 But we, their sons, a pampered race of men,
Are dwindled down to threescore years and ten.
Better to hunt in fields for health unbought
Than fee the doctor for a nauseous draught.
The wise for cure on exercise depend;
95 God never made his work for man to mend.
The tree of knowledge, once in Eden placed,
Was easy found, but was forbid the taste:
O had our grandsire walked without his wife,
He first had sought the better plant of life!
100 Now, both are lost; yet, wandering in the dark,

---

82 **Gibbons** William Gibbons, Dryden's physician   83 **Maurus** Sir
Richard Blackmore, physician and poet   85 **Maro's** Virgil's   87
M-lb–rne Luke Milbourne, critic of Dryden's translation of Virgil

Physicians, for the tree, have found the bark.
They, laboring for relief of humankind,
With sharpened sight some remedies may find;
Th' apothecary train is wholly blind.
From files a random recipe they take,   *105*
And many deaths of one prescription make.
Garth,° generous as his Muse, prescribes and gives;
The shopman sells, and by destruction lives:
Ungrateful tribe! who, like the viper's brood,
From medicine issuing, suck their mother's blood!   *110*
Let these obey, and let the learned prescribe,
That men may die without a double bribe:
Let them but under their superiors kill,
When doctors first have signed the bloody bill;
He scapes the best, who, nature to repair,   *115*
Draws physic from the fields, in draughts of vital air.

You hoard not health for your own private use,
But on the public spend the rich produce;
When, often urged, unwilling to be great,
Your country calls you from your loved retreat,   *120*
And sends to senates, charged with common care,
Which none more shuns, and none can better bear.
Where could they find another formed so fit,
To poise with solid sense a sprightly wit?
Were these both wanting, (as they both abound,)   *125*
Where could so firm integrity be found?

Well-born, and wealthy, wanting no support,
You steer betwixt the country and the court;
Nor gratify whate'er the great desire,
Nor grudging give what public needs require.   *130*
Part must be left, a fund when foes invade;
And part employed to roll the watery trade:
Ev'n Canaan's happy land, when worn with toil,
Required a sabbath year to mend the meager soil.

Good senators (and such are you) so give,   *135*
That Kings may be supplied, the people thrive.
And he, when want requires, is truly wise,
Who slights not foreign aids, nor overbuys,
But on our native strength, in time of need, relies.

107 **Garth** Sir Samuel Garth, physician and poet

140 Munster° was bought, we boast not the success;
Who fights for gain, for greater makes his peace.
   Our foes, compelled by need, have peace embraced;
The peace both parties want is like to last:
Which if secure, securely we may trade;
145 Or, not secure, should never have been made.
Safe in ourselves, while on ourselves we stand,
The sea is ours, and that defends the land.
Be, then, the naval stores the nation's care,
New ships to build, and battered to repair.
150   Observe the war, in every annual course;
What has been done was done with British force:
Namur° subdued is England's palm alone;
The rest besieged, but we constrained the town:
We saw th' event that followed our success;
155 France, though pretending arms, pursued the peace;
Obliged, by one sole treaty, to restore
What twenty years of war had won before.
Enough for Europe has our Albion fought:
Let us enjoy the peace our blood has bought.
160 When once the Persian king was put to flight,
The weary Macedons refused to fight,
Themselves their own mortality confessed,
And left the son of Jove to quarrel for the rest.
   Even victors are by victories undone;
165 Thus Hannibal, with foreign laurels won,   }
To Carthage was recalled, too late to keep his own. }
While sore of battle, while our wounds are green,
Why should we tempt the doubtful die° again?
In wars renewed, uncertain of success;
170 Sure of a share, as umpires of the peace.
   A patriot both the king and country serves;
Prerogative and privilege preserves:
Of each our laws the certain limit show;
One must not ebb, nor t'other overflow.

140 **Munster** Bishop of Munster, an ally unfaithful to the British
152 **Namur** Belgian battle won by William III   168 **die** cast of the
dice

Betwixt the Prince and Parliament we stand;   *175*
The barriers of the state on either hand:
May neither overflow, for then they drown the land!
When both are full, they feed our blest abode;
Like those that watered once the Paradise of God.

Some overpoise of sway by turns they share;   *180*
In peace the people, and the Prince in war:
Consuls of moderate power in calms were made;
When the Gauls came, one sole dictator swayed.

Patriots, in peace, assert the people's right;
With noble stubbornness resisting might: *185*
No lawless mandates from the court receive,
Nor lend by force, but in a body give.
Such was your generous grandsire; free to grant
In Parliaments that weighed their Prince's want:
But so tenacious of the common cause,   *190*
As not to lend the King against his laws;
And, in a loathsome dungeon doomed to lie,
In bonds retained his birthright liberty,
And shamed oppression, till it set him free.

O true descendant of a patriot line,   *195*
Who, while thou sharest their luster, lendest 'em thine,
Vouchsafe this picture of thy soul to see;
'T is so far good, as it resembles thee.
The beauties to th' original I owe;
Which when I miss, my own defects I show: *200*
Nor think the kindred Muses thy disgrace;
A poet is not born in every race.
Two of a house few ages can afford;
One to perform, another to record.
Praiseworthy actions are by thee embraced;   *205*
And 't is my praise, to make thy praises last.
For even when death dissolves our human frame,
The soul returns to heav'n, from whence it came;
Earth keeps the body, verse preserves the fame.

Sigismonda and Guiscardo

from Boccace

While Norman Tancred in Salerno reigned,
The title of a gracious Prince he gained;
Till, turned a tyrant in his latter days,
He lost the luster of his former praise;
5 And, from the bright meridian where he stood
Descending, dipped his hands in lovers' blood.
    This Prince, of Fortune's favor long possessed,
Yet was with one fair daughter only blest;
And blest he might have been with her alone,
10 But O! how much more happy had he none!
She was his care, his hope, and his delight,
Most in his thought, and ever in his sight;
Next, nay beyond his life, he held her dear;
She lived by him, and now he lived in her.
15 For this, when ripe for marriage, he delayed
Her nuptial bands, and kept her long a maid,
As envying any else should share a part
Of what was his, and claiming all her heart.
At length, as public decency required,
20 And all his vassals eagerly desired,
With mind averse, he rather underwent
His people's will than gave his own consent.
So was she torn as from a lover's side,
And made almost in his despite a bride.
25   Short were her marriage joys, for in the prime
Of youth her lord expired before his time;
And, to her father's court in little space)
Restored anew, she held a higher place; }
More loved, and more exalted into grace.)
30 This Princess, fresh and young, and fair and wise,
The worshipped idol of her father's eyes,
Did all her sex in every grace exceed,

And had more wit beside than women need.
  Youth, health, and ease, and most an amorous⎫
    mind,   ⎬
To second nuptials had her thoughts inclined,   ⎬ 35
And former joys had left a secret sting behind.   ⎭
But prodigal in every other grant,
Her sire left unsupplied her only want;
And she, betwixt her modesty and pride,
Her wishes, which she could not help, would hide.   40
  Resolved at last to lose no longer time,
And yet to please herself without a crime,
She cast her eyes around the court, to find
A worthy subject suiting to her mind,
To him in holy nuptials to be tied,   45
A seeming widow, and a secret bride.
Among the train of courtiers one she found
With all the gifts of bounteous nature crowned,
Of gentle blood; but one whose niggard fate
Had set him far below her high estate.   50
Guiscard his name was called, of blooming age,
Now squire to Tancred, and before his page:
To him, the choice of all the shining crowd,
Her heart the noble Sigismonda vowed.
  Yet hitherto she kept her love concealed,   55
And with close glances every day beheld
The graceful youth; and every day increased
The raging fire that burned within her breast.
Some secret charm did all his acts attend,
And what his fortune wanted, hers could mend;   60
Till, as the fire will force its outward way,
Or, in the prison pent, consume the prey;
So long her earnest eyes on his were set,
At length their twisted rays° together met;
And he, surprised with humble joy, surveyed   65
One sweet regard, shot by the royal maid:
Not well assured, while doubtful hopes he nursed,
A second glance came gliding like the first;
And he, who saw the sharpness of the dart,
Without defense received it in his heart.   70

64 **twisted rays** interchanging glances

In public though their passion wanted speech,
Yet mutual looks interpreted for each;
Time, ways, and means of meeting were denied;
But all those wants ingenious Love supplied.
75 Th' inventive god, who never fails his part,
Inspires the wit when once he warms the heart.
　　When Guiscard next was in the circle seen,
Where Sigismonda held the place of Queen,
A hollow cane within her hand she brought,
80 But in the concave had enclosed a note.
With this she seemed to play, and, as in sport,
Tossed to her love, in presence of the court:
"Take it," she said, "and when your needs require,
This little brand will serve to light your fire."
85 He took it with a bow, and soon divined
The seeming toy was not for naught designed;
But when retired, so long with curious eyes
He viewed the present, that he found the prize.
Much was in little writ, and all conveyed ⎫
90 With cautious care, for fear to be betrayed ⎬
By some false confident, or favorite maid. ⎭
The time, the place, the manner how to meet,
Were all in punctual order plainly writ;
But since a trust must be, she thought it best ⎫
95 To put it out of laymen's power at least; ⎬
And for their solemn vows prepared a priest. ⎭
　　Guiscard (her secret purpose understood)
With joy prepared to meet the coming good;
Nor pains nor danger was resolved to spare,
100 But use the means appointed by the fair.
　　Near the proud palace of Salerno stood
A mount of rough ascent, and thick with wood.
Through this a cave was dug with vast expense;
The work it seemed of some suspicious Prince,
105 Who, when abusing power with lawless might,
From public justice would secure his flight.
The passage made by many a winding way
Reached ev'n the room in which the tyrant lay.
Fit for his purpose, on a lower floor
110 He lodged, whose issue was an iron door,

From whence, by stairs descending to the ground,
In the blind grot a safe retreat he found.
Its outlet ended in a brake o'ergrown
With brambles, choked by time, and now unknown.
A rift there was, which from the mountain's height   115
Conveyed a glimmering and malignant light,
A breathing-place to draw the damps away,
A twilight of an intercepted day.
The tyrant's den, whose use though lost to fame,
Was now th' apartment of the royal dame;   120
The cavern, only to her father known,
By him was to his darling daughter shown.
    Neglected long she let the secret rest,
Till love recalled it to her laboring breast,
And hinted as the way by Heav'n designed,   125
The teacher, by the means he taught, to blind.
What will not women do, when need inspires
Their wit, or love their inclination fires!
Though jealousy of state th' invention found,
Yet love refined upon the former ground.   130
That way, the tyrant had reserved to fly
Pursuing hate, now served to bring two lovers nigh.
    The dame, who long in vain had kept the key,
Bold by desire, explored the secret way;
Now tried the stairs, and, wading through the night,   135
Searched all the deep recess, and issued into light.
All this her letter had so well explained,
Th' instructed youth might compass what remained;
The cavern mouth alone was hard to find,
Because the path, disused, was out of mind: 140
But in what quarter of the copse it lay,
His eye by certain level could survey.
Yet (for the wood perplexed° with thorns he knew)
A frock of leather o'er his limbs he drew;
And thus provided, searched the brake around,   145
Till the choked entry of the cave he found.
    Thus, all prepared, the promised hour arrived,
So long expected, and so well contrived:
With Love to friend, th' impatient lover went,
143 **perplexed** tangled

150 Fenced from the thorns, and trod the deep descent.
The conscious° priest, who was suborned before,
Stood ready posted at the postern door;
The maids in distant rooms were sent to rest,
And nothing wanted but th' invited guest.
155 He came, and knocking thrice, without delay,
The longing lady heard, and turned the key;
At once invaded him with all her charms,
And the first step he made was in her arms.
The leathern outside, boisterous as it was,
160 Gave way, and bent beneath her strict embrace;
On either side the kisses flew so thick,
That neither he nor she had breath to speak.
The holy man, amazed at what he saw,
Made haste to sanctify the bliss by law,
165 And muttered fast the matrimony o'er,
For fear committed sin should get before.
His work performed, he left the pair alone, ⎫
Because he knew he could not go too soon; ⎬
His presence odious, when his task was done. ⎭
170 What thoughts he had beseems not me to say; ⎫
Though some surmise he went to fast and pray, ⎬
And needed both to drive the tempting thoughts away. ⎭
    The foe once gone, they took their full delight;
'T was restless rage and tempest all the night;
175 For greedy Love each moment would employ,
And grudged the shortest pauses of their joy.
    Thus were their loves auspiciously begun,
And thus with secret care were carried on;
The stealth itself did appetite restore,
180 And looked so like a sin, it pleased the more.
    The cave was now become a common way;
The wicket, often opened, knew the key:
Love rioted secure, and, long enjoyed,
Was ever eager, and was never cloyed.
185   But as extremes are short, of ill and good,
And tides at highest mark regorge the flood;
So Fate, that could no more improve their joy,
Took a malicious pleasure to destroy.

151 **conscious** privy to a secret

Tancred, who fondly loved, and whose delight
Was placed in his fair daughter's daily sight,   190
Of custom, when his state affairs were done,
Would pass his pleasing hours with her alone;
And, as a father's privilege allowed,
Without attendance of th' officious° crowd.
It happened once, that when in heat of day   195
He tried to sleep, as was his usual way,
The balmy slumber fled his wakeful eyes,
And forced him, in his own despite, to rise.
Of sleep forsaken, to relieve his care,
He sought the conversation of the fair;   200
But with her train of damsels she was gone,
In shady walks the scorching heat to shun.
He would not violate that sweet recess,
And found besides a welcome heaviness
That seized his eyes; and slumber, which forgot,   205
When called before, to come, now came unsought.
From light retired, behind his daughter's bed,
He for approaching sleep composed his head;
A chair was ready, for that use designed,
So quilted, that he lay at ease reclined,   210
The curtains closely drawn, the light to screen,
As if he had contrived to lie unseen:
Thus covered with an artificial night,
Sleep did his office soon, and sealed his sight.
With Heav'n averse, in this ill-omened hour   215
Was Guiscard summoned to the secret bower,
And the fair nymph, with expectation fired,
From her attending damsels was retired:
For, true to love, she measured time so right,
As not to miss one moment of delight.   220
The garden, seated on the level floor,
She left behind, and, locking every door,
Thought all secure; but little did she know,
Blind to her fate, she had enclosed her foe.
Attending Guiscard, in his leathern frock,   225
Stood ready, with his thrice-repeated knock:
Thrice with a doleful sound the jarring grate
194 officious dutiful

Rung deaf, and hollow, and presaged their fate.
The door unlocked, to known delight they haste,
230 And panting in each other's arms, embraced,
Rush to the conscious° bed, a mutual freight,
And heedless press it with their wonted weight.

The sudden bound awaked the sleeping sire,
And showed a sight no parent can desire;
235 His opening eyes at once with odious view
The love discovered, and the lover knew.
He would have cried; but, hoping that he dreamt,
Amazement tied his tongue, and stopped th' attempt.
Th' ensuing moment all the truth declared,
240 But now he stood collected and prepared;
For malice and revenge had put him on his guard.

So, like a lion that unheeded lay,
Dissembling sleep, and watchful to betray,
With inward rage he meditates his prey.

245 The thoughtless pair, indulging their desires,
Alternate, kindled, and then quenched their fires;
Nor thinking in the shades of death they played,
Full of themselves, themselves alone surveyed,
And, too secure, were by themselves betrayed.

250 Long time dissolved in pleasure thus they lay,
Till nature could no more suffice their play;
Then rose the youth, and through the cave again
Returned; the Princess mingled with her train.

Resolved his unripe vengeance to defer,
255 The royal spy, when now the coast was clear,
Sought not the garden, but retired unseen,
To brood in secret on his gathered spleen,
And methodize revenge: to death he grieved;
And, but he saw the crime, had scarce believed.

260 Th' appointment for th' ensuing night he heard,
And therefore in the cavern had prepared
Two brawny yeomen of his trusty guard.

Scarce had unwary Guiscard set his foot
Within the farmost entrance of the grot,
265 When these in secret ambush ready lay,
And rushing on the sudden seized the prey.

231 **conscious** knowledgeable

Encumbered with his frock, without defense,
An easy prize, they led the prisoner thence,
And, as commanded, brought before the Prince.
The gloomy sire, too sensible of wrong   *270*
To vent his rage in words, restrained his tongue,
And only said: "Thus servants are preferred,
And, trusted, thus their sovereigns they reward.
Had I not seen, had not these eyes received
Too clear a proof, I could not have believed."   *275*
    He paused and choked the rest. The youth, who
        saw
His forfeit life abandoned to the law,
The judge th' accuser, and th' offense to him
Who had both power and will t' avenge the crime,
No vain defense prepared, but thus replied: *280*
"The faults of Love by Love are justified.
With unresisted might the Monarch reigns,
He levels mountains, and he raises plains;
And, not regarding difference of degree,
Abased your daughter, and exalted me."   *285*
    This bold return with seeming patience heard,
The prisoner was remitted to the guard.
The sullen tyrant slept not all the night,
But, lonely walking by a winking light,
Sobbed, wept, and groaned, and beat his withered
        breast,   *290*
But would not violate his daughter's rest;
Who long expecting lay, for bliss prepared,
Listening for noise, and grieved that none she heard;
Oft rose, and oft in vain employed the key,
And oft accused her lover of delay,   *295*
And passed the tedious hours in anxious thoughts
        away.
    The morrow came, and at his usual hour
Old Tancred visited his daughter's bower;
Her cheek (for such his custom was) he kissed,
Then blessed her kneeling, and her maids dismissed.   *300*
The royal dignity thus far maintained,
Now left in private, he no longer feigned;
But all at once his grief and rage appeared,

And floods of tears ran trickling down his beard.
305   "O Sigismonda," he began to say:
Thrice he began, and thrice was forced to stay, }
Till words with often trying found their way: }
"I thought, O Sigismonda, (but how blind
Are parents' eyes, their children's faults to find!)
310 Thy virtue, birth, and breeding were above
A mean desire, and vulgar sense of love;
Nor less than sight and hearing could convince }
So fond a father, and so just a prince, }
Of such an unforeseen and unbelieved offense. }
315 Then what indignant sorrow must I have,
To see thee lie subjected to my slave!
A man so smelling of the people's lee,°
The court received him first for charity;
And since with no degree of honor graced,
320 But only suffered where he first was placed:
A grovelling insect still, and so designed
By Nature's hand, nor born of noble kind;
A thing, by neither man nor woman prized,
And scarcely known enough to be despised.
325 To what has Heav'n reserved my age? Ah! why
Should man, when Nature calls, not choose to die,
Rather than stretch the span of life, to find
Such ills as Fate has wisely cast behind,
For those to feel, whom fond desire to live
330 Makes covetous of more than life can give!
Each has his share of good; and when 't is gone,
The guest, though hungry, cannot rise too soon.
But I, expecting more, in my own wrong
Protracting life, have lived a day too long.
335 If yesterday could be recalled again,
Ev'n now would I conclude my happy reign;
But 't is too late, my glorious race is run,
And a dark cloud o'ertakes my setting sun.
Hadst thou not loved, or loving saved the shame,
340 If not the sin, by some illustrious name,
This little comfort had relieved my mind,
'T was frailty, not unusual to thy kind;
317 **lee** dregs

But thy low fall beneath thy royal blood
Shows downward appetite to mix with mud.
Thus not the least excuse is left for thee,   345
Nor the least refuge for unhappy me.
    "For him I have resolved: whom by surprise
I took, and scarce can call it in disguise;
For such was his attire, as, with intent
Of nature, suited to his mean descent.   350
The harder question yet remains behind,   )
What pains a parent and a prince can find   }
To punish an offense of this degenerate kind.)
    "As I have loved, and yet I love thee more
Than ever father loved a child before;   355
So that indulgence draws me to forgive:
Nature, that gave thee life, would have thee live.
But, as a public parent of the state,
My justice, and thy crime, requires thy fate.
Fain would I choose a middle course to steer;   360
Nature's too kind, and justice too severe.
Speak for us both, and to the balance bring,
On either side, the father and the king.
Heav'n knows, my heart is bent to favor thee;
Make it but scanty weight, and leave the rest to me."   365
    Here stopping with a sigh, he poured a flood
Of tears, to make his last expression good.
    She, who had heard him speak, nor saw alone
The secret conduct of her love was known,
But he was taken who her soul possessed,   370
Felt all the pangs of sorrow in her breast:
And little wanted, but a woman's heart,
With cries and tears, had testified her smart;
But inborn worth, that fortune can control,
New strung, and stiffer bent her softer soul;   375
The heroine assumed the woman's place,
Confirmed her mind, and fortified her face.
Why should she beg, or what could she pretend,
When her stern father had condemned her friend?
Her life she might have had; but her despair   380
Of saving his had put it past her care:
Resolved on fate, she would not lose her breath,

But, rather than not die, solicit death.
Fixed on this thought, she not, as women use,
385 Her fault by common frailty would excuse,
But boldly justified her innocence,
And, while the fact was owned, denied th' offense.
Then with dry eyes, and with an open look,
She met his glance midway, and then undaunted
      spoke:
390 "Tancred, I neither am disposed to make
Request for life, nor offered life to take;
Much less deny the deed; but least of all
Beneath pretended justice weakly fall.
My words to sacred truth shall be confined,
395 My deeds shall show the greatness of my mind.
That I have loved, I own; that still I love,
I call to witness all the powers above.
Yet more I own: to Guiscard's love I give
The small remaining time I have to live;
400 And if beyond this life desire can be,
Not fate itself shall set my passion free.
    "This first avowed; nor folly warped my mind,
Nor the frail texture of the female kind
Betrayed my virtue; for too well I knew
405 What honor was, and honor had his due:
Before the holy priest my vows were tied;
So came I not a strumpet, but a bride.
This for my fame, and for the public voice:
Yet more, his merits justified my choice;
410 Which had they not, the first election thine,
That bond dissolved, the next is freely mine.
Or, grant I erred (which yet I must deny,)
Had parents power even second vows to tie,
Thy little care to mend my widowed nights
415 Has forced me to recourse of marriage rites,
To fill an empty side, and follow known delights. }
What have I done in this, deserving blame?
State-laws may alter; Nature's are the same:
Those are usurped on helpless womankind,
Made without our consent, and wanting power to
420   bind.

"Thou, Tancred, better shouldst have understood,
That as thy father gave thee flesh and blood,
So gavest thou me: not from the quarry hewed,
But of a softer mold, with sense endued;
Ev'n softer than thy own, of suppler kind,   *425*
More exquisite of taste, and more than man refined.
Nor needest thou by thy daughter to be told,
Though now thy sprightly blood with age be cold,
Thou hast been young; and canst remember still,
That when thou hadst the power, thou hadst the will;   *430*
And from the past experience of thy fires
Canst tell with what a tide our strong desires
Come rushing on in youth, and what their rage
    requires.

"And grant thy youth was exercised in arms,
When love no leisure found for softer charms;   *435*
My tender age in luxury was trained,
With idle ease and pageants entertained;
My hours my own, my pleasures unrestrained.
So bred, no wonder if I took the bent
That seemed even warranted by thy consent;   *440*
For, when the father is too fondly kind,
Such seed he sows, such harvest shall he find.
Blame then thyself, as reason's law requires
(Since Nature gave, and thou fomentest my fires.)
If still those appetites continue strong,   *445*
Thou mayest consider I am yet but young;
Consider too that, having been a wife,
I must have tasted of a better life,
And am not to be blamed, if I renew,
By lawful means, the joys which then I knew.   *450*
Where was the crime, if pleasure I procured,
Young, and a woman, and to bliss inured?
That was my case, and this is my defense:
I pleased myself, I shunned incontinence,
And, urged by strong desires, indulged my sense.   *455*
"Left to myself, I must avow, I strove
From public shame to screen my secret love,
And, well acquainted with thy native pride,
Endeavored, what I could not help, to hide;
For which a woman's wit an easy way supplied.   *460*

How this, so well contrived, so closely laid,
Was known to thee, or by what chance betrayed,
Is not my care; to please thy pride alone,
I could have wished it had been still unknown.
465   "Nor took I Guiscard by blind fancy led,
Or hasty choice, as many women wed;
But with deliberate care, and ripened thought,
At leisure first designed, before I wrought:
On him I rested, after long debate,
470 And not without considering, fixed my fate.
His flame was equal, though by mine inspired;
(For so the difference of our birth required;)
Had he been born like me, like me his love
Had first begun what mine was forced to move:
475 But thus beginning, thus we persevere;
Our passions yet continue what they were,
Nor length of trial makes our joys the less sincere.
  "At this my choice, though not by thine allowed
(Thy judgment herding with the common crowd,)
480 Thou takest unjust offense; and, led by them,
Dost less the merit than the man esteem.
Too sharply, Tancred, by thy pride betrayed,
Hast thou against the laws of kind inveighed;
For all th' offense is in opinion placed,
485 Which deems high birth by lowly choice debased.
This thought alone with fury fires thy breast
(For holy marriage justifies the rest,)
That I have sunk the glories of the state,
And mixed my blood with a plebeian mate;
490 In which I wonder thou shouldst oversee
Superior causes, or impute to me
The fault of Fortune, or the Fates' decree.
Or call it Heav'n's imperial power alone,
Which moves on springs of justice, though unknown;
495 Yet this we see, though ordered for the best,
The bad exalted, and the good oppressed;
Permitted laurels grace the lawless brow,
Th' unworthy raised, the worthy cast below.
  "But leaving that, search we the secret springs,

And backward trace the principles of things: *500*
There shall we find, that when the world began,
One common mass composed the mold of man;
One paste of flesh on all degrees bestowed,
And kneaded up alike with moistening blood.
The same Almighty Power inspired the frame   *505*
With kindled life, and formed the souls the same;
The faculties of intellect and will
Dispensed with equal hand, disposed with equal skill;
Like liberty indulged, with choice of good or ill.
Thus born alike, from virtue first began   *510*
The difference that distinguished man from man:
He claimed no title from descent of blood,
But that which made him noble made him good;
Warmed with more particles of heav'nly flame,
He winged his upward flight, and soared to fame,   *515*
The rest remained below, a tribe without a name.
  "This law, though custom now diverts the course,
As Nature's institute, is yet in force;
Uncancelled, though disused: and he, whose mind
Is virtuous, is alone of noble kind;   *520*
Though poor in fortune, of celestial race;
And he commits the crime, who calls him base.
  "Now lay the line, and measure all thy court
By inward virtue, not external port;
And find whom justly to prefer above   *525*
The man on whom my judgment placed my love:
So shalt thou see his parts and person shine;
And thus compared, the rest a base degenerate line.
Nor took I, when I first surveyed thy court,
His valor, or his virtues, on report;   *530*
But trusted what I ought to trust alone,
Relying on thy eyes, and not my own.
Thy praise (and thine was then the public voice)
First recommended Guiscard to my choice.
Directed thus by thee, I looked, and found   *535*
A man, I thought, deserving to be crowned;
First by my father pointed to my sight,
Nor less conspicuous by his native light;
His mind, his mien, the features of his face,

540 Excelling all the rest of human race.
    These were thy thoughts, and thou couldst judge
        aright,
    Till interest made a jaundice in thy sight.
        "Or should I grant thou didst not rightly see,
    Then thou wert first deceived, and I deceived by thee.
545 But if thou shalt allege, through pride of mind,
    Thy blood with one of base condition joined,
    'T is false; for 't is not baseness to be poor;
    His poverty augments thy crime the more;
    Upbraids thy justice with the scant regard
550 Of worth: whom Princes praise, they should reward.
    Are these the Kings entrusted by the crowd
    With wealth, to be dispensed for common good?
    The people sweat not for their King's delight,
    T' enrich a pimp, or raise a parasite:
555 Theirs is the toil; and he who well has served
    His country, has his country's wealth deserved.
        "Even mighty monarchs oft are meanly born,
    And kings by birth to lowest rank return;
    All subject to the power of giddy chance,
560 For Fortune can depress, or can advance:
    But true nobility is of the mind,
    Not given by chance, and not to chance resigned.
        "For the remaining doubt of thy decree,
    What to resolve, and how dispose of me,
565 Be warned to cast that useless care aside,
    Myself alone will for myself provide.
    If in thy doting and decrepit age,
    Thy soul, a stranger in thy youth to rage,
    Begins in cruel deeds to take delight,
570 Gorge with my blood thy barbarous appetite,
    For I so little am disposed to pray
    For life, I would not cast a wish away.
    Such as it is, th' offense is all my own;
    And what to Guiscard is already done,
575 Or to be done, is doomed by thy decree; ⎞
    That, if not executed first by thee,   ⎬
    Shall on my person be performed by me.   ⎠
        "Away! with women weep, and leave me here,

Fixed like a man, to die without a tear;
Or save, or slay us both this present hour,   580
'T is all that fate has left within thy power."
    She said; nor did her father fail to find,
In all she spoke, the greatness of her mind;
Yet thought she was not obstinate to die,
Nor deemed the death she promised was so nigh.   585
Secure in this belief, he left the dame,
Resolved to spare her life and save her shame;
But that detested object to remove,
To wreak his vengeance, and to cure her love.
    Intent on this, a secret order signed   590
The death of Guiscard to his guards enjoined;
Strangling was chosen, and the night the time,
A mute revenge, and blind as was the crime.
His faithful heart, a bloody sacrifice,
Torn from his breast, to glut the tyrant's eyes,   595
Closed the severe command: for (slaves to pay)
What kings decree, the soldier must obey:
Waged against foes; and, when the wars are o'er,
Fit only to maintain despotic power;
Dangerous to freedom, and desired alone   600
By kings who seek an arbitrary throne.
Such were these guards; as ready to have slain
The prince himself, allured with greater gain:
So was the charge performed with better will,
By men inured to blood and exercised in ill.   605
    Now, though the sullen sire had eased his mind,
The pomp of his revenge was yet behind,
A pomp prepared to grace the present he designed.
A goblet rich with gems and rough with gold,
Of depth and breadth the precious pledge to hold,   610
With cruel care he chose: the hollow part
Enclosed, the lid concealed the lover's heart.
Then of his trusted mischiefs one he sent,
And bade him with these words the gift present:
"Thy father sends thee this to cheer thy breast,   615
And glad thy sight with what thou lovest the best;
As thou hast pleased his eyes and joyed his mind
With what he loved the most of humankind."

Ere this the royal dame, who well had weighed
620 The consequence of what her sire had said,
Fixed on her fate, against th' expected hour,
Procured the means to have it in her power.
For this she had distilled, with early care,
The juice of simples° friendly to despair,
625 A magazine of death, and thus prepared,
Secure° to die, the fatal message heard:
Then smiled severe, nor with a troubled look
Or trembling hand the funeral present took;
Even kept her countenance, when the lid removed
630 Disclosed the heart, unfortunately loved.
She needed not be told within whose breast
It lodged; the message had explained the rest.
Or not amazed, or hiding her surprise,
She sternly on the bearer fixed her eyes;
635 Then thus: "Tell Tancred, on his daughter's part,
The gold, though precious, equals not the heart:
But he did well to give his best; and I,
Who wished a worthier urn, forgive his poverty."
At this she curbd a groan, that else had come,
640 And pausing, viewed the present in the tomb;
Then, to the heart adored devoutly glued
Her lips, and raising it, her speech renewed:
"Even from my day of birth, to this, the bound
Of my unhappy being, I have found
645 My father's care and tenderness expressed;
But this last act of love excels the rest:
For this so dear a present, bear him back
The best return that I can live to make."
The messenger dispatched, again she viewed
650 The loved remains, and sighing thus pursued:
"Source of my life, and lord of my desires,
In whom I lived, with whom my soul expires!
Poor heart, no more the spring of vital heat,
Curst be the hands that tore thee from thy seat!
655 The course is finished which thy fates decreed,
And thou from thy corporeal prison freed:
Soon hast thou reached the goal with mended pace,
624 **simples** herbs   626 **Secure** unafraid

A world of woes dispatched in little space.
Forced by thy worth, thy foe, in death become
Thy friend, has lodged thee in a costly tomb.   660
There yet remained thy funeral exequies,
The weeping tribute of thy widow's eyes,
And those, indulgent Heav'n has found the way
That I, before my death, have leave to pay.
My father even in cruelty is kind,   665
Or Heav'n has turned the malice of his mind }
To better uses than his hate designed;
And made th' insult, which in his gift appears,
The means to mourn thee with my pious tears;
Which I will pay thee down, before I go,   670
And save myself the pains to weep below,
If souls can weep. Though once I meant to meet
My fate with face unmoved, and eyes unwet,
Yet since I have thee here in narrow room,
My tears shall set thee first afloat within thy tomb: 675
Then (as I know thy spirit hovers nigh)
Under thy friendly conduct will I fly
To regions unexplored, secure° to share }
Thy state; nor Hell shall punishment appear; }
And Heav'n is double Heav'n, if thou art there."   680
    She said; her brimful eyes, that ready stood,
And only wanted will to weep a flood,
Released their watery store, and poured amain,
Like clouds low hung, a sober shower of rain;
Mute solemn sorrow, free from female noise,   685
Such as the majesty of grief destroys;
For, bending o'er the cup, the tears she shed
Seemed by the posture to discharge her head,
O'erfilled before; and oft (her mouth applied
To the cold heart) she kissed at once and cried.   690
Her maids, who stood amazed, nor knew the cause
Of her complaining, nor whose heart it was;
Yet all due measures of her mourning kept,
Did office at the dirge, and by infection wept;
And oft enquired th' occasion of her grief   695
(Unanswered but by sighs,) and offered vain relief.
678 secure unafraid

At length, her stock of tears already shed,
She wiped her eyes, she raised her drooping head,
And thus pursued: "O ever faithful heart,
700 I have performed the ceremonial part,
The decencies of grief; it rests behind,
That, as our bodies were, our souls be joined;
To thy whate'er abode my shade convey,
And as an elder ghost, direct the way."
705 She said; and bade the vial to be brought,
Where she before had brewed the deadly draught.
First pouring out the medicinable bane,
The heart her tears had rinsed she bathed again;
Then down her throat the death securely throws,
710 And quaffs a long oblivion of her woes.
　　This done, she mounts the genial bed°, and there
(Her body first composed with honest care)
Attends the welcome rest; her hands yet hold
Close to her heart the monumental gold;
715 Nor farther word she spoke, but closed her sight,
And quiet sought the covert of the night.
　　The damsels, who the while in silence mourned,
Not knowing, nor suspecting death suborned,
Yet, as their duty was, to Tancred sent,
720 Who, conscious of th' occasion, feared th' event.
Alarmed, and with presaging heart, he came,
And drew the curtains, and exposed the dame
To loathsome light; then with a late relief
Made vain efforts to mitigate her grief.
725 She, what she could, excluding day, her eyes
Kept firmly sealed, and sternly thus replies:
　　"Tancred, restrain thy tears, unsought by me,
And sorrow, unavailing now to thee:
Did ever man before afflict his mind
730 To see th' effect of what himself designed?
Yet if thou hast remaining in thy heart
Some sense of love, some unextinguished part
Of former kindness, largely once professed, ⎫
Let me by that adjure thy hardened breast ⎬
735 Not to deny thy daughter's last request. ⎭

711 **genial bed** marriage bed

The secret love which I so long enjoyed,
And still concealed, to gratify thy pride,
Thou hast disjoined; but, with my dying breath,
Seek not, I beg thee, to disjoin our death:
Where'er his corpse by thy command is laid,   740
Thither let mine in public be conveyed;
Exposed in open view, and side by side,
Acknowledged as a bridegroom and a bride."

    The prince's anguish hindered his reply;
And she, who felt her fate approaching nigh,   745
Seized the cold heart, and heaving to her breast:
"Here, precious pledge," she said, "securely rest."
These accents were her last; the creeping death
Benumbed her senses first, then stopped her breath.

    Thus she for disobedience justly died;   750
The sire was justly punished for his pride;
The youth, least guilty, suffered for th' offense,
Of duty violated to his prince;
Who, late repenting of his cruel deed,
One common sepulcher for both decreed;   755
Entombed the wretched pair in royal state,
And on their monument inscribed their fate.

Ceyx and Alcyone
Out of the Eleventh Book of Ovid's Metamorphoses

CONNECTION OF THIS FABLE WITH THE FORMER

Ceyx, the son of Lucifer (the morning star) and King
of Trachin, in Thessaly, was married to Alcyone,
daughter to Æolus, God of the Winds. Both the
husband and the wife loved each other with an entire affection. Dædalion, the elder brother of Ceyx
(whom he succeeded), having been turned into a
falcon by Apollo, and Chione, Dædalion's daughter,
slain by Diana, Ceyx prepares a ship to sail to
Claros, there to consult the oracle of Apollo, and
(as Ovid seems to intimate) to inquire how the
anger of the gods might be atoned.

THESE prodigies afflict the pious Prince,
But, more perplexed with those that happened since,
He purposes to seek the Clarion god,°
Avoiding Delphos, his more famed abode,
5 Since Phlegyan robbers made unsafe the road.
Yet could he not from her he loved so well,
The fatal voyage, he resolved, conceal:
But when she saw her lord prepared to part,
A deadly cold ran shivering to her heart,
10 Her faded cheeks are changed to boxen° hue,
And in her eyes the tears are ever new.
She thrice assayed to speak; her accents hung,
And faltering died unfinished on her tongue,
Or vanished into sighs; with long delay
15 Her voice returned, and found the wonted way.

3 **Clarian god** Apollo 10 **boxen** the color of boxwood

"Tell me, my lord," she said, "what fault unknown }
Thy once beloved Alcyone has done?
Whether, ah whether is thy kindness gone! }
Can Ceyx then sustain to leave his wife,
And unconcerned forsake the sweets of life?   20
What can thy mind to this long journey move,
Or needest thou absence to renew thy love?
Yet, if thou goest by land, though grief possess
My soul even then, my fears will be the less.
But ah! be warned to shun the watery way,   25
The face is frightful of the stormy sea;
For late I saw adrift disjointed planks,
And empty tombs erected on the banks.
Nor let false hopes to trust betray thy mind,
Because my sire in caves constrains the wind,   30
Can with a breath their clamorous rage appease,
They fear his whistle, and forsake the seas.
Not so, for, once indulged, they sweep the main,
Deaf to the call, or, hearing, hear in vain;
But, bent on mischief, bear the waves before,   35
And, not content with seas, insult° the shore;
When ocean, air, and earth, at once engage,
And rooted forests fly before their rage:
At once the clashing clouds to battle move,
And lightnings run across the fields above.   40
I know them well, and marked their rude comport,
While yet a child, within my father's court:
In times of tempest they command alone,
And he but sits precarious on the throne.
The more I know, the more my fears augment,   45
And fears are oft prophetic of th' event.
But if not fears or reasons will prevail,
If fate has fixed thee obstinate to sail,
Go not without thy wife, but let me bear }
My part of danger with an equal share, }   50
And present, what I suffer, only fear: }
Then o'er the bounding billows shall we fly,
Secure to live together, or to die."
    These reasons moved her starlike husband's heart,

36 insult leap upon

55 But still he held his purpose to depart:
For, as he loved her equal to his life,
He would not to the seas expose his wife;
Nor could be wrought his voyage to refrain,
But sought by arguments to soothe her pain:
60 Nor these availed; at length he lights on one.
With which so difficult a cause he won:
"My love, so short an absence cease to fear,
For, by my father's holy flame, I swear,
Before two moons their orb with light adorn,
65 If Heav'n allow me life, I will return."
　　This promise of so short a stay prevails;
He soon equips the ship, supplies the sails,
And gives the word to launch; she trembling views
This pomp of death, and parting tears renews:
70 Last, with a kiss, she took a long farewell,
Sighed, with a sad presage, and swooning fell.
While Ceyx seeks delays, the lusty crew,
Raised on their banks, their oars in order drew ⎫
To their broad breasts; the ship with fury flew. ⎬
75 　　The Queen, recovered, rears her humid eyes,
And first her husband on the poop espies,
Shaking his hand at distance on the main;
She took the sign, and shook her hand again.
Still as the ground recedes, contracts her view
80 With sharpened sight, till she no longer knew
The much-loved face; that comfort lost supplies
With less, and with the galley feeds her eyes;
The galley borne from view by rising gales,
She followed with her sight the flying sails:
85 When even the flying sails were seen no more,
Forsaken of all sight, she left the shore.
　　Then on her bridal bed her body throws,
And sought in sleep her wearied eyes to close;
Her husband's pillow, and the widowed part
90 Which once he pressed, renewed the former smart.
　　And now a breeze from shore began to blow,
The sailors ship their oars, and cease to row;
Then hoist their yards atrip,° and all their sails
93 **atrip** aloft

Let fall, to court the wind, and catch the gales:
By this the vessel half her course had run,   95
And as much rested till the rising sun;
Both shores were lost to sight, when at the close
Of day a stiffer gale at east arose:
The sea grew white, the rolling waves from far,
Like heralds first denounce° the watery war.   100
   This seen, the master soon began to cry:
"Strike, strike the topsail; let the mainsheet fly,
And furl your sails." The winds repel the sound,
And in the speaker's mouth the speech is drowned.
Yet of their own accord, as danger taught,   105
Each in his way, officiously they wrought;
Some stow their oars, or stop the leaky sides;
Another bolder yet the yard bestrides,
And folds the sails; a fourth, with labor, laves
Th' intruding seas, and waves ejects on waves.   110
   In this confusion while their work they ply,
The winds augment the winter of the sky,
And wage intestine wars; the suffering seas
Are tossed and mingled as their tyrants please.
The master would command, but, in despair   115
Of safety, stands amazed with stupid care;
Nor what to bid, or what forbid, he knows,
Th' ungoverned tempest to such fury grows:
Vain is his force, and vainer is his skill,
With such a concourse comes the flood of ill.   120
The cries of men are mixed with rattling shrouds;
Seas dash on seas, and clouds encounter clouds:
At once from east to west, from pole to pole,
The forky lightnings flash, the roaring thunders roll.
   Now waves on waves ascending scale the skies,   125
And in the fires above the water fries.°
When yellow sands are sifted from below,
The glittering billows give a golden show;
And when the fouler bottom spews the black,
The Stygian dye the tainted waters take: 130
Then frothy white appear the flatted seas,
And change their color, changing their disease.

100 **denounce** proclaim   126 **fries** foams, seethes

Like various fits the Trachin° vessel finds,
And now sublime she rides upon the winds;
135 As from a lofty summit looks from high,
And from the clouds beholds the nether sky;
Now from the depth of Hell they lift their sight,
And at a distance see superior light.
The lashing billows make a loud report,
140 And beat her sides, as battering rams a fort:
Or as a lion, bounding in his way,
With force augmented bears against his prey,
Sidelong to seize; or, unappalled with fear,
Springs on the toils and rushes on the spear:
145 So seas impelled by winds with added power
Assault the sides, and o'er the hatches tower.
    The planks (their pitchy covering washed away)
Now yield, and now a yawning breach display:
The roaring waters with a hostile tide
150 Rush through the ruins of her gaping side.
Meantime in sheets of rain the sky descends,
And ocean, swelled with waters, upwards tends;
One rising, falling one, the heav'ns and sea
Meet at their confines, in the middle way:
155 The sails are drunk with showers, and drop with rain;
Sweet waters mingle with the briny main.
No star appears to lend his friendly light;
Darkness and tempest make a double night.
But flashing fires disclose the deep by turns,
160 And, while the lightnings blaze, the water burns.
    Now all the waves their scattered force unite,
And, as a soldier, foremost in the fight,
Makes way for others, and, an host alone,
Still presses on, and urging gains the town;
165 So, while th' invading billows come abreast,
The hero tenth° advanced before the rest,
Sweeps all before him with impetuous sway,
And from the walls descends upon the prey;
Part following enter, part remain without,
170 With envy hear their fellows' conquering shout,

133 **Trachin** from a town in Thessalia   166 **The hero tenth** (the Latin
decumana, "tenth," was used to signify perfection)

And mount on others' backs, in hope to share
The city, thus become the seat of war.
  An universal cry resounds aloud,
The sailors run in heaps, a helpless crowd;
Art fails, and courage falls, no succor near;   *175*
As many waves, as many deaths appear.
  One weeps, and yet despairs of late relief;
One cannot weep (his fears congeal his grief,)
But stupid, with dry eyes expects his fate;
One with loud shrieks laments his lost estate,   *180*
And calls those happy whom their funerals wait.
This wretch with prayers and vows the gods implores,
And even the skies he cannot see, adores.
That other on his friends his thoughts bestows,
His careful father, and his faithful spouse.   *185*
The covetous worldling in his anxious mind
Thinks only on the wealth he left behind.
  All Ceyx his Alcyone employs;
For her he grieves, yet in her absence joys:
His wife he wishes, and would still be near,   *190*
Not her with him, but wishes him with her.
Now with last looks he seeks his native shore,
Which fate has destined him to see no more:
He sought, but in the dark tempestuous night
He knew not whither to direct his sight.   *195*
So whirl the seas, such darkness blinds the sky,
That the black night receives a deeper dye.
  The giddy ship ran round; the tempest tore
Her mast, and overboard the rudder bore.
One billow mounts, and with a scornful brow,   *200*
Proud of her conquest gained, insults the waves
    below;
Nor lighter falls, than if some giant tore
Pindus and Athos,° with the freight they bore,
And tossed on seas: pressed with the ponderous blow,
Down sinks the ship within th' abyss below: *205*
Down with the vessel sink into the main
The many, never more to rise again.
Some few on scattered planks with fruitless care

203 **Pindus . . . Athos** great mountains in Greece

Lay hold, and swim, but while they swim, despair.
210   Even he, who late a scepter did command,
Now grasps a floating fragment in his hand,
And while he struggles on the stormy main,
Invokes his father, and his wife's, in vain;
But yet his consort is his greatest care;
215 Alcyone he names amidst his prayer,
Names as a charm against the waves and wind;
Most in his mouth, and ever in his mind:
Tired with his toil, all hopes of safety past,
From prayers to wishes he descends at last:
220 That his dead body, wafted to the sands,
Might have its burial from her friendly hands.
As oft as he can catch a gulp of air,
And peep above the seas, he names the fair,
And even when plunged beneath, on her he raves,
225 Murmuring Alcyone below the waves:
At last a falling billow stops his breath,
Breaks o'er his head, and whelms him underneath.
Bright Lucifer unlike himself appears
That night, his heav'nly form obscured with tears,
230 And since he was forbid to leave the skies,
He muffled with a cloud his mournful eyes.
    Meantime Alcyone (his fate unknown)
Computes how many nights he had been gone,
Observes the waning moon with hourly view,
235 Numbers her age, and wishes for a new;
Against the promised time provides with care,
And hastens in the woof the robes he was to wear;
And for herself employs another loom,
New-dressed to meet her lord returning home,
240 Flattering her heart with joys that never were to come.
She fumed the temples with an odorous flame,
And oft before the sacred altars came,
To pray for him, who was an empty name.
All powers implored, but far above the rest,
245 To Juno she her pious vows addressed,
Her much-loved lord from perils to protect
And safe o'er seas his voyage to direct:
Then prayed that she might still possess his heart,

And no pretending rival share a part.
This last petition heard of all her prayer,   250
The rest, dispersed by winds, were lost in air.
    But she,° the goddess of the nuptial bed,
Tired with her vain devotions for the dead,
Resolved the tainted hand should be repelled,
Which incense offered, and her altar held: 255
Then Iris thus bespoke: "Thou faithful maid,
By whom thy Queen's commands are well conveyed,
Haste to the house of Sleep, and bid the god,
Who rules the night by visions with a nod,
Prepare a dream, in figure and in form   260
Resembling him who perished in the storm;
This form before Alcyone present,
To make her certain of the sad event."
    Endued with robes of various hue she flies,
And flying draws an arch (a segment of the skies);   265
Then leaves her bending bow, and from the steep
Descends to search the silent house of Sleep.
    Near the Cimmerians,° in his dark abode
Deep in a cavern, dwells the drowsy god;°
Whose gloomy mansion nor the rising sun   270
Nor setting, visits, nor the lightsome noon:
But lazy vapors round the region fly,
Perpetual twilight, and a doubtful sky;
No crowing cock does there his wings display,
Nor with his horny bill provoke the day;   275
Nor watchful dogs, nor the more wakeful geese,
Disturb with nightly noise the sacred peace:
Nor beast of nature, nor the tame, are nigh,
Nor trees with tempests rocked, nor human cry;
But safe repose without an air of breath   280
Dwells here, and a dumb quiet next to death.
    An arm of Lethe,° with a gentle flow
Arising upwards from the rock below
The palace moats, and o'er the pebbles creeps,
And with soft murmurs calls the coming sleeps;   285

252 **she** Juno   268 **Cimmerians** people in the land of perpetual night
269 **drowsy god** Sleep   282 **Lethe** river of forgetfulness in Hades

Around its entry nodding poppies grow,
And all cool simples° that sweet rest bestow;
Night from the plants their sleepy virtue drains,
And passing, sheds it on the silent plains:
290 No door there was th' unguarded house to keep,
On creaking hinges turned, to break his sleep.

But in the gloomy court was raised a bed,
Stuffed with black plumes, and on an ebon stead:
Black was the covering too, where lay the god,
295 And slept supine, his limbs displayed° abroad:
About his head fantastic visions fly,
Which various images of things supply,
And mock their forms; the leaves on trees not more,
Nor bearded ears in fields, nor sands upon the shore.

300 The virgin entering bright indulged° the day
To the brown° cave, and brushed the dreams away:
The god disturbed with this new glare of light
Cast sudden on his face, unsealed his sight,
And raised his tardy head, which sunk again,
305 And sinking on his bosom knocked his chin;
At length shook off himself; and asked the dame
(And asking yawned) for what intent she came.

To whom the goddess thus: "O sacred Rest,
Sweet pleasing Sleep, of all the powers the best!
310 O peace of mind, repairer of decay,
Whose balms renew the limbs to labors of the day, ⎱
Care shuns thy soft approach, and sullen flies away! ⎰
Adorn a dream, expressing human form,
The shape of him who suffered in the storm,
315 And send it flitting to the Trachin court,
The wreck of wretched Ceyx to report:
Before his Queen bid the pale specter stand,
Who begs a vain relief at Juno's hand."
She said, and scarce awake her eyes could keep,
320 Unable to support the fumes of sleep:
But fled, returning by the way she went,
And swerved along her bow with swift ascent.

The god, uneasy till he slept again,

287 **simples** herbs   295 **displayed** exposed to view   300 **indulged**
let in   301 **brown** dark

Resolved at once to rid himself of pain;
And, though against his custom, called aloud,   325
Exciting Morpheus from the sleepy crowd:
Morpheus of all his numerous train expressed
The shape of man, and imitated best;
The walk, the words, the gesture could supply,
The habit mimic, and the mien bely;   330
Plays well, but all his action is confined,
Extending not beyond our human kind.
Another birds, and beasts, and dragons apes,
And dreadful images, and monster shapes:
This demon Icelos in Heav'n's high hall   335
The gods have named, but men Phobetor call.
A third is Phantasus, whose actions roll
On meaner thoughts, and things devoid of soul;
Earth, fruits, and flowers he represents in dreams,
And solid rocks unmoved, and running streams: 340
These three to kings and chiefs their scenes display,
The rest before th' ignoble commons play.
Of these the chosen Morpheus is dispatched:
Which done, the lazy monarch, overwatched,
Down from his propping elbow drops his head,   345
Dissolved in sleep, and shrinks within his bed.
    Darkling° the demon glides, for flight prepared,
So soft that scarce his fanning wings are heard.
To Trachin, swift as thought, the flitting shade
Through air his momentary journey made: 350
Then lays aside the steerage of his wings,
Forsakes his proper form, assumes the King's;
And pale as death, despoiled of his array, ⎫
Into the Queen's apartment takes his way, ⎬
And stands before the bed at dawn of day. ⎭   355
Unmoved his eyes, and wet his beard appears; ⎫
And shedding vain, but seeming real tears; ⎬
The briny water dropping from his hairs: ⎭
Then staring on her, with a ghastly look
And hollow voice, he thus the Queen bespoke: 360
    "Know'st thou not me? Not yet, unhappy wife?
Or are my features perished with my life?
347 **Darkling** in the dark

Look once again, and, for thy husband lost,
Lo, all that's left of him, thy husband's ghost!
365 Thy vows for my return were all in vain;
The stormy south o'ertook us in the main;
And never shalt thou see thy living lord again.
Bear witness, Heav'n, I called on thee in death,
And while I called, a billow stopped my breath:
370 Think not that flying fame reports my fate;
I present, I appear, and my own wreck relate.
Rise, wretched widow, rise, nor undeplored
Permit my ghost to pass the Stygian ford:
But rise, prepared in black, to mourn thy perished
      lord."
375   Thus said the player god; and adding art
Of voice and gesture, so performed his part,
She thought (so like her love the shade appears)
That Ceyx spake the words, and Ceyx shed the tears.
She groaned, her inward soul with grief oppressed;
380 She sighed, she wept, and sleeping beat her breast:
Then stretched her arms t' embrace his body bare,
Her clasping arms enclose but empty air.
At this, not yet awake, she cried, "O stay,
One is our fate, and common is our way!"
385 So dreadful was the dream, so loud she spoke,
That, starting sudden up, the slumber broke:
Then cast her eyes around, in hope to view
Her vanished lord, and find the vision true:
For now the maids, who waited her commands,
390 Ran in with lighted tapers in their hands.
Tired with the search, not finding what she seeks,
With cruel blows she pounds her blubbered cheeks:
Then from her beaten breast the linen tare,
And cut the golden caul that bound her hair.
395 Her nurse demands the cause; with louder cries
She prosecutes her griefs, and thus replies:
    "No more Alcyone; she suffered death
With her loved lord, when Ceyx lost his breath:
No flattery, no false comfort, give me none,
400 My shipwrecked Ceyx is for ever gone.
I saw, I saw him manifest in view,

His voice, his figure, and his gestures knew.
His luster lost, and every living grace,
Yet I retained the features of his face;
Though with pale cheeks, wet beard, and dropping
    hair,   405
None but my Ceyx could appear so fair:
I would have strained° him with a strict embrace,
But through my arms he slipped, and vanished from
    the place:
There, ev'n just there he stood;" and as she spoke,
Where last the specter was, she cast her look: 410
Fain would she hope, and gazed upon the ground,
If any printed footsteps might be found.
    Then sighed and said: "This I too well foreknew,
And my prophetic fear presaged too true:
'T was what I begged, when with a bleeding heart   415
I took my leave, and suffered thee to part;
Or I to go along, or thou to stay,
Never, ah never to divide our way!
Happier for me, that all our hours assigned
Together we had lived; e'en not in death disjoined!   420
So had my Ceyx still be living here,
Or with my Ceyx I had perished there.
Now I die absent, in the vast profound,
And me without myself the seas have drowned:
The storms were not so cruel; should I strive   425
To lengthen life, and such a grief survive;
But neither will I strive, nor wretched thee
In death forsake, but keep thee company.
If not one common sepulcher contains
Our bodies, or one urn our last remains,   430
Yet Ceyx and Alcyone shall join,
Their names remembered in one common line."
    No farther voice her mighty grief affords,
For sighs come rushing in betwixt her words,
And stopped her tongue, but what her tongue denied,   435
Soft tears, and groans, and dumb complaints supplied.
    'T was morning; to the port she takes her way,
And stands upon the margin of the sea:

407 **strained** restrained

That place, that very spot of ground she sought,
440 Or thither by her destiny was brought,
Where last he stood; and while she sadly said:
" 'T was here he left me, lingering here delayed }
His parting kiss; and there his anchors weighed.")
    Thus speaking, while her thoughts past actions trace,
445 And call to mind, admonished by the place,
Sharp at her utmost ken she cast her eyes,
And somewhat floating from afar descries;
It seemed a corpse adrift, to distant sight,
But at a distance who could judge aright?
450 It wafted nearer yet, and then she knew
That what before she but surmised, was true:
A corpse it was, but whose it was, unknown,
Yet moved, howe'er, she made the case her own;
Took the bad omen of a shipwrecked man,
455 As for a stranger wept, and thus began:
    "Poor wretch, on stormy seas to lose thy life,
Unhappy thou, but more thy widowed wife!"
At this she paused; for now the flowing tide
Had brought the body nearer to the side:
460 The more she looks, the more her fears increase
At nearer sight, and she's herself the less.
Now driven ashore, and at her feet it lies,
She knows too much, in knowing whom she sees:
Her husband's corpse: at this she loudly shrieks:
465 " 'T is he, 't is he," she cries, and tears her cheeks,
Her hair, her vest, and, stooping to the sands,
About his neck she cast her trembling hands.
    "And is it thus, O dearer than my life,
Thus, thus returnest thou to thy longing wife!"
470 She said, and to the neighboring mole° she strode,
(Raised there to break th' incursions of the flood)
Headlong from hence to plunge herself she springs,
But shoots along supported on her wings,
A bird new-made about the banks she plies,
475 Not far from shore, and short excursions tries;
Nor seeks in air her humble flight to raise,
470 **mole** massive structure

Content to skim the surface of the seas:
Her bill, though slender, sends a creaking noise,
And imitates a lamentable voice.
Now lighting where the bloodless body lies,   480
She with a funeral note renews her cries.
At all her stretch her little wings she spread,
And with her feathered arms embraced the dead:
Then flickering to his pallid lips, she strove
To print a kiss, the last essay of love.   485
Whether the vital touch revived the dead,
Or that the moving waters raised his head
To meet the kiss, the vulgar doubt alone;
For sure a present miracle was shown.
The gods their shapes to winter-birds translate,°   490
But both obnoxious° to their former fate.
The conjugal affection still is tied,
And still the mournful race is multipled;
They bill, they tread; Alcyone compressed,
Seven days sits brooding on her floating nest,   495
A wintry Queen: her sire at length is kind,
Calms every storm, and hushes every wind;
Prepares his empire for his daughter's ease,
And for his hatching nephews smooths the seas.

490 **translate** transform   491 **obnoxious** liable to harm

The Fable of Acis, Polyphemus, and Galatea
from the Thirteenth Book of
Ovid's Metamorphoses

Galatea relates the story

Acis, the lovely youth, whose loss I mourn,
From Faunus and the nymph Symethis born,
Was both his parents' pleasure; but to me
Was all that love could make a lover be.
5   The gods our minds in mutual bands did join;
I was his only joy, as he was mine.
Now sixteen summers the sweet youth had seen,
And doubtful down began to shade his chin;
When Polyphemus first disturbed our joy,
10   And loved me fiercely, as I loved the boy.
Ask not which passion in my soul was higher,
My last aversion, or my first desire:
Nor this the greater was, nor that the less:
Both were alike, for both were in excess.
15   Thee, Venus, thee, both heav'n and earth obey;
Immense thy power, and boundless is thy sway.
The Cyclops, who defied th' ethereal throne,
And thought no thunder louder than his own;
The terror of the woods, and wilder far
20   Than wolves in plains, or bears in forests are;
Th' inhuman host, who made his bloody feasts
On mangled members of his butchered guests,
Yet felt the force of love and fierce desire,
And burnt for me with unrelenting fire.

Forgot his caverns, and his woolly care,   25
Assumed the softness of a lover's air;
And combed, with teeth of rakes, his rugged hair.
Now with a crooked scythe his beard he sleeks,
And mows the stubborn stubble of his cheeks;
Now in the crystal stream he looks to try   30
His simagres,° and rolls his glaring eye.
His cruelty and thirst of blood are lost,
And ships securely sail along the coast.

The prophet Telemus (arrived by chance
Where Etna's summits to the sea's advance,   35
Who marked the tracts of every bird that flew,
And sure presages from their flying drew)
Foretold the Cyclops that Ulysses' hand
In his broad eye should thrust a flaming brand.
The giant, with a scornful grin, replied,   40
"Vain augur, thou hast falsely prophesied;
Already Love his flaming brand has tossed;
Looking on two fair eyes, my sight I lost."
Thus, warned in vain, with stalking pace he strode,
And stamped the margin of the briny flood   45
With heavy steps; and weary, sought again
The cool retirement of his gloomy den.

A promontory, sharpening by degrees,
Ends in a wedge, and overlooks the seas:
On either side, below, the water flows: 50
This airy walk the giant lover chose.
Here on the midst he sate; his flocks, unled,
Their shepherd followed, and securely fed.
A pine so burly, and of length so vast,
That sailing ships required it for a mast,   55
He wielded for a staff, his steps to guide;
But laid it by, his whistle while he tried.
A hundred reeds, of a prodigious growth,
Scarce made a pipe proportioned to his mouth;
Which when he gave it wind, the rocks around,   60
And watery plains, the dreadful hiss resound.
I heard the ruffian shepherd rudely blow,
Where, in a hollow cave, I sat below;

31 **simagres** grimaces

On Acis' bosom I my head reclined:
65   And still preserve the poem in my mind.
"O lovely Galatea, whiter far
Than falling snows and rising lilies are;
More flowery than the meads, as crystal bright,
Erect as alders, and of equal height;
70   More wanton than a kid, more sleek thy skin
Than orient shells that on the shores are seen.
Than apples fairer, when the boughs they lade,
Pleasing as winter suns or summer shade:
More grateful to the sight than goodly planes;°
75   And softer to the touch than down of swans;
Or curds new turned: and sweeter to the taste
Than swelling grapes that to the vintage haste:
More clear than ice, or running streams, that stray
Through garden plots, but ah! more swift than they.
80   "Yet, Galatea, harder to be broke   ⎫
Than bullocks, unreclaimed to bear the yoke, ⎬
And far more stubborn than the knotted oak: ⎭
Like sliding streams, impossible to hold;
Like them fallacious, like their fountains cold;
85   More warping than the willow, to decline
My warm embrace, more brittle than the vine;
Immovable, and fixed in thy disdain;
Rough as these rocks, and of a harder grain.
More violent than is the rising flood;
90   And the praised peacock is not half so proud.
Fierce as the fire, and sharp as thistles are,
And more outrageous than a mother bear:
Deaf as the billows to the vows I make;
And more revengeful than a trodden snake.
95   In swiftness fleeter than the flying hind,
Or driven tempests, or the driving wind:
All other faults with patience I can bear;
But swiftness is the vice I only fear.
"Yet, if you knew me well, you would not shun
100 My love, but to my wished embraces run:
Would languish in your turn, and court my stay;
And much repent of your unwise delay.

74 **planes** plane-trees

"My palace, in the living rock, is made   ⎫
By Nature's hand; a spacious pleasing shade,   ⎬
Which neither heat can pierce, nor cold invade. ⎭   *105*
My garden filled with fruits you may behold,
And grapes in clusters, imitating gold;
Some blushing bunches of a purple hue:
And these, and those, are all reserved for you.
Red strawberries, in shades, expecting stand,   *110*
Proud to be gathered by so white a hand.
Autumnal cornels° latter fruit provide,
And plums to tempt you, turn their glossy side;
Not those of common kinds, but such alone
As in Phæacian orchards might have grown;   *115*
Nor chestnuts shall be wanting to your food,
Nor garden fruits, nor wildings of the wood;
The laden boughs for you alone shall bear;
And yours shall be the product of the year.
   "The flocks you see, are all my own, beside ⎫   *120*
The rest that woods and winding valleys hide, ⎬
And those that folded in the caves abide.   ⎭
Ask not the numbers of my growing store;
Who knows how many, knows he has no more.
Nor will I praise my cattle; trust not me,   *125*
But judge yourself, and pass your own decree:
Behold their swelling dugs; the sweepy weight
Of ewes that sink beneath the milky freight;
In the warm folds their tender lambkins lie,
Apart from kids that call with human cry.   *130*
New milk in nut-brown bowls is duly served
For daily drink; the rest for cheese reserved.
Nor are these household dainties all my store: ⎫
The fields and forests will afford us more;   ⎬
The deer, the hare, the goat, the savage boar, ⎭   *135*
All sorts of venison; and of birds the best;
A pair of turtles° taken from the nest.
I walked the mountains, and two cubs I found
Whose dam had left 'em on the naked ground,
So like, that no distinction could be seen;   *140*
So pretty, they were presents for a queen;

112 **cornels** cherry trees   137 **turtles** turtledoves

And so they shall: I took 'em both away;
And keep, to be companions of your play.
    "O raise, fair nymph, your beauteous face above
145 The waves; nor scorn my presents, and my love.
Come, Galatea, come, and view my face;   )
I late beheld it in the watery glass,   }
And found it lovelier than I feared it was.)
Survey my towering stature, and my size:
150 Not Jove, the Jove you dream that rules the skies,
Bears such a bulk, or is so largely spread.
My locks, the plenteous harvest of my head,
Hang o'er my manly face; and dangling down
As with a shady grove my shoulders crown.
155 Nor think, because my limbs and body bear
A thickset underwood of bristling hair,
My shape deformed; what fouler sight can be
Than the bald branches of a leafless tree?
Foul is the steed, without a flowing mane;
160 And birds, without their feathers and their train.
Wool decks the sheep; and man receives a grace
From bushy limbs, and from a bearded face.
My forehead with a single eye is filled,
Round as a ball, and ample as a shield.
165 The glorious lamp of heav'n, the radiant sun,
Is Nature's eye; and she 's content with one.
Add, that my father sways your seas, and I,
Like you, am of the watery family.
I make you his, in making you my own;
170 You I adore, and kneel to you alone:
Jove, with his fabled thunder, I despise,
And only fear the lightning of your eyes.
Frown not, fair nymph; yet I could bear to be
Disdained, if others were disdained with me.
175 But to repulse the Cyclops, and prefer
The love of Acis, heav'ns! I cannot bear.
But let the stripling please himself; nay more,
Please you, though that 's the thing I most abhor;
The boy shall find, if e'er we cope in fight,
180 These giant limbs endued with giant might.
His living bowels, from his belly torn,

And scattered limbs, shall on the flood be borne:
Thy flood, ungrateful nymph; and fate shall find
That way for thee and Acis to be joined.
For O! I burn with love, and thy disdain 185
Augments at once my passion, and my pain.
Translated Etna flames within my heart,
And thou, inhuman, wilt not ease my smart."
    Lamenting thus in vain, he rose, and strode
With furious paces to the neighboring wood. 190
Restless his feet, distracted was his walk;
Mad were his motions, and confused his talk:
Mad as the vanquished bull, when forced to yield
His lovely mistress, and forsake the field.
    Thus far unseen I saw: when fatal chance 195
His looks directing, with a sudden glance,
Acis and I were to his sight betrayed;
Where, naught suspecting, we securely play'd.
From his wide mouth a bellowing cry he cast,
"I see, I see; but this shall be your last!" 200
A roar so loud made Etna to rebound;
And all the Cyclops labored in the sound.
Affrighted with his monstrous voice, I fled,
And in the neighboring ocean plunged my head.
Poor Acis turned his back, and: "Help," he cried, 205
"Help, Galatea! help, my parent gods,
And take me dying to your deep abodes!"
The Cyclops followed; but he sent before
A rib, which from the living rock he tore:
Though but an angle reached him of the stone, 210
The mighty fragment was enough alone
To crush all Acis; 't was too late to save,
But what the fates allowed to give, I gave:
That Acis to his lineage should return;
And roll, among the river gods, his urn. 215
Straight issued from the stone a stream of blood,
Which lost the purple, mingling with the flood.
Then like a troubled torrent it appeared:
The torrent, too, in little space was cleared.
The stone was cleft, and through the yawning chink 220
New reeds arose, on the new river's brink.

The rock, from out its hollow womb, disclosed
A sound like water in its course opposed:
When (wondrous to behold) full in the flood
225 Up starts a youth, and navel high he stood.
Horns from his temples rise; and either horn
Thick wreaths of reeds (his native growth) adorn.
Were not his stature taller than before,
His bulk augmented, and his beauty more,
230 His color blue, for Acis he might pass:
And Acis changed into a stream he was.
But mine no more; he rolls along the plains
With rapid motion, and his name retains.

Helen to Paris°
by the Right Honorable the Earl of Mulgrave and Mr. Dryden

THE ARGUMENT

Helen, having received the foregoing epistle from
Paris, returns the following answer: wherein she
seems at first to chide him for his presumption in
writing as he had done, which could only proceed
from his low opinion of her virtue; then owns herself to be sensible of the passion which he had
expressed for her, though she much suspect his constancy; and at last discovers her inclinations to be
favorable to him: the whole letter showing the extreme artifice of womankind.

When loose epistles violate chaste eyes,
She half consents, who silently denies.
How dares a stranger, with designs so vain,
Marriage and hospitable rights profane?
Was it for this, your fleet did shelter find   5
From swelling seas, and every faithless wind?
(For though a distant country brought you forth,
Your usage here was equal to your worth.)
Does this deserve to be rewarded so?
Did you come here a stranger, or a foe?   10
Your partial judgment may perhaps complain,
And think me barbarous for my just disdain.
Ill-bred then let me be, but not unchaste,
Nor my clear fame with any spot defaced.
Though in my face there 's no affected frown,   15
Nor in my carriage a feigned niceness shown,

° Translated from Ovid's **Heroides**, XVII

I keep my honor still without a stain,
Nor has my love made any coxcomb vain.
Your boldness I with admiration see;
20 What hope had you to gain a Queen like me?
Because a hero° forced me once away,
Am I thought fit to be a second prey?
Had I been won, I had deserved your blame,
But sure my part was nothing but the shame:
25 Yet the base theft to him no fruit did bear,
I scaped unhurt by anything but fear.
Rude force might some unwilling kisses gain,
But there was all he ever could obtain.
You on such terms would ne'er have let me go;
30 Were he like you, we had not parted so.
Untouched the youth restored me to my friends,
And modest usage made me some amends;
'T is virtue to repent a vicious deed:
Did he repent, that Paris might succeed?
35 Sure 't is some fate that sets me above wrongs,
Yet still exposes me to busy tongues.
I'll not complain; for who 's displeased with love,
If it sincere, discreet, and constant prove?
But that I fear; not that I think you base,
40 Or doubt the blooming beauties of my face,
But all your sex is subject to deceive,
And ours alas, too willing to believe.
Yet others yield, and love o'ercomes the best
But why should I not shine above the rest?
45 Fair Leda's° story seems at first to be
A fit example ready found for me;
But she was cozened by a borrowed shape,
And under harmless feathers felt a rape.
If I should yield, what reason could I use?
50 By what mistake the loving crime excuse?
Her fault was in her powerful lover lost,
But of what Jupiter have I to boast?
Though you to heroes and to Kings succeed,

21 **hero** Theseus, son of Neptune, once ran away with Helen   45
Leda's mother of Castor and Pollux, sired by Jove in the form of a
swan

Our famous race does no addition need,
And great alliances but useless prove   55
To one that's come herself from mighty Jove.
Go then, and boast in some less haughty place
Your Phrygian blood, and Priam's ancient race,
Which I would show I valued, if I durst;
You are the fifth from Jove, but I the first.   60
The crown of Troy is powerful, I confess,
But I have reason to think ours no less.
Your letter, filled with promises of all
That men can good, or women pleasant call,
Gives expectation such an ample field,   65
As would move goddesses themselves to yield.
But if I e'er offend great Juno's laws,
Yourself shall be the dear, the only cause;
Either my honor I'll to death maintain,
Or follow you, without mean thoughts of gain.   70
Not that so fair a present I despise;
We like the gift, when we the giver prize.
But 't is your love moves me, which made you take
Such pains, and run such hazards for my sake.
I have perceived (though I dissembled too)   75
A thousand things that love has made you do;
Your eager eyes would almost dazzle mine,
In which, wild man, your wanton thoughts would
     shine.
Sometimes you 'd sigh, sometimes disordered stand,
And with unusual ardor press my hand;   80
Contrive just after me to take the glass,
Nor would you let the least occasion pass,
Which oft I feared, I did not mind alone,
And blushing sate for things which you have done:
Then murmured to myself: "He 'll for my sake   85
Do anything"—I hope 't was no mistake.
Oft have I read within this pleasing grove,
Under my name, those charming words, "I love."
I, frowning, seemed not to believe your flame;
But now, alas, am come to write the same.   90
If I were capable to do amiss,
I could not but be sensible of this.

For O, your face has such peculiar charms,
That who can hold from flying to your arms?
95 But what I ne'er can have without offense,
May some blest maid possess with innocence.
Pleasure may tempt, but virtue more should move;
O learn of me to want the thing you love!
What you desire is sought by all mankind:
100 As you have eyes, so others are not blind.
Like you they see, like you my charms adore,
They wish not less, but you dare venture more.
O, had you then upon our coasts been brought,
My virgin love when thousand rivals sought,
105 You had I seen, you should have had my voice;
Nor could my husband justly blame my choice!
For both our hopes, alas, you come too late!
Another now is master of my fate.
More to my wish I could have lived with you,
110 And yet my present lot can undergo.
Cease to solicit a weak woman's will,
And urge not her you love to so much ill.
But let me live contented as I may,
And make not my unspotted fame your prey.
115 Some right you claim, since naked to your eyes
Three goddesses disputed beauty's prize;
One offered valor, t'other crowns, but she
Obtained her cause, who, smiling, promised me.
But first, I am not of belief so light,
120 To think such nymphs would show you such a sight.
Yet, granting this, the other part is feigned:
A bribe so mean your sentence had not gained.
With partial eyes I should myself regard,
To think that Venus made me her reward:
125 I humbly am content with human praise;
A goddess's applause would envy raise.
But be it as you say, for, 't is confessed,
The men who flatter highest please us best.
That I suspect it, ought not to displease;
130 For miracles are not believed with ease.
One joy I have, that I had Venus' voice;
A greater yet, that you confirmed her choice;

That proffered laurels, promised sovereignty,
Juno and Pallas you contemned for me.
Am I your empire then, and your renown?   *135*
What heart of rock, but must by this be won?
And yet bear witness, O you powers above,
How rude I am in all the arts of love!
My hand is yet untaught to write to men;
This is th' essay of my unpracticed pen: *140*
Happy those nymphs, whom use has perfect made!
I think all crime, and tremble at a shade.
Even while I write, my fearful conscious eyes
Look often back, misdoubting a surprise.
For now the rumor spreads among the crowd,   *145*
At court in whispers, but in town aloud.
Dissemble you, whate'er you hear 'em say: }
To leave off loving were your better way, }
Yet if you will dissemble it, you may. }
Love secretly; the absence of my lord   *150*
More freedom gives, but does not all afford:
Long is his journey, long will be his stay;
Called by affairs of consequence away.
To go, or not, when unresolved he stood,
I bid him make what swift return he could: *155*
Then kissing me, he said: "I recommend
All to thy care, but most my Trojan friend."
I smiled at what he innocently said,
And only answered: "You shall be obeyed."
Propitious winds have borne him far from hence,   *160*
But let not this secure your confidence.
Absent he is, yet absent he commands:
You know the proverb: "Princes have long hands."
My fame 's my burden, for the more I 'm praised,
A juster ground of jealousy is raised.   *165*
Were I less fair, I might have been more blest:
Great beauty through great danger is possessed.
To leave me here his venture was not hard,
Because he thought my virtue was my guard.
He feared my face, but trusted to my life,   *170*
The beauty doubted, but believed the wife.
You bid me use th' occasion while I can,

Put in our hands by the good easy man.
I would, and yet I doubt, 'twixt love and fear;
175 One draws me from you, and one brings me near.
Our flames are mutual, and my husband 's gone,
The nights are long; I fear to lie alone.
One house contains us, and weak walls divide,
And you 're too pressing to be long denied.
180 Let me not live, but everything conspires
To join our loves, and yet my fear retires.
You court with words, when you should force employ,
A rape is requisite to shame-faced joy.
Indulgent to the wrongs which we receive,
185 Our sex can suffer what we dare not give.
What have I said? for both of us 't were best,
Our kindling fires if each of us suppressed.
The faith of strangers is too prone to change,
And, like themselves, their wandering passions range.
190 Hypsipyle,° and the fond Minoian maid,°
Were both by trusting of their guests betrayed.
How can I doubt that other men deceive,
When you yourself did fair Œnone° leave?
But lest I should upbraid your treachery,
195 You make a merit of that crime to me.
Yet grant you were to faithful love inclined,
Your weary Trojans wait but for a wind.
Should you prevail while I assign the night,
Your sails are hoisted, and you take your flight:
200 Some bawling mariner our love destroys,
And breaks asunder our unfinished joys.
But I with you may leave the Spartan port,
To view the Trojan wealth and Priam's court.
Shown while I see, I shall expose my fame,
205 And fill a foreign country with my shame.
In Asia what reception shall I find?
And what dishonor leave in Greece behind?
What will your brothers, Priam, Hecuba,
And what will all your modest matrons say?

190 **Hypsipyle** queen of Lemnos who received the Argonauts 190
Minoian maid Ariadne   193 **Œnone** the nymph whom Paris deserted
for Helen

Ev'n you, when on this action you reflect,   210
My future conduct justly may suspect:
And whate'er stranger lands upon your coast,
Conclude me, by your own example, lost.
I from your rage a strumpet's name shall hear,
While you forget what part in it you bear.   215
You, my crime's author, will my crime upbraid:
Deep under ground, O let me first be laid!
You boast the pomp and plenty of your land,
And promise all shall be at my command;
Your Trojan wealth, believe me, I despise;   220
My own poor native land has dearer ties.
Should I be injured on your Phrygian shore,
What help of kindred could I there implore?
Medea was by Jason's flattery won:
I may, like her, believe, and be undone.   225
Plain honest hearts, like mine, suspect no cheat,
And love contributes to its own deceit.
The ships, about whose sides loud tempests roar,
With gentle winds were wafted from the shore.
Your teeming mother° dreamt a flaming brand   230
Sprung from her womb consumed the Trojan land.
To second this, old prophecies conspire,
That Ilium shall be burnt with Grecian fire.
Both give me fear; nor is it much allayed,
That Venus is obliged our loves to aid.   235
For they, who lost their cause, revenge will take,
And for one friend two enemies you make.
Nor can I doubt, but, should I follow you,
The sword would soon our fatal crime pursue:
A wrong so great my husband's rage would rouse,   240
And my relations would his cause espouse.
You boast your strength and courage; but, alas!
Your words receive small credit from your face.
Let heroes in the dusty field delight:
Those limbs were fashioned for another fight.   245
Bid Hector sally from the walls of Troy,
A sweeter quarrel should your arms employ.
Yet fears like these should not my mind perplex,

230 **Your . . . mother** Hecuba

Were I as wise as many of my sex.
250 But time and you may bolder thoughts inspire;
And I perhaps may yield to your desire.
You last demand a private conference:
These are your words, but I can guess your sense.
Your unripe hopes their harvest must attend:
255 Be ruled by me, and time may be your friend.
This is enough to let you understand,
For now my pen has tired my tender hand:
My woman knows the secret of my heart,
And may hereafter better news impart.

Horace,
The Twenty-ninth Ode of the Third Book

PARAPHRASED IN PINDARIC VERSE, AND INSCRIBED
TO THE RIGHT HONORABLE LAURENCE, EARL OF
ROCHESTER

I

Descended of an ancient line,
    That long the Tuscan scepter swayed,
Make haste to meet the generous wine,
    Whose piercing is for thee delayed:
The rosy wreath is ready made;   *5*
    And artful hands prepare
The fragrant Syrian oil, that shall perfume thy hair.

II

When the wine sparkles from afar,
    And the well-natured friend cries, "Come away!"
Make haste, and leave thy business and thy care,   *10*
    No mortal interest can be worth thy stay.

III

Leave for a while thy costly country seat;
    And, to be great indeed, forget
The nauseous pleasures of the great:
    Make haste and come: *15*
Come, and forsake thy cloying store;
    Thy turret that surveys, from high,
The smoke, and wealth, and noise of Rome;
    And all the busy pageantry

20   That wise men scorn, and fools adore:
Come, give thy soul a loose, and taste the pleasures
        of the poor.

IV

Sometimes 't is grateful to the rich to try
A short vicissitude, and fit of poverty:
        A savory dish, a homely treat,
25   Where all is plain, where all is neat,
        Without the stately spacious room,
The Persian carpet, or the Tyrian loom,
Clear up the cloudy foreheads of the great.

V

The sun is in the Lion mounted high;
30   The Syrian star
                Barks from afar,
And with his sultry breath infects the sky;
The ground below is parched, the heav'ns above us
        fry.
The shepherd drives his fainting flock
35   Beneath the covert of a rock,
        And seeks refreshing rivulets nigh:
The Sylvans° to their shades retire,
Those very shades and streams new shades and
        streams require,
And want a cooling breeze of wind to fan the raging
        fire.

VI

40   Thou, what befits the new lord Mayor,
        And what the city faction dare,
        And what the Gallic arms will do,
        And what the quiver-bearing foe,
        Art anxiously inquisitive to know;
45   But God has, wisely, hid from human sight
        The dark decrees of future fate,

37 **Sylvans** wood deities

And sown their seeds in depth of night;
He laughs at all the giddy turns of state,
When mortals search too soon, and fear too late.

VII

Enjoy the present smiling hour,   50
   And put it out of Fortune's power:
The tide of business, like the running stream,
   Is sometimes high, and sometimes low,
A quiet ebb, or a tempestuous flow,
     And always in extreme.   55
   Now with a noiseless gentle course
   It keeps within the middle bed;
   Anon it lifts aloft the head,
And bears down all before it with impetuous force:
   And trunks of trees come rolling down,   60
   Sheep and their folds together drown:
Both house and homestead into seas are borne,
And rocks are from their old foundations torn,
And woods, made thin with winds, their scattered
   honors mourn.

VIII

Happy the man, and happy he alone,   65
   He, who can call today his own:
   He, who secure within, can say
"Tomorrow do thy worst, for I have lived today.
   Be fair, or foul, or rain, or shine,
The joys I have possessed, in spite of fate, are mine.   70
   Not Heav'n itself upon the past has power;
But what has been, has been, and I have had my
   hour."

IX

Fortune, that with malicious joy
   Does man her slave oppress,
Proud of her office to destroy,   75
   Is seldom pleased to bless.

Still various and unconstant still,
But with an inclination to be ill;
Promotes, degrades, delights in strife,
80   And makes a lottery of life.
I can enjoy her while she 's kind;
But when she dances in the wind,
And shakes her wings, and will not stay,
I puff the prostitute away:
85 The little or the much she gave, is quietly resigned;
Content with poverty, my soul I arm;
And virtue, though in rags, will keep me warm.

X

What is 't to me,
Who never sail in her unfaithful sea,
90   If storms arise, and clouds grow black;
If the mast split, and threaten wrack?
Then let the greedy merchant fear
For his ill-gotten gain;
And pray to gods that will not hear,
95 While the debating winds and billows bear
His wealth into the main.
For me, secure from Fortune's blows,
(Secure of what I cannot lose)
In my small pinnace° I can sail,
100   Contemning all the blustering roar;
And running with a merry gale,
With friendly stars my safety seek,
Within some little winding creek,
And see the storm ashore.

99 **pinnace** a smaller version of a full-rigged ship

Lucretius,

The Beginning of the First Book

Delight of humankind, and gods above,
Parent of Rome, propitious Queen of Love,°
Whose vital power, air, earth, and sea supplies,
And breeds whate'er is born beneath the rolling
    skies:
For every kind, by thy prolific might,   *5*
Springs, and beholds the regions of the light.
Thee, Goddess, thee the clouds and tempests fear,
And at thy pleasing presence disappear:
For thee the land in fragrant flowers is dressed,
For thee the ocean smiles, and smooths her wavy
    breast;   *10*
And Heav'n itself with more serene and purer light is
    blest.
For when the rising spring adorns the mead,
And a new scene of nature stands displayed,
When teeming buds and cheerful greens appear,
And western gales unlock the lazy year,   *15*
The joyous birds thy welcome first express,
Whose native songs thy genial fire° confess;
Then savage beasts bound o'er their slighted food,
Strook° with thy darts, and tempt the raging flood.
All nature is thy gift; earth, air, and sea: *20*
Of all that breathes, the various progeny,
Stung with delight, is goaded on by thee.
O'er barren mountains, o'er the flowery plain,
The leavy forest, and the liquid main,
Extends thy uncontrolled and boundless reign.   *25*
Through all the living regions dost thou move,

2 **Queen of Love** Venus   17 **genial fire** creating power   19 **Strook**
struck

And scatterest, where thou goest, the kindly seeds of
    love.
  Since then the race of every living thing
Obeys thy power; since nothing new can spring
30 Without thy warmth, without thy influence bear,
Or beautiful, or lovesome can appear;
Be thou my aid, my tuneful song inspire,
And kindle with thy own productive fire;
While all thy province, Nature, I survey,
35 And sing to Memmius° an immortal lay
Of heav'n and earth, and everywhere thy wondrous
    power display:
To Memmius, under thy sweet influence born,
Whom thou with all thy gifts and graces dost adorn.
The rather, then, assist my Muse and me,
40 Infusing verses worthy him and thee.
Meantime on land and sea let barbarous discord
    cease,
And lull the listening world in universal peace.
To thee mankind their soft repose must owe,
For thou alone that blessing canst bestow;
45 Because the brutal business of the war
Is managed by thy dreadful servant's care:
Who oft retires from fighting fields, to prove
The pleasing pains of thy eternal love:
And panting on thy breast, supinely lies,
While with thy heavenly form he feeds his famished
50   eyes:
Sucks in with open lips thy balmy breath,
By turns restored to life, and plunged in pleasing
    death.
There while thy curling limbs about him move,
Involved and fettered in the links of love,
55 When, wishing all, he nothing can deny,
Thy charms in that auspicious moment try;
With winning eloquence our peace implore,
And quiet to the weary world restore.

Lucretius,
The Latter Part of the Third Book

AGAINST THE FEAR OF DEATH

What has this bugbear death to frighten man,
If souls can die, as well as bodies can?
For, as before our birth we felt no pain,
When Punic arms infested land and main,
When heav'n and earth were in confusion hurled,   *5*
For the debated empire of the world,
Which awed with dreadful expectation lay,
Sure to be slaves, uncertain who should sway:
So, when our mortal frame shall be disjoined,
The lifeless lump uncoupled from the mind,   *10*
From sense of grief and pain we shall be free;
We shall not feel, because we shall not *be*.
Though earth in seas, and seas in heav'n were lost,
We should not move, we only should be tossed.
Nay, ev'n suppose when we have suffered fate,   *15*
The soul could feel in her divided state,
What's that to us? for we are only we
While souls and bodies in one frame agree.
Nay, though our atoms should revolve by chance,
And matter leap into the former dance;   *20*
Though time our life and motion could restore,
And make our bodies what they were before,
What gain to us would all this bustle bring?
The new-made man would be another thing.
When once an interrupting pause is made,   *25*
That individual being is decayed.
We, who are dead and gone, shall bear no part
In all the pleasures, nor shall feel the smart
Which to that other mortal shall accrue,

30   Whom of our matter time shall mold anew.
    For backward if you look on that long space
    Of ages past, and view the changing face
    Of matter, tossed and variously combined
    In sundry shapes, 't is easy for the mind
35   From thence t' infer, that seeds of things have been
    In the same order as they now are seen:
    Which yet our dark remembrance cannot trace,
    Because a pause of life, a gaping space,
    Has come betwixt, where memory lies dead,
    And all the wandering motions from the sense are
40   fled.
    For whosoe'er shall in misfortunes live,
    Must *be,* when those misfortunes shall arrive;
    And since the man who *is* not, feels not woe
    (For death exempts him, and wards off the blow,
45   Which we, the living, only feel and bear)
    What is there left for us in death to fear?
    When once that pause of life has come between,
    'T is just the same as we had never been.
      And therefore if a man bemoan his lot,
50   That after death his moldering limbs shall rot,
    Or flames, or jaws of beasts devour his mass,
    Know, he 's an unsincere, unthinking ass.
    A secret sting remains within his mind,
    The fool is to his own cast offals kind.
55   He boasts no sense can after death remain,)
    Yet makes himself a part of life again,   }
    As if some other He could feel the pain.)
    If, while he live, this thought molest his head,
    "What wolf or vulture shall devour me dead?"
60   He wastes his days in idle grief, nor can
    Distinguish 'twixt the body and the man:
    But thinks himself can still himself survive;
    And, what when dead he feels not, feels alive.
    Then he repines that he was born to die,
65   Nor knows in death there is no other He,
    No living He remains his grief to vent,
    And o'er his senseless carcass to lament.
    If after death 't is painful to be torn

By birds, and beasts, then why not so to burn,
Or drenched in floods of honey, to be soaked;   *70*
Imbalm'd, to be at once preserved and choked;
Or on an airy mountain's top to lie,
Exposed to cold and heav'n's inclemency;
Or crowded in a tomb to be oppressed
With monumental marble on thy breast?   *75*
   But to be snatched from all thy household joys,
From thy chaste wife, and thy dear prattling boys,
Whose little arms about thy legs are cast,
And climbing for a kiss prevent their mother's haste,
Inspiring secret pleasure through thy breast—   *80*
All these shall be no more: thy friends oppressed
Thy care and courage now no more shall free:
"Ah wretch!" thou criest, "ah! miserable me!
One woeful day sweeps children, friends, and wife,
And all the brittle blessings of my life!"   *85*
Add one thing more, and all thou sayest is true;
Thy want and wish of them is vanished too,
Which, well considered, were a quick relief
To all thy vain imaginary grief.
For thou shalt sleep, and never wake again,   *90*
And quitting life, shalt quit thy living pain.
But we thy friends shall all those sorrows find, ⎫
Which in forgetful death thou leavest behind; ⎬
No time shall dry our tears, nor drive thee ⎭
   from our mind.
The worst that can befall thee, measured right,   *95*
Is a sound slumber, and a long good-night.
Yet thus the fools, that would be thought the wits,
Disturb their mirth with melancholy fits,
When healths go round, and kindly brimmers flow,
Till the fresh garlands on their foreheads glow,   *100*
They whine, and cry: "Let us make haste to live.
Short are the joys that human life can give."
Eternal preachers, that corrupt the draught,
And pall the god that never thinks, with thought;
Idiots with all that thought, to whom the worst   *105*
Of death is want of drink, and endless thirst,
Or any fond desire as vain as these.

For even in sleep, the body wrapped in ease,
Supinely lies, as in the peaceful grave;
110 And wanting nothing, nothing can it crave.
Were that sound sleep eternal, it were death;
Yet the first atoms then, the seeds of breath,
Are moving near to sense; we do but shake
And rouse that sense, and straight we are awake.
115 Then death to us, and death's anxiety,
Is less than nothing, if a less could be.
For then our atoms, which in order lay,
Are scattered from their heap, and puffed away,
And never can return into their place,
120 When once the pause of life has left an empty space.
    And last, suppose great Nature's voice should call
To thee, or me, or any of us all,
"What dost thou mean, ungrateful wretch, thou vain,
Thou mortal thing, thus idly to complain,
125 And sigh and sob that thou shalt be no more?
For if thy life were pleasant heretofore,
If all the bounteous blessings I could give   ⎫
Thou hast enjoyed; if thou hast known to live,   ⎬
And pleasure not leaked through thee like a sieve; ⎭
130 Why dost thou not give thanks as at a plenteous feast,
Crammed to the throat with life, and rise and take
        thy rest?
But if my blessings thou hast thrown away,
If indigested joys passed through, and would not stay,
Why dost thou wish for more to squander still?
135 If life be grown a load, a real ill,
And I would all thy cares and labors end,
Lay down thy burden, fool, and know thy friend.
To please thee, I have emptied all my store,   ⎫
I can invent and can supply no more,   ⎬
140 But run the round again, the round I ran before. ⎭
Suppose thou art not broken yet with years,
Yet still the selfsame scene of things appears,
And would be ever, couldst thou ever live;
For life is still but life, there 's nothing new to give."
145 What can we plead against so just a bill?
We stand convicted, and our cause goes ill.

But if a wretch, a man oppressed by fate,
Should beg of Nature to prolong his date,
She speaks aloud to him with more disdain:
"Be still, thou martyr fool, thou covetous of pain."   150
But if an old decrepit sot lament;
"What, thou," she cries, "who hast outlived content!
Dost thou complain, who hast enjoyed my store?
But this is still th' effect of wishing more!
Unsatisfied with all that Nature brings;   155
Loathing the present, liking absent things;
From hence it comes, thy vain desires at strife
Within themselves, have tantalized thy life,
And ghastly death appeared before thy sight,
Ere thou hadst gorged thy soul and senses with
    delight.   160
Now leave those joys, unsuiting to thy age,
To a fresh comer, and resign the stage."
    Is Nature to be blamed if thus she chide?
No, sure; for 't is her business to provide,
Against this ever-changing frame's decay,   165
New things to come, and old to pass away.
One being, worn, another being makes;
Changed, but not lost; for Nature gives and takes:
New matter must be found for things to come,
And these must waste like those, and follow Nature's
    doom.   170
All things, like thee, have time to rise and rot;
And from each other's ruin are begot;
For life is not confined to him or thee;
'T is given to all for use, to none for property.
    Consider former ages past and gone,   175
Whose circles ended long ere thine begun,
Then tell me, fool, what part in them thou hast.
Thus mayest thou judge the future by the past.
What horror see'st thou in that quiet state?
What bugbear dreams to fright thee after fate?   180
No ghost, no goblins, that still passage keep,
But all is there serene, in that eternal sleep.
For all the dismal tales that poets tell
Are verified on earth, and not in hell.

185 No Tantalus° looks up with fearful eye,
    Or dreads th' impending rock to crush him from on
       high;
    But fear of chance on earth disturbs our easy hours,
    Or vain imagined wrath of vain imagined powers.
    No Tityus° torn by vultures lies in hell;
190 Nor could the lobes of his rank liver swell
    To that prodigious mass for their eternal meal.
    Not though his monstrous bulk had covered o'er
    Nine spreading acres, or nine thousand more;
    Not though the globe of earth had been the giant's
       floor:
195 Nor in eternal torments could he lie;
    Nor could his corpse sufficient food supply.
    But he 's the Tityus, who by love oppressed,
    Or tyrant passion preying on his breast,
    And ever-anxious thoughts, is robbed of rest.
200 The Sisyphus° is he, whom noise and strife
    Seduce from all the soft retreats of life,
    To vex the government, disturb the laws;
    Drunk with the fumes of popular applause,
    He courts the giddy crowd to make him great,
    And sweats and toils in vain, to mount the sovereign
205   seat.
    For still to aim at power, and still to fail,
    Ever to strive, and never to prevail,
    What is it, but, in reason's true account,
    To heave the stone against the rising mount?
210 Which urged, and labored, and forced up with pain,
    Recoils and rolls impetuous down, and smokes along
      the plain.
    Then still to treat thy ever-craving mind
    With every blessing, and of every kind,
    Yet never fill thy ravening appetite;
215 Though years and seasons vary thy delight,
    Yet nothing to be seen of all the store,

185 **Tantalus** son of Zeus, tortured by being forced to stand in water
that receded whenever he attempted to drink   189 **Tityus** son of
Zeus, tortured by vultures gnawing at his liver   200 **Sisyphus** son of
Aeolus, condemned to roll a great stone up a hill which constantly
fell back

But still the wolf within thee barks for more;
This is the fable's moral, which they tell
Of fifty foolish virgins damned in hell
To leaky vessels, which the liquor spill;   220
To vessels of their sex, which none could ever fill.
As for the Dog, the Furies, and their snakes,
The gloomy caverns, and the burning lakes,
And all the vain infernal trumpery,
They neither are, nor were, nor e'er can be.   225
But here on earth the guilty have in view
The mighty pains to mighty mischiefs due:
Racks, prisons, poisons, the Tarpeian rock,°
Stripes, hangmen, pitch, and suffocating smoke,
And last, and most, if these were cast behind,   230
Th' avenging horror of a conscious mind,
Whose deadly fear anticipates the blow,
And sees no end of punishment and woe;
But looks for more, at the last gasp of breath:
This makes a hell on earth, and life a death.   235
    Meantime, when thoughts of death disturb thy
      head,
Consider, Ancus,° great and good, is dead;
Ancus thy better far, was born to die,
And thou, dost thou bewail mortality?
So many monarchs with their mighty state,   240
Who ruled the world, were overruled by fate.
That haughty king, who lorded o'er the main,
And whose stupendous bridge did the wild waves
      restrain
(In vain they foamed, in vain they threatened wrack,
While his proud legions marched upon their back)   245
Him death, a greater monarch, overcame;
Nor spared his guards the more, for their immortal
      name.
The Roman chief, the Carthaginian dread,   ⎫
Scipio, the thunderbolt of war, is dead,   ⎬
And like a common slave, by fate in triumph led.   ⎭   250
The founders of invented arts are lost;

228 **Tarpeian rock** cliff from which ancient Roman criminals were
hurled   237 **Ancus** fourth king of Rome

And wits, who made eternity their boast.
Where now is Homer, who possessed the throne?
Th' immortal work remains, the mortal author's gone.
255 Democritus, perceiving age invade,
His body weakened, and his mind decayed,
Obeyed the summons with a cheerful face;
Made haste to welcome death, and met him half the
race.
That stroke even Epicurus could not bar,
260 Though he in wit surpassed mankind as far
As does the midday sun the midnight star.
And thou, dost thou disdain to yield thy breath,
Whose very life is little more than death?
More than one half by lazy sleep possessed;
265 And when awake, thy soul but nods at best,
Day-dreams and sickly thoughts revolving in thy
breast.
Eternal troubles haunt thy anxious mind,
Whose cause and cure thou never hopest to find;
But still uncertain, with thyself at strife,
270 Thou wanderest in the labyrinth of life.
    O, if the foolish race of man, who find
A weight of cares still pressing on their mind,
Could find as well the cause of this unrest,
And all this burden lodged within the breast,
275 Sure they would change their course, nor live as now,
Uncertain what to wish or what to vow.
Uneasy both in country and in town,
They search a place to lay their burden down.
One, restless in his palace, walks abroad,
280 And vainly thinks to leave behind the load.
But straight returns, for he 's as restless there,
And finds there 's no relief in open air.
Another to his villa would retire,
And spurs as hard as if it were on fire;
285 No sooner entered at his country door,
But he begins to stretch, and yawn, and snore;
Or seeks the city which he left before.

Thus every man o'erworks his weary will,
To shun himself, and to shake off his ill;
The shaking fit returns, and hangs upon him still.   *290*
No prospect of repose, nor hope of ease;
The wretch is ignorant of his disease;
Which known would all his fruitless trouble spare,
For he would know the world not worth his care;
Then would he search more deeply for the cause,   *295*
And study Nature well, and Nature's laws:
For in this moment lies not the debate,
But on our future, fixed, eternal state;
That never-changing state, which all must keep,
Whom death has doomed to everlasting sleep.   *300*

Why are we then so fond of mortal life,
Beset with dangers, and maintained with strife?
A life which all our care can never save;
One fate attends us, and one common grave.
Besides, we tread but a perpetual round;   *305*
We ne'er strike out, but beat the former ground,
And the same mawkish joys in the same track
        are found.
For still we think an absent blessing best,
Which cloys, and is no blessing when possessed;
A new arising wish expels it from the breast.   *310*
The feverish thirst of life increases still;
We call for more and more, and never have our fill:
Yet know not what tomorrow we shall try,
What dregs of life in the last draught may lie.
Nor, by the longest life we can attain,   *315*
One moment from the length of death we gain;
For all behind belongs to his eternal reign.
When once the Fates have cut the mortal thread,
The man as much to all intents is dead,
Who dies today, and will as long be so,   *320*
As he who died a thousand years ago.

Virgil:
The Seventh Pastoral,
or, Meliboeus°

Beneath a holm° repaired two jolly swains;
Their sheep and goats together grazed the plains,
Both young Arcadians, both alike inspired
To sing, and answer as the song required.
5 Daphnis, as umpire, took the middle seat,
And fortune thither led my weary feet.
For while I fenced my myrtles from the cold,
The father of my flock had wandered from the fold.
Of Daphnis I inquired; he, smiling, said:
10 "Dismiss your fear;" and pointed where he fed;
"And, if no greater cares disturb your mind,
Sit here with us, in covert of the wind.
Your lowing heifers, of their own accord,
At watering time will seek the neighboring ford.
15 Here wanton Mincius° winds along the meads,
And shades his happy banks with bending reeds.
And see, from yon old oak that mates the skies,
How black the clouds of swarming bees arise."
What should I do! Nor was Alcippe nigh,
20 Nor absent Phyllis could my care supply,
To house, and feed by hand my weaning lambs,
And drain the strutting udders of their dams.

° **Meliboeus** (Virgil may be representing himself under this name in this pastoral, but the other persons may be fictional. Alcippe and Phyllis represent either mistresses or servants of the singers) **1 holm** oak **15 Mincius** river near Mantua

Great was the strife betwixt the singing swains;
And I preferred my pleasure to my gains.
Alternate rhyme the ready champions chose: 25
These Corydon rehearsed, and Thyrsis those.

CORYDON

Ye Muses, ever fair, and ever young,
Assist my numbers, and inspire my song.
With all my Codrus,° O inspire my breast!
For Codrus, after Phœbus, sings the best.   30
Or, if my wishes have presumed too high,
And stretched their bounds beyond mortality,
The praise of artful numbers I resign,
And hang my pipe upon the sacred pine.

THYRSIS

Arcadian swains, your youthful poet crown   35
With ivy wreaths, though surly Codrus frown:
Or, if he blast my Muse with envious praise,
Then fence my brows with amulets of bays,
Lest his ill arts, or his malicious tongue,
Should poison, or bewitch my growing song.   40

CORYDON

These branches of a stag, this tusky boar
(The first essay of arms untried before)
Young Micon offers, Delia,° to thy shrine:
But speed his hunting with thy power divine;
Thy statue then of Parian stone° shall stand;   45
Thy legs in buskins with a purple band.

THYRSIS

This bowl of milk, these cakes (our country fare),   ⎫
For thee, Priapus,° yearly we prepare,   ⎬
Because a little garden is thy care;   ⎭

29 **Codrus** a contemporary poet   43 **Delia** Diana, the moon   45
Parian stone marble of Paros   48 **Priapus** son of Dionysus, protector
of vineyards and gardens

50   But if the falling lambs increase my fold,
      Thy marble statue shall be turned to gold.

CORYDON

      Fair Galatea,° with thy silver feet,
      O, whiter than the swan, and more than Hybla°
          sweet;
      Tall as a poplar, taper as the bole,
55   Come, charm thy shepherd, and restore my soul!
      Come, when my lated sheep at night return,
      And crown the silent hours, and stop the rosy morn!

THYRSIS

      May I become as abject in thy sight
      As seaweed on the shore, and black as night:
60   Rough as a bur; deformed like him who chaws
      Sardinian herbage to contract his jaws;
      Such and so monstrous let thy swain appear,
      If one day's absence looks not like a year.
      Hence from the field, for shame: the flock deserves
65   No better feeding while the shepherd starves.

CORYDON

      Ye mossy springs, inviting easy sleep,
      Ye trees, whose leafy shades those mossy fountains
          keep,
      Defend my flock! The summer heats are near,
      And blossoms on the swelling vines appear.

THYRSIS

70   With heapy fires our cheerful hearth is crowned;
      And firs for torches in the woods abound:

52 **Galatea** a sea-nymph   53 **Hybla** the ancient name of the city of
Megara

We fear not more the winds and wintry cold,
Than streams the banks, or wolves the bleating fold.

CORYDON

Our woods, with juniper and chestnuts crowned,
With falling fruits and berries paint the ground;   *75*
And lavish Nature laughs, and strows her stores
   around.
But if Alexis from our mountains fly,
Ev'n running rivers leave their channels dry.

THYRSIS

Parched are the plains, and frying is the field,
Nor withering vines their juicy vintage yield.   *80*
But if returning Phyllis bless the plain,
The grass revives, the woods are green again,
And Jove descends in showers of kindly rain.

CORYDON

The poplar is by great Alcides° worn:
The brows of Phœbus his own bays adorn.   *85*
The branching vine the jolly Bacchus loves;
The Cyprian Queen° delights in myrtle groves.
With hazel Phyllis crowns her flowing hair;
And, while she loves that common wreath to wear,
Nor bays, nor myrtle boughs, with hazel shall com-
  pare.   *90*

THYRSIS

The towering ash is fairest in the woods;
In gardens pines, and poplars by the floods:
But, if my Lycidas° will ease my pains,
And often visit our forsaken plains,
To him the towering ash shall yield in woods,   *95*
In gardens pines, and poplars by the floods.

84 **Alcides** Hercules   87 **Cyprian Queen** Venus   93 **Lycidas** poetic
name for a friend of Virgil's

MELIBŒUS

These rhymes I did to memory commend,
When vanquished Thyrsis did in vain contend,
Since when 't is Corydon among the swains,
100 Young Corydon without a rival reigns.

Virgil:
The Fourth Book of The Æneid°

But anxious cares already seized the Queen:
She fed within her veins a flame unseen;
The hero's valor, acts, and birth inspire
Her soul with love, and fan the secret fire.
His words, his looks, imprinted in her heart,   5
Improve the passion, and increase the smart.
Now, when the purple morn had chased away
The dewy shadows, and restored the day,
Her sister first with early care she sought,
And thus in mournful accents eased her thought: 10
  "My dearest Anna, what new dreams affright
My laboring soul! what visions of the night
Disturb my quiet, and distract my breast
With strange ideas of our Trojan guest!
His worth, his actions, and majestic air,   15
A man descended from the gods declare.
Fear ever argues a degenerate kind,
His birth is well asserted by his mind.
Then, what he suffered, when by Fate betrayed,
What brave attempts for falling Troy he made!   20
Such were his looks, so gracefully he spoke,
That, were I not resolved against the yoke
Of hapless marriage, never to be curst
With second love, so fatal was my first,

°The story of the *Æneid* begins with the account of a Trojan fleet,
after a voyage of seven years, setting sail for Italy. A storm drives
several of the ships upon the coast of Africa, one of them the ship
of Aeneas. Venus, the mother of Aeneas, conveys him in a cloud to
the city of Carthage where the Queen, Dido, entertains him. Venus
causes her to conceive a passion for her son, and Dido keeps Aeneas
there, asking him to tell the story of his adventures since the siege of
Troy. The fourth book takes up after he has come to the end of the
story.

25 To this one error I might yield again;
    For since Sichæus° was untimely slain,
    This only man is able to subvert
    The fixed foundations of my stubborn heart.
    And, to confess my frailty, to my shame, ⎫
30 Somewhat I find within, if not the same,   ⎬
    Too like the sparkles of my former flame. ⎭
    But first let yawning earth a passage rend,
    And let me through the dark abyss descend;
    First let avenging Jove, with flames from high, ⎫
35 Drive down this body to the nether sky,   ⎬
    Condemned with ghosts in endless night to lie,   ⎭
    Before I break the plighted faith I gave!
    No, he who had my vows shall ever have;   ⎫
    For whom I loved on earth, I worship in the grave." ⎬
40   She said; the tears ran gushing from her eyes,
    And stopped her speech. Her sister thus replies:
    "O dearer than the vital air I breathe,
    Will you to grief your blooming years bequeath,
    Condemned to waste in woes your lonely life,
45 Without the joys of mother or of wife?
    Think you these tears, this pompous train of woe,
    Are known or valued by the ghosts below?
    I grant, that while your sorrows yet were green,
    It well became a woman, and a Queen,
50 The vows of Tyrian Princes to neglect,
    To scorn Hyarbas,° and his love reject,
    With all the Libyan lords of mighty name;
    But will you fight against a pleasing flame!
    This little spot of land, which Heav'n bestows,
55 On every side is hemmed with warlike foes;
    Getulian cities here are spread around,
    And fierce Numidians there your frontiers bound;
    Here lies a barren waste of thirsty land,
    And there the Syrtes° raise the moving sand:
60 Barcæan troops besiege the narrow shore,
    And from the sea Pygmalion threatens more.

26 **Sichæus** the husband of Dido whom her brother, Pygmalion, slew
51 **Hyarbas** son of Jupiter Ammon   59 **Syrtes** an inhospitable bar-
barian tribe

Propitious Heav'n, and gracious Juno, lead
This wandering navy to your needful aid:
How will your empire spread, your city rise,
From such a union, and with such allies! 65
Implore the favor of the powers above,
And leave the conduct of the rest to love.
Continue still your hospitable way,
And still invent occasions of their stay,
Till storms and winter winds shall cease to threat, 70
And planks and oars repair their shattered fleet."

These words, which from a friend and sister came,
With ease resolved the scruples of her fame,
And added fury to the kindled flame.
Inspired with hope, the project they pursue; 75
On every altar sacrifice renew;
A chosen ewe of two years old they pay
To Ceres, Bacchus, and the God of Day:
Preferring Juno's power, for Juno ties
The nuptial knot and makes the marriage joys. 80
The beauteous Queen before her altar stands,
And holds the golden goblet in her hands.
A milk-white heifer she with flowers adorns,
And pours the ruddy wine betwixt her horns;
And, while the priests with prayer the gods invoke, 85
She feeds their altars with Sabæan° smoke,
With hourly care the sacrifice renews,
And anxiously the panting entrails views.
What priestly rites, alas! what pious art,
What vows avail to cure a bleeding heart! 90
A gentle fire she feeds within her veins,
Where the soft god secure in silence reigns.

Sick with desire, and seeking him she loves,
From street to street the raving Dido roves.
So when the watchful shepherd, from the blind, 95
Wounds with a random shaft the careless hind,
Distracted with her pain she flies the woods,
Bounds o'er the lawn, and seeks the silent floods,
With fruitless care; for still the fatal dart

86 Sabæan Sabæa, a city in Arabia Felix famous for frankincense
and myrrh

100 Sticks in her side, and rankles in her heart.
And now she leads the Trojan chief along
The lofty walls, amidst the busy throng;
Displays her Tyrian wealth, and rising town,
Which Love, without his labor, makes his own.
105 This pomp she shows, to tempt her wandering guest;
Her faltering tongue forbids to speak the rest.
When day declines, and feasts renew the night,
Still on his face she feeds her famished sight;
She longs again to hear the Prince relate
110 His own adventures and the Trojan fate.
He tells it o'er and o'er; but still in vain,
For still she begs to hear it once again.
The hearer on the speaker's mouth depends,
And thus the tragic story never ends.
115   Then, when they part, when Phœbe's paler light
Withdraws, and falling stars to sleep invite,
She last remains, when every guest is gone,
Sits on the bed he pressed, and sighs alone;
Absent, her absent hero sees and hears;
120 Or in her bosom young Ascanius bears,
And seeks the father's image in the child,
If love by likeness might be so beguiled.
    Meantime the rising towers are at a stand;
No labors exercise the youthful band,
125 Nor use of arts, nor toils of arms they know;
The mole° is left unfinished to the foe;
The mounds, the works, the walls, neglected lie,
Short of their promised heighth, that seemed to threat
    the sky.
    But when imperial Juno, from above,
130 Saw Dido fettered in the chains of Love,
Hot with the venom which her veins inflamed,
And by no sense of shame to be reclaimed,
With soothing words to Venus she begun:
"High praises, endless honors, you have won,
135 And mighty trophies, with your worthy son!
Two gods a silly woman have undone.

126 **mole** massive structure of stone

Nor am I ignorant, you both suspect°
This rising city, which my hands erect:
But shall celestial discord never cease?
'T is better ended in a lasting peace.   *140*
You stand possessed of all your soul desired;
Poor Dido with consuming love is fired.
Your Trojan with my Tyrian let us join, ⎫
So Dido shall be yours, Æneas mine: ⎬
One common kingdom, one united line. ⎭   *145*
Eliza shall a Dardan lord obey,°
And lofty Carthage for a dower convey."
Then Venus, who her hidden fraud descried, ⎫
Which would the scepter of the world misguide ⎬
To Libyan shores, thus artfully replied: ⎭   *150*
"Who, but a fool, would wars with Juno choose,
And such alliance and such gifts refuse,
If Fortune with our joint desires comply?
The doubt is all from Jove and destiny:
Lest he forbid, with absolute command,   *155*
To mix the people in one common land.
Or will the Trojan and the Tyrian line
In lasting leagues and sure succession join?
But you, the partner of his bed and throne,
May move his mind; my wishes are your own."   *160*
   "Mine," said imperial Juno, "be the care;
Time urges, now, to perfect this affair:
Attend my counsel, and the secret share.
When next the Sun his rising light displays,
And gilds the world below with purple rays,   *165*
The Queen, Æneas, and the Tyrian court
Shall to the shady woods, for sylvan game, resort.
There, while the huntsmen pitch their toils around,
And cheerful horns from side to side resound,
A pitchy cloud shall cover all the plain   *170*
With hail, and thunder, and tempestuous rain:
The fearful train shall take their speedy flight,
Dispersed, and all involved in gloomy night:

137 **suspect** look upon with ill will   146 **Eliza . . . obey** Dido shall
be subjected to a Trojan lord (Juno is here speaking of Aeneas with
contempt)

One cave a grateful shelter shall afford
175 To the fair Princess, and the Trojan lord.
I will myself the bridal bed prepare,
If you, to bless the nuptials, will be there:
So shall their loves be crowned with due delights,
And Hymen shall be present at the rites."
180 The Queen of Love consents, and closely smiles
At her vain project, and discovered wiles.

The rosy morn was risen from the main,
And horns and hounds awake the princely train:
They issue early through the city gate,
185 Where the more wakeful huntsmen ready wait,
With nets, and toils, and darts, beside the force
Of Spartan dogs, and swift Massylian horse.
The Tyrian peers and officers of state
For the slow Queen in antechambers wait;
190 Her lofty courser, in the court below,
Who his majestic rider seems to know,
Proud of his purple trappings, paws the ground,
And champs the golden bit, and spreads the foam
         around.
The Queen at length appears: on either hand
195 The brawny guards in martial order stand.
A flowered simar° with golden fringe she wore,
And at her back a golden quiver bore;
Her flowing hair a golden caul restrains,
A golden clasp the Tyrian robe sustains.
200 Then young Ascanius, with a sprightly grace,
Leads on the Trojan youth to view the chase.
But far above the rest in beauty shines
The great Æneas, when the troop he joins;
Like fair Apollo, when he leaves the frost
205 Of wintery Xanthus, and the Lycian coast,
When to his native Delos he resorts,
Ordains the dances, and renews the sports:
Where painted Scythians, mixed with Cretan bands,
Before the joyful altars join their hands.
210 Himself, on Cynthus walking, sees below
The merry madness of the sacred show.
196 **simar** loose outer garment

Green wreaths of bays his length of hair inclose,
A golden fillet binds his awful brows;
His quiver sounds: not less the Prince is seen
In manly presence, or in lofty mien.   215
    Now had they reached the hills, and stormed the seat
Of savage beasts, in dens, their last retreat.
The cry pursues the mountain goats; they bound
From rock to rock, and keep the craggy ground;
Quite otherwise the stags, a trembling train, ⎫   220
In herds unsingled, scour the dusty plain,   ⎬
And a long chase in open view maintain.   ⎭
The glad Ascanius, as his courser guides,
Spurs through the vale, and these and those outrides.
His horse's flanks and sides are forced to feel   225
The clanking lash, and goring of the steel.
Impatiently he views the feeble prey,
Wishing some nobler beast to cross his way,
And rather would the tusky boar attend,
Or see the tawny lion downward bend.   230
    Meantime, the gathering clouds obscure the skies;
From pole to pole the forky lightning flies;
The rattling thunders roll; and Juno pours
A wintry deluge down, and sounding showers.
The company, dispersed, to coverts ride,   235
And seek the homely cots, or mountain's hollow side.
The rapid rains, descending from the hills,
To rolling torrents raise the creeping rills.
The Queen and Prince, as Love or Fortune guides,
One common cavern in her bosom hides.   240
Then first the trembling earth the signal gave,
And flashing fires enlighten all the cave:
Hell from below, and Juno from above,
And howling nymphs, were conscious to their love.
From this ill-omened hour in time arose   245
Debate and death, and all succeeding woes.
    The Queen, whom sense of honor could not move,
No longer made a secret of her love,
But called it marriage, by that specious name
To veil the crime and sanctify the shame.   250
    The loud report through Libyan cities goes;

Fame, the great ill, from small beginnings grows:
Swift from the first; and every moment brings
New vigor to her flights, new pinions to her wings.
255 Soon grows the pigmy to gigantic size;
Her feet on earth, her forehead in the skies.
Enraged against the gods, revengeful Earth
Produced her last of the Titanian birth.
Swift is her walk, more swift her wingèd haste:
260 A monstrous phantom, horrible and vast;
As many plumes as raise her lofty flight,
So many piercing eyes enlarge her sight;
Millions of opening mouths to Fame belong,
And every mouth is furnished with a tongue,
And round with listening ears the flying plague is
265   hung.
She fills the peaceful universe with cries;
No slumbers ever close her wakeful eyes;
By day, from lofty towers her head she shows,
And spreads through trembling crowds disastrous
        news;
270 With court informers haunts, and royal spies;
Things done relates, not done she feigns, and mingles
        truth with lies.
Talk is her business, and her chief delight
To tell of prodigies and cause affright.
She fills the people's ears with Dido's name,
275 Who, lost to honor and the sense of shame,
Admits into her throne and nuptial bed
A wandering guest, who from his country fled:
Whole days with him she passes in delights,
And wastes in luxury long winter nights.
280 Forgetful of her fame and royal trust,
Dissolved in ease, abandoned to her lust.
    The goddess widely spreads the loud report,
And flies at length to King Hyarba's court.
When first possessed with this unwelcome news,
285 Whom did he not of men and gods accuse?
This Prince, from ravished Garamantis born,
A hundred temples did with spoils adorn,
In Ammon's honor, his celestial sire;

A hundred altars fed with wakeful fire;
And, through his vast dominions, priests ordained,   290
Whose watchful care these holy rites maintained.
The gates and columns were with garlands crowned,
And blood of victim beasts enriched the ground.

He, when he heard a fugitive could move
The Tyrian Princess, who disdained his love,   295
His breast with fury burned, his eyes with fire,
Mad with despair, impatient with desire.
Then on the sacred altars pouring wine,
He thus with prayers implored his sire divine:
"Great Jove! propitious to the Moorish race,   300
Who feast on painted beds, with offerings grace
Thy temples, and adore thy power divine
With blood of victims, and with sparkling wine,
Seest thou not this? or do we fear in vain
Thy boasted thunder, and thy thoughtless reign?   305
Do thy broad hands the forky lightnings lance?
Thine are the bolts, or the blind work of chance?
A wandering woman builds, within our state,
A little town, bought at an easy rate;
She pays me homage, and my grants allow   310
A narrow space of Libyan lands to plow;
Yet scorning me, by passion blindly led,
Admits a banished Trojan to her bed!
And now this other Paris, with his train
Of conquered cowards, must in Afric reign!   315
(Whom, what they are, their looks and garb confess,
Their locks with oil perfumed, their Lydian dress.)
He takes the spoil, enjoys the princely dame;
And I, rejected I, adore an empty name."

His vows, in haughty terms, he thus preferred,   320
And held his altar's horns. The mighty Thunderer
    heard,
Then cast his eyes on Carthage, where he found
The lustful pair in lawless pleasure drowned,
Lost in their loves, insensible of shame,
And both forgetful of their better fame.   325
He calls Cyllenius, and the god attends,
By whom his menacing command he sends:

"Go, mount the western winds, and cleave the sky;
Then, with a swift descent, to Carthage fly:
330 There find the Trojan chief, who wastes his days
In slothful riot and inglorious ease,
Nor minds the future city, given by fate.°
To him this message from my mouth relate.
'Not so fair Venus hoped, when twice she won
335 Thy life with prayers, nor promised such a son.
Hers was a hero, destined to command
A martial race, and rule the Latian land,
Who should his ancient line from Teucer draw,
And on the conquered world impose the law.'
340 If glory cannot move a mind so mean,
Nor future praise from fading pleasure wean,
Yet why should he defraud his son of fame,
And grudge the Romans their immortal name!
What are his vain designs! what hopes he more
345 From his long lingering on a hostile shore,
Regardless to redeem his honor lost,
And for his race to gain th' Ausonian coast!
Bid him with speed the Tyrian court forsake;
With this command the slumbering warrior wake."
350   Hermes obeys; with golden pinions binds
His flying feet, and mounts the western winds:
And whether o'er the seas or earth he flies,
With rapid force they bear him down the skies.
But first he grasps within his awful hand
355 The mark of sovereign power, his magic wand;
With this he draws the ghosts from hollow graves,
With this he drives them down the Stygian waves;
With this he seals in sleep the wakeful sight,
And eyes, though closed in death, restores to light.
360 Thus armed, the god begins his airy race,
And drives the racking clouds along the liquid space.
Now sees the tops of Atlas, as he flies,
Whose brawny back supports the starry skies;
Atlas, whose head, with piny forests crowned,

332 **future city . . . fate** fate was to lead him to Lavinium, Alba Longa,
and Rome (Jove is rebuking Aeneas for failing to remember the glory
that was promised him)

Is beaten by the winds, with foggy vapors bound.   365
Snows hide his shoulders; from beneath his chin
The founts of rolling streams their race begin;
A beard of ice on his large breast depends.
Here, poised upon his wings, the god descends.
Then, rested thus, he from the towering height   370
Plunged downward, with precipitated flight,
Lights on the seas, and skims along the flood.
As waterfowl, who seek their fishy food,
Less, and yet less, to distant prospect show;
By turns they dance aloft, and dive below: 375
Like these, the steerage of his wings he plies,
And near the surface of the water flies,
Till having passed the seas, and crossed the sands,
He closed his wings, and stooped on Libyan lands:
Where shepherds once were housed in homely sheds,   380
Now towers within the clouds advance their heads.
Arriving there, he found the Trojan prince
New ramparts raising for the town's defense.
A purple scarf, with gold embroidered o'er
(Queen Dido's gift) about his waist he wore;   385
A sword, with glittering gems diversified,
For ornament, not use, hung idly by his side.
   Then thus, with wingèd words, the god began,
Resuming his own shape: "Degenerate man,
Thou woman's property, what makest thou here,   390
These foreign walls and Tyrian towers to rear,
Forgetful of thy own? All-powerful Jove,
Who sways the world below and Heav'n above,
Has sent me down with this severe command:
What means thy lingering in the Libyan land?   395
If glory cannot move a mind so mean,
Nor future praise from flitting pleasure wean,
Regard the fortunes of thy rising heir;
The promised crown let young Ascanius wear,
To whom th' Ausonian scepter, and the state   400
Of Rome's imperial name is owed by fate."
So spoke the god; and, speaking, took his flight,
Involved in clouds, and vanished out of sight.
   The pious Prince was seized with sudden fear;

405 Mute was his tongue, and upright stood his hair.
Revolving in his mind the stern command,
He longs to fly, and loathes the charming land.
What should he say? or how should he begin?)
What course, alas! remains to steer between }
410 Th' offended lover and the powerful Queen?)
This way and that he turns his anxious mind,
And all expedients tries, and none can find.
Fixed on the deed, but doubtful of the means,
After long thought to this advice he leans:
415 Three chiefs he calls, commands them to repair
The fleet, and ship their men with silent care;
Some plausible pretense he bids them find,
To color what in secret he designed.
Himself, meantime, the softest hours would choose,
420 Before the love-sick lady heard the news;
And move her tender mind, by slow degrees,
To suffer what the sovereign power decrees:
Jove will inspire him, when, and what to say.
They hear with pleasure, and with haste obey.
425   But soon the Queen perceives the thin disguise
(What arts can blind a jealous woman's eyes!)
She was the first to find the secret fraud,
Before the fatal news was blazed abroad.
Love the first motions of the lover hears,
430 Quick to presage, and even in safety fears.
Nor impious Fame was wanting to report)
The ships repaired, the Trojans' thick resort, }
And purpose to forsake the Tyrian court.)
Frantic with fear, impatient of the wound,
435 And impotent of mind, she roves the city round.
Less wild the Bacchanalian dames appear,
When, from afar, their nightly god they hear,
And howl about the hills, and shake the wreathy spear.
At length she finds the dear perfidious man;
440 Prevents his formed excuse, and thus began:
"Base and ungrateful! could you hope to fly,
And undiscovered scape a lover's eye?
Nor could my kindness your compassion move,
Nor plighted vows, nor dearer bands of love?

Or is the death of a despairing Queen   445
Nor worth preventing, though too well foreseen?
Even when the wintry winds command your stay,
You dare the tempests, and defy the sea.
False as you are, suppose you were not bound
To lands unknown, and foreign coasts to sound;   450
Were Troy restored, and Priam's happy reign,
Now durst you tempt, for Troy, the raging main?
See whom you fly! am I the foe you shun?
Now, by those holy vows, so late begun,
By this right hand (since I have nothing more   455
To challenge, but the faith you gave before;)
I beg you by these tears too truly shed,
By the new pleasures of our nuptial bed;
If ever Dido, when you most were kind,
Were pleasing in your eyes, or touched your mind;   460
By these my prayers, if prayers may yet have place,
Pity the fortunes of a falling race.
For you I have provoked a tyrant's hate,
Incensed the Libyan and the Tyrian state;
For you alone I suffer in my fame,   465
Bereft of honor, and exposed to shame.
Whom have I now to trust, ungrateful guest?
(That only name remains of all the rest!)
What have I left? or whither can I fly?
Must I attend Pygmalion's cruelty!   470
Or till Hyarba shall in triumph lead
A Queen that proudly scorned his proffered bed!
Had you deferred, at least, your hasty flight,
And left behind some pledge of our delight,
Some babe to bless the mother's mournful sight,   475
Some young Æneas, to supply your place,
Whose features might express his father's face;
I should not then complain to live bereft
Of all my husband, or be wholly left."

Here paused the Queen. Unmoved he holds his eyes,   480
By Jove's command; nor suffered love to rise,
Though heaving in his heart; and thus at length
        replies:
"Fair Queen, you never can enough repeat

Your boundless favors, or I own my debt;
485 Nor can my mind forget Eliza's° name,
While vital breath inspires this mortal frame.
This only let me speak in my defense,
I never hoped a secret flight from hence,
Much less pretended to the lawful claim
490 Of sacred nuptials, or a husband's name.
For if indulgent Heav'n would leave me free,
And not submit my life to fate's decree,
My choice would lead me to the Trojan shore, ⎫
Those relics to review, their dust adore,   ⎬
495 And Priam's ruined palace to restore.   ⎭
But now the Delphian oracle commands,
And fate invites me to the Latian lands.
That is the promised place to which I steer,
And all my vows are terminated there.
500 If you, a Tyrian, and a stranger born,
With walls and towers a Libyan town adorn,
Why may not we—like you, a foreign race—
Like you, seek shelter in a foreign place?
As often as the night obscures the skies
505 With humid shades, or twinkling stars arise,
Anchises' angry ghost in dreams appears;
Chides my delay, and fills my soul with fears:
And young Ascanius justly may complain
Of his defrauded fate and destined reign.
510 Ev'n now the herald of the gods appeared:
Waking I saw him, and his message heard.
From Jove he came commissioned, heav'nly bright
With radiant beams, and manifest to sight.
The sender and the sent I both attest:
515 These walls he entered, and those words expressed.
Fair Queen, oppose not what the gods command;
Forced by my fate, I leave your happy land."
   Thus while he spoke, already she began,
With sparkling eyes, to view the guilty man:
520 From head to foot surveyed his person o'er,
Nor longer these outrageous threats forebore.
"False as thou art, and, more than false, forsworn!

485 **Eliza's** another name by which Dido was known

Not sprung from noble blood, nor goddess-born,
But hewn from hardened entrails of a rock!
And rough Hyrcanian tigers gave thee suck.   525
Why should I fawn? what have I worse to fear?
Did he once look, or lent a listening ear,
Sighed when I sobbed, or shed one kindly tear?—
All symptoms of a base ungrateful mind,
So foul, that, which is worse, 't is hard to find.   530
Of man's injustice why should I complain?
The gods, and Jove himself, behold in vain
Triumphant treason; yet no thunder flies,
Nor Juno views my wrongs with equal eyes;
Faithless is earth, and faithless are the skies!   535
Justice is fled, and Truth is now no more!
I saved the shipwracked exile on my shore;
With needful food his hungry Trojans fed;
I took the traitor to my throne and bed:
Fool that I was—'t is little to repeat   540
The rest—I stored and rigged his ruined fleet.
I rave, I rave! A god's command he pleads,
And makes Heav'n accessary to his deeds.
Now Lycian lots, and now the Delian god,
Now Hermes is employed from Jove's abode,   545
To warn him hence; as if the peaceful state
Of heav'nly powers were touched with human fate!
But go! thy flight no longer I detain.
Go seek thy promised kingdom through the main!
Yet if the Heav'ns will hear my pious vow,   550
The faithless waves, not half so false as thou,
Or secret sands, shall sepulchers afford
To thy proud vessels, and their perjured lord.
Then shalt thou call on injured Dido's name;
Dido shall come in a black sulphury flame,   555
When death has once dissolved her mortal frame.
Shall smile to see the traitor vainly weep,
Her angry ghost, arising from the deep,
Shall haunt thee waking, and disturb thy sleep.
At least my shade thy punishment shall know,   560
And Fame shall spread the pleasing news below."
　　Abruptly here she stops; then turns away

Her loathing eyes, and shuns the sight of day.
Amazed he stood, revolving in his mind
565 What speech to frame, and what excuse to find.
Her fearful maids their fainting mistress led,
And softly laid her on her ivory bed.
    But good Æneas, though he much desired
To give that pity which her grief required,
570 Though much he mourned, and labored with his love,
Resolved at length, obeys the will of Jove:
Reviews his forces; they with early care
Unmoor their vessels, and for sea prepare.
The fleet is soon afloat, in all its pride,
575 And well-calked galleys in the harbor ride.
Then oaks for oars they felled; or, as they stood,
Of its green arms despoiled the growing wood,
Studious of flight. The beach is covered o'er
With Trojan bands, that blacken all the shore:
580 On every side are seen, descending down,
Thick swarms of soldiers, loaden from the town.
Thus, in battalia, march embodied ants,
Fearful of winter, and of future wants,
T' invade the corn, and to their cells convey
585 The plundered forage of their yellow prey.
The sable troops, along the narrow tracks,
Scarce bear the weighty burthen on their backs:
Some set their shoulders to the ponderous grain; ⎫
Some guard the spoil; some lash the lagging train; ⎬
590 All ply their several tasks, and equal toil sustain. ⎭
    What pangs the tender breast of Dido tore,
When, from the tower, she saw the covered shore,
And heard the shouts of sailors from afar,
Mixed with the murmurs of the watery war!
595 All-powerful Love, what changes canst thou cause
In human hearts, subjected to thy laws!
Once more her haughty soul the tyrant bends;
To prayers and mean submissions she descends.
No female arts or aids she left untried,
600 Nor counsels unexplored, before she died.
"Look, Anna! look! the Trojans crowd to sea;
They spread their canvas, and their anchors weigh.

The shouting crew their ships with garlands bind,
Invoke the sea gods, and invite the wind.
Could I have thought this threatening blow so near,   *605*
My tender soul had been forewarned to bear.
But do not you my last request deny,
With yon perfidious man your interest try,
And bring me news, if I must live or die.
You are his favorite, you alone can find   *610*
The dark recesses of his inmost mind:
In all his trusted secrets you have part,
And know the soft approaches to his heart.
Haste then, and humbly seek my haughty foe;
Tell him, I did not with the Grecians go,   *615*
Nor did my fleet against his friends employ,
Nor swore the ruin of unhappy Troy,
Nor moved with hands profane his father's dust:
Why should he then reject a suit so just?
Whom does he shun, and whither would he fly?   *620*
Can he this last, this only prayer deny?
Let him at least his dangerous flight delay,
Wait better winds, and hope a calmer sea.
The nuptials he disclaims I urge no more:
Let him pursue the promised Latian shore.   *625*
A short delay is all I ask him now;
A pause of grief, an interval from woe,
Till my soft soul be tempered to sustain
Accustomed sorrows, and inured to pain.
If you in pity grant this one request,   *630*
My death shall glut the hatred of his breast."
This mournful message pious Anna bears,
And seconds with her own her sister's tears:
But all her arts are still employed in vain;
Again she comes, and is refused again.   *635*
His hardened heart nor prayers nor threatenings
      move;
Fate, and the god, had stopped his ears to love.
    As when the winds their airy quarrel try,
Justling° from every quarter of the sky,
This way and that the mountain oak they bend,   *640*

639 Justling driving forcefully

His boughs they shatter, and his branches rend;
With leaves and falling mast they spread the ground;
The hollow valleys echo to the sound:
Unmoved, the royal plant their fury mocks,
645 Or shaken, clings more closely to the rocks;
Far as he shoots his towering head on high,
So deep in earth his fixed foundations lie.
No less a storm the Trojan hero bears;
Thick messages and loud complaints he hears,
650 And bandied words, still beating on his ears.
Sighs, groans, and tears proclaim his inward pains;
But the firm purpose of his heart remains.

The wretched Queen, pursued by cruel fate,
Begins at length the light of Heav'n to hate:
655 And loathes to live. Then dire portents she sees,
To hasten on the death her soul decrees.
Strange to relate: for when before the shrine
She pours in sacrifice the purple wine,
The purple wine is turned to putrid blood,
660 And the white offered milk converts to mud.
This dire presage, to her alone revealed,
From all, and even her sister, she concealed.
A marble temple stood within the grove,
Sacred to death, and to her murthered love;
665 That honored chapel she had hung around
With snowy fleeces, and with garlands crowned:
Oft, when she visited this lonely dome,
Strange voices issued from her husband's tomb;
She thought she heard him summon her away,
670 Invite her to his grave, and chide her stay.
Hourly 't is heard, when with a boding note
The solitary screech owl strains her throat,
And on a chimney's top, or turret's height,
With songs obscene disturbs the silence of the night.
675 Besides, old prophecies augment her fears;
And stern Æneas in her dreams appears,
Disdainful as by day: she seems, alone,
To wander in her sleep, through ways unknown,
Guideless and dark; or, in a desert plain,
680 To seek her subjects, and to seek in vain.

Like Pentheus, when, distracted with his fear,
He saw two suns, and double Thebes appear;
Or mad Orestes, when his mother's ghost
Full in his face infernal torches tossed,
And shook her snaky locks: he shuns the sight,   685
Flies o'er the stage, surprised with mortal fright;
The Furies guard the door and intercept his flight.
    Now, sinking underneath a load of grief,
From death alone she seeks her last relief;
The time and means resolved within her breast,   690
She to her mournful sister thus addressed
(Dissembling hope, her cloudy front she clears,
And a false vigor in her eyes appears):
"Rejoice!" she said. "Instructed from above,
My lover I shall gain, or lose my love.   695
Nigh rising Atlas, next the falling sun,
Long tracts of Ethiopian climates run:
There a Massylian priestess I have found,
Honored for age, for magic arts renowned:
Th' Hesperian temple was her trusted care;   700
'T was she supplied the wakeful dragon's fare.
She poppy seeds in honey taught to steep,
Reclaimed his rage, and soothed him into sleep.
She watched the golden fruit; her charms unbind
The chains of love, or fix them on the mind.   705
She stops the torrents, leaves the channel dry,
Repels the stars, and backward bears the sky.
The yawning earth rebellows to her call,
Pale ghosts ascend, and mountain ashes fall.
Witness, ye gods, and thou my better part,   710
How loth I am to try this impious art!
Within the secret court, with silent care,
Erect a lofty pile, exposed in air:
Hang on the topmost part the Trojan vest,
Spoils, arms, and presents, of my faithless guest.   715
Next, under these, the bridal bed be placed,
Where I my ruin in his arms embraced:
All relics of the wretch are doomed to fire;
For so the priestess and her charms require."
    Thus far she said, and farther speech forbears;   720

A mortal paleness in her face appears:
Yet the mistrustless Anna could not find
The secret funeral in these rites designed;
Nor thought so dire a rage possessed her mind.

725 Unknowing of a train concealed so well,
She feared no worse than when Sichæus° fell;
Therefore obeys. The fatal pile they rear,
Within the secret court, exposed in air.
The cloven holms° and pines are heaped on high,
730 And garlands on the hollow spaces lie.
Sad cypress, vervain, yew, compose the wreath,
And every baleful green denoting death.
The Queen, determined to the fatal deed,
The spoils and sword he left, in order spread,
735 And the man's image on the nuptial bed.
    And now (the sacred altars placed around)
The priestess enters, with her hair unbound,
And thrice invokes the powers below the ground.
Night, Erebus, and Chaos she proclaims,
740 And threefold Hecate, with her hundred names,
And three Dianas: next, she sprinkles round
With feigned Avernian drops the hallowed ground;
Culls hoary simples, found by Phœbe's light,
With brazen sickles reaped at noon of night;
745 Then mixes baleful juices in the bowl,
And cuts the forehead of a newborn foal,
Robbing the mother's love. The destined Queen
Observes, assisting at the rites obscene:
A leavened cake in her devoted hands
750 She holds, and next the highest altar stands:
One tender foot was shod, her other bare;
Girt was her gathered gown, and loose her hair.
Thus dressed, she summoned, with her dying breath,
The Heav'ns and planets conscious of her death,
755 And every power, if any rules above,
Who minds, or who revenges, injured love.
    'T was dead of night, when weary bodies close
Their eyes in balmy sleep and soft repose:
The winds no longer whisper through the woods,

726 **Sichæus** Dido's husband   729 **holms** holm-oaks

Nor murmuring tides disturb the gentle floods.   760
The stars in silent order moved around;
And Peace, with downy wings, was brooding on the
      ground.
The flocks and herds, and parti-colored fowl,
Which haunt the woods, or swim the weedy pool,
Stretched on the quiet earth securely lay,   765
Forgetting the past labors of the day.
All else of Nature's common gift partake;
Unhappy Dido was alone awake.
Nor sleep nor ease the furious queen can find,
Sleep fled her eyes, as quiet fled her mind.   770
Despair, and rage, and love divide her heart;
Despair and rage had some, but love the greater part.
      Then thus she said within her secret mind:
"What shall I do? what succor can I find?
Become a suppliant to Hyarba's° pride,   775
And take my turn, to court and be denied?
Shall I with this ungrateful Trojan go,
Forsake an empire, and attend a foe?
Himself I refuged, and his train relieved;
'T is true; but am I sure to be received?   780
Can gratitude in Trojan souls have place?
Laomedon still lives in all his race!
Then, shall I seek alone the churlish crew,
Or with my fleet their flying sails pursue?
What force have I but those whom scarce before   785
I drew reluctant from their native shore?
Will they again embark at my desire,
Once more sustain the seas, and quit their second
      Tyre?
Rather with steel thy guilty breast invade,
And take the fortune thou thyself hast made.   790
Your pity, sister, first seduced my mind,
Or seconded too well what I designed.
These dear-bought pleasures had I never known,
Had I continued free, and still my own;
Avoiding love, I had not found despair,   795
But shared with savage beasts the common air.

775 **Hyarba's** son of Jupiter Ammon

Like them, a lonely life I might have led,
Not mourned the living, nor disturbed the dead."
These thoughts she brooded in her anxious breast.
800 On board, the Trojan found more easy rest.
Resolved to sail, in sleep he passed the night;
And ordered all things for his early flight.
　　To whom once more the wingèd god appears;
His former youthful mien and shape he wears,
805 And with this new alarm invades his ears.
"Sleepest thou, O goddess-born! and canst thou drown
Thy needful cares, so near a hostile town?
Beset with foes, nor hearest the western gales
Invite thy passage, and inspire thy sails?
810 She harbors in her heart a furious hate,
And thou shalt find the dire effects too late;
Fixed on revenge, and obstinate to die.
Haste swiftly hence, while thou hast power to fly.
The sea with ships will soon be covered o'er,
815 And blazing firebrands kindle all the shore.
Prevent her rage, while night obscures the skies,
And sail before the purple morn arise.
Who knows what hazards thy delay may bring?
Woman's a various and a changeful thing."
820 Thus Hermes in the dream; then took his flight
Aloft in air unseen, and mixed with night.
　　Twice warned by the celestial messenger,
The pious Prince arose with hasty fear;
Then roused his drowsy train without delay,
825 "Hast to your banks; your crooked anchors weigh,
And spread your flying sails, and stand to sea.
A god commands: he stood before my sight,
And urged us once again to speedy flight.
O sacred power, what power soe'er thou art,
830 To thy blest orders I resign my heart.
Lead thou the way; protect thy Trojan bands,
And prosper the design thy will commands."
He said; and, drawing forth his flaming sword,
His thundering arm divides the many-twisted cord.
835 An emulating zeal inspires his train:
They run; they snatch; they rush into the main.

With headlong haste they leave the desert shores,
And brush the liquid seas with laboring oars.
  Aurora now had left her saffron bed,
And beams of early light the heav'ns o'er-spread,   *840*
When, from a tower, the Queen, with wakeful eyes,
Saw day point upward from the rosy skies.
She looked to seaward; but the sea was void,
And scarce in ken the sailing ships descried.
Stung with despite, and furious with despair,   *845*
She struck her trembling breast, and tore her hair.
"And shall th' ungrateful traitor go," she said,
"My land forsaken, and my love betrayed?
Shall we not arm? not rush from every street,
To follow, sink, and burn his perjured fleet?   *850*
Haste, haul my galleys out! pursue the foe!
Bring flaming brands! set sail, and swiftly row!
What have I said? where am I? Fury turns
My brain; and my distempered bosom burns.
Then, when I gave my person and my throne,   *855*
This hate, this rage, had been more timely shown.
See now the promised faith, the vaunted name,
The pious man, who, rushing through the flame,
Preserved his gods, and to the Phrygian shore
The burthen of his feeble father bore!   *860*
I should have torn him piecemeal; strowed in floods
His scattered limbs, or left exposed in woods;
Destroyed his friends and son; and from the fire,
Have set the reeking boy before the sire.
Events are doubtful, which on battles wait: *865*
Yet where's the doubt, to souls secure° of fate?
My Tyrians, at their injured Queen's command,
Had tossed their fires amid the Trojan band:
At once extinguished all the faithless name;
And I myself, in vengeance of my shame,   } *870*
Had fallen upon the pile, to mend the funeral flame.
Thou Sun, who viewest at once the world below;
Thou Juno, guardian of the nuptial vow;
Thou Hecate, hearken from thy dark abodes!
Ye Furies, fiends, and violated gods,   *875*

866 **secure** unafraid

All powers invoked with Dido's dying breath,
Attend her curses, and avenge her death!
If so the Fates ordain, and Jove commands,
Th' ungrateful wretch should find the Latian lands,
880 Yet let a race untamed, and haughty foes,
His peaceful entrance with dire arms oppose;
Oppressed with numbers in th' unequal field,
His men discouraged, and himself expelled,
Let him for succor sue from place to place,
885 Torn from his subjects, and his son's embrace.
First, let him see his friends in battle slain,
And their untimely fate lament in vain;
And when, at length, the cruel war shall cease,
On hard conditions may he buy his peace.
890 Nor let him then enjoy supreme command;)
But fall, untimely, by some hostile hand, }
And lie unburied on the barren sand!   )
These are my prayers, and this my dying will;
And you, my Tyrians, every curse fulfil.
895 Perpetual hate and mortal wars proclaim,
Against the Prince, the people, and the name.
These grateful offerings on my grave bestow;
Nor league, nor love, the hostile nations know!
Now, and from hence, in every future age,
When rage excites your arms, and strength supplies
900   the rage,
Rise some avenger of our Libyan blood,
With fire and sword pursue the perjured brood:
Our arms, our seas, our shores, opposed to theirs;
And the same hate descend on all our heirs!"
905   This said, within her anxious mind she weighs
The means of cutting short her odious days.
Then to Sichæus' nurse she briefly said
(For, when she left her country, hers was dead):
"Go, Barce, call my sister. Let her care
910 The solemn rites of sacrifice prepare:
The sheep, and all th' atoning offerings bring,
Sprinkling her body from the crystal spring
With living drops; then let her come, and thou
With sacred fillets bind thy hoary brow.

Thus will I pay my vows to Stygian Jove,   *915*
And end the cares of my disastrous love.
Then cast the Trojan image on the fire,
And as that burns, my passion shall expire."
　　The nurse moves onward, with officious care,
And all the speed her aged limbs can bear.   *920*
But furious Dido, with dark thoughts involved,
Shook at the mighty mischief she resolved.
With livid spots distinguished was her face;
Red were her rolling eyes, and discomposed her pace;
Ghastly she gazed, with pain she drew her breath,   *925*
And Nature shivered at approaching death.
　　Then swiftly to the fatal place she passed,
And mounts the funeral pile with furious haste;
Unsheathes the sword the Trojan left behind
(Not for so dire an enterprise designed).   *930*
But when she viewed the garments loosely spread,
Which once he wore, and saw the conscious bed,
She paused, and with a sigh the robes embraced;
Then on the couch her trembling body cast,
ceive a soul, of mortal anguish eased: *935*
"Dear pledges of my love, while Heav'n so pleased,
Receive a soul, of mortal anguish eased:
My fatal course is finished; and I go
A glorious name, among the ghosts below.
A lofty city by my hands is raised,   *940*
Pygmalion punished, and my lord appeased.
What could my fortune have afforded more,
Had the false Trojan never touched my shore!"
Then kissed the couch; and, "Must I die," she said,
"And unrevenged? 'T is doubly to be dead!   *945*
Yet even this death with pleasure I receive
On any terms, 't is better than to live.
These flames, from far, may the false Trojan view;
These boding omens his base flight pursue!"
　　She said, and struck; deep entered in her side   *950*
The piercing steel, with reeking purple dyed:
Clogged in the wound the cruel weapon stands;
The spouting blood came streaming on her hands.
Her sad attendants saw the deadly stroke,

955 And with loud cries the sounding palace shook.
Distracted from the fatal sight they fled,
And through the town the dismal rumor spread.
First from the frighted court the yell began;
Redoubled, thence from house to house it ran:
960 The groans of men, with shrieks, laments, and cries
Of mixing women, mount the vaulted skies.
Not less the clamor, than if ancient Tyre,
Or the new Carthage, set by foes on fire
The rolling ruin, with their loved abodes,
965 Involved the blazing temples of their gods.
    Her sister hears; and furious with despair,
She beats her breast, and rends her yellow hair,
And calling on Eliza's name aloud,
Runs breathless to the place, and breaks the crowd.
970 "Was all that pomp of woe for this prepared;
These fires, this funeral pile, these altars reared?
Was all this train of plots contrived," said she,
"All only to deceive unhappy me?
Which is the worst? Didst thou in death pretend
975 To scorn thy sister, or delude thy friend?
Thy summoned sister, and thy friend, had come;
One sword had served us both, one common tomb.
Was I to raise the pile, the powers invoke,
Not to be present at the fatal stroke?
980 At once thou hast destroyed thyself and me,
Thy town, thy senate, and thy colony!
Bring water, bathe the wound; while I in death
Lay close my lips to hers, and catch the flying breath."
This said, she mounts the pile with eager haste,
985 And in her arms the gasping Queen embraced:
Her temples chafed; and her own garments tore,
To stanch the streaming blood, and cleanse the gore.
Thrice Dido tried to raise her drooping head,
And fainting thrice, fell grovelling on the bed.
990 Thrice oped her heavy eyes, and sought the light, ⎫
But having found it, sickened at the sight; ⎬
And closed her lids at last in endless night. ⎭
    Then Juno, grieving that she should sustain
A death so lingering, and so full of pain,

Sent Iris down, to free her from the strife   995
Of laboring Nature, and dissolve her life.
For since she died, not doomed by Heav'n's decree,
Or her own crime, but human casualty,
And rage of love, that plunged her in despair,
The Sisters had not cut the topmost hair,   1000
Which Proserpine and they can only know;
Nor made her sacred to the shades below.
Downward the various goddess took her flight,
And drew a thousand colors from the light;
Then stood above the dying lover's head,   1005
And said: "I thus devote thee to the dead.
This offering to th' infernal gods I bear."
Thus while she spoke, she cut the fatal hair;
The struggling soul was loosed, and life dissolved in
    air.

CRITICAL PROSE

From *Of Dramatic Poesy* (1668)

"The Dramatic Unities"

He had no sooner said this, but all desired the favor of him to give the definition of a play; and they were the more importunate, because neither Aristotle, nor Horace, nor any other, who writ of that subject, had ever done it.

Lisideius, after some modest denials, at last confessed he had a rude notion of it; indeed, rather a description than a definition; but which served to guide him in his private thoughts, when he was to make a judgment of what others writ: that he conceived a play ought to be, *A just and lively image of human nature, representing its passions and humors, and the changes of fortune to which it is subject, for the delight and instruction of mankind.*

This definition, though Crites raised a logical objection against it—that it was only *a genere et fine* [with respect to genus and purpose], and so not altogether perfect, was yet well received by the rest: and after they had given order to the water-men to turn their barge, and row softly, that they might take the cool of the evening in their return, Crites, being desired by the company to begin, spoke on behalf of the Ancients in this manner:—

"If confidence presage a victory, Eugenius, in his own opinion, has already triumphed over the Ancients: nothing

322

seems more easy to him, than to overcome those whom
it is our greatest praise to have imitated well; for we do
not only build upon their foundation, but by their models.
Dramatic Poesy had time enough, reckoning from Thespis
(who first invented it) to Aristophanes, to be born, to
grow up, and to flourish in maturity. It has been observed
of arts and sciences, that in one and the same century
they have arrived to great perfection; and no wonder,
since every age has a kind of universal genius, which
inclines those that live in it to some particular studies:
the work then, being pushed on by many hands, must of
necessity go forward.

"Is it not evident, in these last hundred years, when
the study of philosophy has been the business of all the
virtuosi in Christendom, that almost a new Nature has
been revealed to us? That more errors of the school have
been detected, more useful experiments in philosophy
have been made, more noble secrets in optics, medicine,
anatomy, astronomy, discovered, than in all those cred-
ulous and doting ages from Aristotle to us?—so true it is,
that nothing spreads more fast than science, when rightly
and generally cultivated.

"Add to this, the more than common emulation that
was in those times of writing well; which though it be
found in all ages and all persons that pretend to the same
reputation, yet Poesy, being then in more esteem than
now it is, had greater honors decreed to the professors of
it, and consequently the rivalship was more high between
them; they had judges ordained to decide their merit, and
prizes to reward it; and historians have been diligent to
record of Æschylus, Euripides, Sophocles, Lycophron,
and the rest of them, both who they were that vanquished
in these wars of the theater, and how often they were
crowned: while the Asian kings and Grecian commonwealths scarce afforded them a nobler subject than the
unmanly luxuries of a debauched court, or giddy intrigues
of a factious city:—*Alit æmulatio ingenia* (says Paterculus), *et nunc invidia, nunc admiratio incitationem ac-
cendit:* Emulation is the spur of wit; and sometimes envy,
sometimes admiration, quickens our endeavors.

"But now, since the rewards of honor are taken away, that virtuous emulation is turned into direct malice; yet so slothful, that it contents itself to condemn and cry down others, without attempting to do better: 'tis a reputation too unprofitable, to take the necessary pains for it; yet, wishing they had it, that desire is incitement enough to hinder others from it. And this, in short, Eugenius, is the reason why you have now so few good poets, and so many severe judges. Certainly, to imitate the Ancients well, much labor and long study is required; which pains, I have already shown, our poets would want encouragement to take, if yet they had ability to go through with it. Those Ancients have been faithful imitators and wise observers of that Nature which is so torn and ill represented in our plays; they have handed down to us a perfect resemblance of her; which we, like ill copiers, neglecting to look on, have rendered monstrous, and disfigured. But that you may know how much you are indebted to those your masters, and be ashamed to have so ill requited them, I must remember you, that all the rules by which we practice the drama at this day (either such as relate to the justness and symmetry of the plot, or the episodical ornaments, such as descriptions, narrations, and other beauties, which are not essential to the play), were delivered to us from the observations which Aristotle made, of these poets, who either lived before him, or were his contemporaries: we have added nothing of our own, except we have the confidence to say our wit is better; of which none boast in this our age but such as understand not theirs. Of that book which Aristotle has left us [*On the Poetics*], Horace his *Art of Poetry* is an excellent comment, and, I believe, restores to us that Second Book of his concerning *Comedy,* which is wanting in him.

"Out of these two have been extracted the famous Rules, which the French call *Des Trois Unités,* or, The Three Unities, which ought to be observed in every regular play; namely, of Time, Place, and Action.

"The Unity of Time they comprehend in twenty-four hours, the compass of a natural day, or as near it as it can be contrived; and the reason of it is obvious to every one,—that the time of the feigned action, or fable of the play, should be proportioned as near as can be to the duration of that time in which it is represented: since, therefore, all plays are acted on the theater in the space of time much within the compass of twenty-four hours, that play is to be thought the nearest imitation of nature whose plot or action is confined within that time; and by the same rule which concludes this general proportion of time it follows that all the parts of it are (as near as may be) to be equally subdivided; as namely, that one act take not up the supposed time of half a day, which is out of proportion to the rest; since the other four are then to be straitened within the compass of the remaining half: for it is unnatural that one act, which being spoke or written is not longer than the rest, should be supposed longer by the audience; 'tis therefore the poet's duty to take care that no act should be imagined to exceed the time in which it is represented on the stage; and that the intervals and inequalities of time be supposed to fall out between the acts.

"This rule of time, how well it has been observed by the Ancients, most of their plays will witness; you see them in their tragedies (wherein to follow this rule is certainly most difficult), from the very beginning of their plays, falling close into that part of the story which they intend for the action or principal object of it, leaving the former part to be delivered by narration: so that they set the audience, as it were, at the post where the race is to be concluded; and saving them the tedious expectation of seeing the poet set out and ride the beginning of the course, they suffer you not to behold him till he is in sight of the goal and just upon you.

"For the second Unity, which is that of Place, the Ancients meant by it, that the scene ought to be continued through the play, in the same place where it was laid in the beginning: for the stage on which it is represented being but one and the same place, it is unnatural to conceive it many, and those far distant from one another. I will not deny but by the variation of painted scenes, the fancy, which in these cases will contribute to its own deceit, may sometimes imagine it several places with some appearance of probability; yet it still carries the greater likelihood of truth if those places be supposed so near each other as in the same town or city; which may all be comprehended under the larger denomination of one place; for a greater distance will bear no proportion to the shortness of time which is allotted in the acting, to pass from one of them to another; for the observation of this, next to the Ancients, the French are to be most commended. They tie themselves so strictly to the Unity of Place that you never see in any of their plays a scene changed in the middle of an act: if the act begins in a garden, a street, or chamber, 'tis ended in the same place; and that you may know it to be the same, the stage is so supplied with persons, that it is never empty all the time: he who enters second, has business with him who was on before; and before the second quits the stage, a third appears who has business with him. This Corneille calls *la liaison des scènes,* the continuity or joining of the scenes; and 'tis a good mark of a well-contrived play, when all the persons are known to each other, and every one of them has some affairs with all the rest.

"As for the third Unity, which is that of Action, the Ancients meant no other by it than what the logicians do by their *finis,* the end or scope of any action; that which is the first in intention, and last in execution: now the poet is to aim at one great and complete action, to the carrying on of which all things in his play, even the very obstacles, are to be subservient; and the reason of this is as evident as any of the former.

"For two actions, equally labored and driven on by the writer, would destroy the unity of the poem; it would be no longer one play, but two: not but that there may be many actions in a play, as Ben Jonson has observed in his *Discoveries;* but they must be all subservient to the great one, which our language happily expresses in the name of *under-plots:* such as in Terence's *Eunuch* is the difference and reconcilement of Thais and Phædria, which is not the chief business of the play, but promotes the marriage of Chærea and Chremes's sister, principally intended by the poet. There ought to be but one action, says Corneille, that is, one complete action, which leaves the mind of the audience in a full repose; but this cannot be brought to pass but by many other imperfect actions, which conduce to it, and hold the audience in a delightful suspense of what will be.

"If by these rules (to omit many other drawn from the precepts and practice of the Ancients) we should judge our modern plays, 'tis probable that few of them would endure the trial: that which should be the business of a day, takes up in some of them an age; instead of one action, they are the epitomes of a man's life; and for one spot of ground, which the stage should represent, we are sometimes in more countries than the map can show us.

"But if we allow the Ancients to have contrived well, we must acknowledge them to have writ better. Questionless, we are deprived of a great stock of wit in the loss of Menander among the Greek poets, and of Cæcilius, Afranius, and Varius, among the Romans; we may guess at Menander's excellency by the plays of Terence, who translated some of his; and yet wanted so much of him that he was called by C. Cæsar the half-Menander; and may judge of Varius, by the testimonies of Horace, Martial, and Velleius Paterculus. 'Tis probable that these, could they be recovered, would decide the controversy; but so long as Aristophanes in the old comedy and Plautus in the new are extant, while the tragedies of Euripides, Sophocles, and Seneca, are to be had, I can never see one of those plays which are now written but it increases my admiration of the Ancients. And yet I must acknowledge farther, that to admire them as we ought, we should understand them better than we do. Doubtless many things appear flat to us, whose wit depended on some custom or story, which never came to our knowledge; or perhaps on some criticism in their language, which being so long dead, and only remaining in their books, 'tis not possible they should make us understand perfectly. To read Macrobius, explaining the propriety and elegancy of many words in Virgil, which I had before passed over without consideration as common things, is enough to assure me

that I ought to think the same of Terence; and that in the
purity of his style (which Tully so much valued that he
ever carried his works about him) there is yet left in him
great room for admiration, if I knew but where to place it.
In the meantime I must desire you to take notice that the
greatest man of the last age, Ben Jonson, was willing to
give place to them in all things: he was not only a professed imitator of Horace, but a learned plagiary of all the
others; you track him everywhere in their snow: if Horace, Lucan, Petronius Arbiter, Seneca, and Juvenal, had
their own from him, there are few serious thoughts which
are new in him: you will pardon me, therefore, if I presume he loved their fashion, when he wore their clothes.
But since I have otherwise a great veneration for him, and
you, Eugenius, prefer him above all other poets, I will use
no farther argument to you than his example: I will produce before you Father Ben, dressed in all the ornaments
and colors of the Ancients; you will need no other guide
to our party, if you follow him; and whether you consider
the bad plays of our age, or regard the good plays of the
last, both the best and the worst of the modern poets will
equally instruct you to admire the Ancients."

*　*　*　*　*

"English and French Drama Compared"

"If the question had been stated," replied Lisideius, "who had writ best, the French or English, forty years ago, I should have been of your opinion, and adjudged the honor to our own nation; but since that time" (said he, turning towards Neander), "we have been so long together bad Englishmen that we had not leisure to be good poets. Beaumont, Fletcher, and Jonson (who were only capable of bringing us to that degree of perfection which we have), were just then leaving the world; as if in an age of so much horror, wit and those milder studies of humanity had no farther business among us. But the Muses, who ever follow peace, went to plant in another country: it was then that the great Cardinal Richelieu began to take them into his protection; and that, by his encouragement, Corneille, and some other Frenchmen, reformed their theater (which before was as much below ours, as it now surpasses it and the rest of Europe). But because Crites in his discourse for the Ancients has prevented me, by observing many rules of the stage which the Moderns have borrowed from them, I shall only, in short, demand of you, whether you are not convinced that of all nations the French have best observed them? In the Unity of Time you find them so scrupulous that it yet remains a dispute among their poets, whether the artificial day of twelve hours, more or less, be not meant by Aristotle, rather than the natural one of twenty-four; and consequently, whether all plays ought not to be reduced into that compass. This I can testify, that in all their dramas writ within these last twenty years and upwards, I have not observed any that have extended the time to thirty hours: in the Unity of Place they are full

as scrupulous; for many of their critics limit it to that very spot of ground where the play is supposed to begin; none of them exceed the compass of the same town or city. The Unity of Action in all plays is yet more conspicuous; for they do not burden them with under-plots, as the English do: which is the reason why many scenes of our tragi-comedies carry on a design that is nothing of kin to the main plot; and that we see two distinct webs in a play, like those in ill-wrought stuffs; and two actions, that is, two plays, carried on together, to the confounding of the audience; who, before they are warm in their concernments for one part, are diverted to another; and by that means espouse the interest of neither. From hence likewise it arises that the one half of our actors are not known to the other. They keep their distances, as if they were Montagues and Capulets, and seldom begin an ac-
all to meet upon the stage. There is no theater in the
quaintance till the last scene of the fifth act, when they are
world has anything so absurd as the English tragi-comedy;
'tis a drama of our own invention, and the fashion of it is enough to proclaim it so; here a course of mirth, there another of sadness and passion, and a third of honor, and a duel: thus in two hours and a half, we run through all the fits of Bedlam. The French affords you as much variety on the same day, but they do it not so unseasonably, or *mal à propos,* as we: our poets present you the play and the farce together; and our stages still retain somewhat of the original civility of the Red Bull:

Atque ursum et pugiles media inter carmina poscunt.—

[The little vulgar of the clamorous pit . . .
     When his most interesting scenes appear,
     Call for a prize fight, or a baited bear.—Francis]

The end of tragedies or serious plays, says Aristotle, is to beget admiration, compassion, or concernment; but are not mirth and compassion things incompatible? and is it not evident that the poet must of necessity destroy the former by intermingling of the latter? that is, he must ruin the sole end and object of his tragedy, to introduce somewhat that is forced into it, and is not of the body of it. Would you not think that physician mad, who, having prescribed a purge, should immediately order you to take restringents upon it?"

* * * * *

"Shakespeare, Beaumont and Fletcher, and Jonson"

"To begin, then, with Shakespeare. He was the man who of all Modern, and perhaps Ancient poets, had the largest and most comprehensive soul. All the images of Nature were still present to him, and he drew them, not laboriously, but luckily; when he describes anything, you more than see it, you feel it too. Those who accuse him to have wanted learning, give him the greater commendation: he was naturally learned; he needed not the spectacles of books to read Nature; he looked inwards, and found her there. I cannot say he is everywhere alike; were he so, I should do him injury to compare him with the greatest of mankind. He is many times flat, insipid; his comic wit degenerating into clenches, his serious swelling into bombast. But he is always great when some great occasion is presented to him; no man can say he ever had a fit subject for his wit, and did not then raise himself as high above the rest of poets,

Quantum lenta solent inter viburna cupressi.

[As cypresses rise above the hedgerow thorn.]

The consideration of this made Mr. Hales of Eaton say, that there was no subject of which any poet ever writ, but he would produce it much better done in Shakespeare; and however others are now generally preferred before him, yet the age wherein he lived, which had contemporaries with him Fletcher and Jonson, never equalled them to him in their esteem: and in the last King's court, when Ben's reputation was at highest, Sir John Suckling, and with him the greater part of the courtiers, set our Shakespeare far above him.

"Beaumont and Fletcher, of whom I am next to speak, had, with the advantage of Shakespeare's wit, which was their precedent, great natural gifts, improved by study: Beaumont especially being so accurate a judge of plays, that Ben Jonson, while he lived, submitted all his writings to his censure, and, 'tis thought, used his judgment in correcting, if not contriving, all his plots. What value he had for him, appears by the verses he writ to him: and therefore I need speak no farther of it. The first play that brought Fletcher and him in esteem was their *Philaster:* for before that, they had written two or three very unsuccessfully, as the like is reported of Ben Jonson, before he writ *Every Man in his Humor.* Their plots were generally more regular than Shakespeare's, especially those which were made before Beaumont's death; and they understood and imitated the conversation of gentlemen much better; whose wild debaucheries, and quickness of wit in repartees, no poet before them could paint as they have done. Humor, which Ben Jonson derived from particular persons, they made it not their business to describe: they represented all the passions very lively, but above all, love. I am apt to believe the English language in them arrived to its highest perfection: what words have since been taken in, are rather superfluous than ornamental. Their plays are now the most pleasant and frequent entertainments of the stage; two of theirs being acted through the year for one of Shakespeare's or Jonson's: the reason is, because there is a certain gaiety in their comedies, and pathos in their more serious plays, which suit generally with all men's humors. Shakespeare's language is likewise a little obsolete, and Ben Jonson's wit comes short of theirs.

"As for Jonson, to whose character I am now arrived, if we look upon him while he was himself (for his last plays were but his dotages), I think him the most learned and judicious writer which any theater ever had. He was a most severe judge of himself, as well as others. One cannot say he wanted wit, but rather that he was frugal of it. In his works you find little to retrench or alter. Wit, and language, and humor also in some measure, we had before him; but something of art was wanting to the drama till he came. He managed his strength to more advantage than any who preceded him. You seldom find him making love in any of his scenes, or endeavoring to move the passions; his genius was too sullen and saturnine to do it gracefully, especially when he knew he came after those who had performed both to such an height. Humor was his proper sphere; and in that he delighted most to represent mechanic people. He was deeply conversant in the Ancients, both Greek and Latin, and he borrowed boldly from them: there is scarce a poet or historian among the Roman authors of those times whom he has not translated in *Sejanus* and *Catiline*. But he has done his robberies so openly, that one may see he fears not to be taxed by any law. He invades authors like a monarch; and what would be theft in other poets, is only victory in him. With the spoils of these writers he so represents old Rome to us, in its rites, ceremonies, and customs, that if one of their poets had written either of his tragedies, we had seen less of it than in him. If there was any fault in his language, 'twas that he weaved it too closely and laboriously, in his comedies especially: perhaps, too, he did a little too much Romanize our tongue, leaving the words which he translated almost as much Latin as he found them: wherein, though he learnedly followed their language, he did not enough comply with the idiom of ours. If I would compare him with Shakespeare, I must acknowledge him the more correct poet, but Shakespeare the greater wit. Shakespeare was the Homer, or father of our dramatic poets; Jonson was the Virgil, the pattern of elaborate writing; I admire him, but I love Shakespeare. To conclude of him; as he has given us the most correct plays, so in the precepts which he has laid down in his *Discoveries,* we have as many and profitable rules for perfecting the stage, as any wherewith the French can furnish us."

From *Preface to Sylvæ*
or, *The Second Part of Poetical Miscellanies*
(1685)

"On Translation"

For this last half year I have been troubled with the disease (as I call it) of translation; the cold prose fits of it (which are always the most tedious with me) were spent in the *History of the League;* the hot (which succeeded them) in this volume of Verse Miscellanies. The truth is, I fancied to myself a kind of ease in the change of the paroxysm; never suspecting but the humor would have wasted itself in two or three *Pastorals* of Theocritus, and as many *Odes* of Horace. But finding, or at least thinking I found, something that was more pleasing in them than my ordinary productions, I encouraged myself to renew my old acquaintance with Lucretius and Virgil; and immediately fixed upon some parts of them, which had most affected me in the reading. These were my natural impulses for the undertaking. But there was an accidental motive which was full as forcible, and God forgive him who was the occasion of it. It was my Lord Roscommon's *Essay on Translated Verse,* which made me uneasy till I tried whether or not I was capable of following his rules, and of reducing the speculation into practice. For many a fair precept in poetry is like a seeming demonstration in the mathematics, very specious in the diagram, but failing in the mechanic operation. I think I have generally observed his instructions; I am sure my reason is sufficiently convinced both of their truth and usefulness; which, in other words, is to confess no less a vanity, than to pretend that I have at least in some places made examples to his rules. Yet withal, I must acknowledge, that I have many times exceeded my commission; for I have both added and omitted, and even sometimes very boldly made such expositions of my authors, as no Dutch commentator will forgive me. Perhaps, in such particular passages, I have thought that I discovered some beauty yet undiscovered by those pedants, which none but a poet could have found. Where I have taken away some of their expressions, and cut them shorter, it may possibly be on this consideration, that what was beautiful in the Greek or Latin, would not appear so shining in the English; and where I have enlarged them, I desire the false critics would not always think that those thoughts are wholly mine, but that either they are secretly in the poet, or may be fairly deduced from him; or at least, if both those considerations should fail, that my own is of a piece with his, and that if he were living, and an Englishman, they are such as he would probably have written.

For, after all, a translator is to make his author appear as charming as possibly he can, provided he maintains his character, and makes him not unlike himself. Translation is a kind of drawing after the life, where every one will acknowledge there is a double sort of likeness, a good one and a bad. 'Tis one thing to draw the outlines true, the features like, the proportions exact, the coloring itself perhaps tolerable; and another thing to make all these graceful, by the posture, the shadowings, and, chiefly, by the spirit which animates the whole. I cannot, without some indignation, look on an ill copy of an excellent original. Much less can I behold with patience Virgil, Homer, and some others, whose beauties I have been endeavoring all my life to imitate, so abused, as I may say, to their faces, by a botching interpreter. What English readers, unacquainted with Greek or Latin, will believe me, or any other man, when we commend those authors, and confess we derive all that is pardonable in us from their fountains, if they take those to be the same poets whom our Ogilbys have translated? But I dare assure them that a good poet is no more like himself, in a dull translation, than his carcass would be to his living body. There are many who understand Greek and Latin, and yet are ignorant of their mother tongue. The proprieties and delicacies of the English are known to few; 'tis impossible even for a good wit to understand and practice them, without the help of a liberal education, long reading, and digesting of those few good authors we have amongst us, the knowledge of men and manners, the freedom of habitudes and conversation with the best company of both sexes; and, in short, without wearing off the rust which he contracted, while he was laying in a stock of learning. Thus difficult it is to understand the purity of English, and critically to discern not only good English, and critically to discern not only good writers from bad, and a proper style from a corrupt, but also to distinguish that which is pure in a good author, from that which is vicious and corrupt in him. And for want of all these requisites, or the greatest part of them, most of our ingenious young men take up some cried-up English poet for their model, adore him, and imitate him, as they think, without knowing wherein he is defective, where he is boyish and trifling, wherein either his thoughts are improper to his subjects, or his expressions unworthy of his thoughts, or the turn of both is unharmonious.

Thus it appears necessary that a man should be a nice critic in his mother-tongue, before he attempts to translate a foreign language. Neither is it sufficient, that he be able to judge of words and style; but he must be a master of them too: he must perfectly understand his author's tongue, and absolutely command his own: so that, to be a thorough translator, he must be a thorough poet. Neither is it enough to give his author's sense in good English, in poetical expressions, and in musical numbers; for, though all these are exceeding difficult to perform, there yet remains a harder task; and 'tis a secret of which few translators have sufficiently thought. I have already hinted a word or two concerning it; that is, the maintaining the character of an author, which distinguishes him from all others and makes him appear that individual poet whom you would interpret. For example, not only the thoughts,

but the style and versification of Virgil and Ovid are very
different: yet I see, even in our best poets, who have
translated some parts of them, that they have confounded
their several talents; and, by endeavoring only at the
sweetness and harmony of numbers, have made them both
so much alike, that if I did not know the originals, I
should never be able to judge by the copies, which was
Virgil, and which was Ovid. It was objected against a
late noble painter, that he drew many graceful pictures,
but few of them were like. And this happened to him,
because he always studied himself, more than those who
sat to him. In such translators I can easily distinguish the
hand which performed the work, but I cannot distinguish
their poet from another. Suppose two authors are equally
sweet, yet there is as great distinction to be made in
sweetness, as in that of sugar, and that of honey. I can
make the difference more plain, by giving you (if it be
worth knowing) my own method of proceeding, in my
translations out of four several poets in this volume—
Virgil, Theocritus, Lucretius, and Horace. In each of
these, before I undertook them, I considered the genius
and distinguishing character of my author. I looked on
Virgil as a succinct and grave majestic writer; one who
weighed not only every thought, but every word and
syllable: who was still aiming to crowd his sense into as
narrow a compass as possibly he could; for which reason
he is so very figurative that he requires (I may almost
say) a grammar apart to construe him. His verse is every
where sounding the very thing in your ears, whose sense
it bears: yet the numbers are perpetually varied, to increase the delight of the reader; so that the same sounds
are never repeated twice together. On the contrary, Ovid
and Claudian, though they write in styles differing from
each other, yet have each of them but one sort of music
in their verses. All the versification and little variety of
Claudian is included within the compass of four or five
lines, and then he begins again in the same tenor; perpetually closing his sense at the end of a verse, and that
verse commonly which they call golden, or two substan-
tives and two adjectives, with a verb betwixt them to

keep the peace. Ovid, with all his sweetness, has as little variety of numbers and sound as he: he is always, as it were, upon the hand-gallop, and his verse runs upon carpet ground. He avoids, like the other, all synalæpha's, or cutting off one vowel when it comes before another in the following word: so that, minding only smoothness, he wants both variety and majesty. But to return to Virgil: though he is smooth where smoothness is required, yet he is so far from affecting it, that he seems rather to disdain it; frequently makes use of synalæpha's, and concludes his sense in the middle of his verse. He is every where above conceits of epigrammatic wit, and gross hyperboles: he maintains majesty in the midst of plainness; he shines, but glares not; and is stately without ambition, which is the vice of Lucan. I drew my definition of poetical wit from my particular consideration of him: for propriety of thoughts and words are only to be found in him; and, where they are proper, they will be delightful. Pleasure follows of necessity, as the effect does the cause; and therefore is not to be put into the definition. This exact propriety of Virgil I particularly regarded as a great part of his character; but must confess to my shame, that I have not been able to translate any part of him so well as to make him appear wholly like himself. For where the original is close, no version can reach it in the same compass. Hannibal Caro's, in the Italian, is the nearest, the most poetical, and the most sonorous of any translation of the Æneids: yet, though he takes the advantage of blank verse, he commonly allows two lines for one of Virgil, and does not always hit his sense. Tasso tells us, in his Letters, that Sperone Speroni, a great Italian wit, who was his contemporary, observed of Virgil and Tully, that the Latin orator endeavored to imitate the copiousness of Homer, the Greek poet; and that the Latin poet made it his business to reach the conciseness of Demosthenes, the Greek orator. Virgil therefore, being so very sparing of his words, and leaving so much to be imagined by the reader, can never be translated as he ought, in any modern tongue. To make him copious, is to alter his character; and to translate him line for line is impossible;

because the Latin is naturally a more succinct language than either the Italian, Spanish, French, or even than the English which, by reason of its monosyllables, is far the most compendious of them. Virgil is much the closest of any Roman poet, and the Latin hexameter has more feet than the English heroic.

Besides all this, an author has the choice of his own thoughts and words, which a translator has not; he is confined by the sense of the inventor to those expressions which are the nearest to it. So that Virgil, studying brevity, and having the command of his own language, could bring those words into a narrow compass, which a translator cannot render without circumlocutions. In short, they, who have called him the torture of grammarians, might also have called him the plague of translators; for he seems to have studied not to be translated. I own that, endeavoring to turn his *Nisus* and *Euryalus* as close as I was able, I have performed that Episode too literally; that, giving more scope to *Mezentius* and *Lausus,* that version, which has more of the majesty of Virgil, has less of his conciseness; and all that I can promise for myself is only that I have done both better than Ogleby, and perhaps as well as Caro. So that, methinks, I come like a malefactor, to make a speech upon the gallows, and to warn all other poets, by my sad example, from the sacrilege of translating Virgil. Yet, by considering him so carefully as I did before my attempt, I have made some faint resemblance of him; and, had I taken more time, might possibly have succeeded better; but never so well, as to have satisfied myself.

From A Discourse Concerning the Original and Progress of Satire
(1693)

"The Origin of Satire"

There has been a long dispute among the modern critics, whether the Romans derived their satire from the Grecians, or first invented it themselves. Julius Scaliger and Heinsius are of the first opinion; Casaubon, Rigaltius, Dacier and the publisher of the Dauphin's *Juvenal* maintain the latter. If we take satire in the general signification of the word, as it is used in all modern languages for an invective, it is certain that it is almost as old as verse; and though hymns, which are praises of God, may be allowed to have been before it, yet the defamation of others was not long after it. After God had cursed Adam and Eve in Paradise, the husband and wife excused themselves by laying the blame on one another, and gave a beginning to those conjugal dialogues in prose which the poets have perfected in verse. The third chapter of Job is one of the first instances of this poem in Holy Scripture, unless we will take it higher, from the latter end of the second—where his wife advises him to curse his Maker.

The original, I confess, is not much to the honor of satire; but here it was Nature, and that depraved! When it became an art, it bore better fruit. Only we have learnt thus much already, that scoffs and reviling are of the growth of all nations; and consequently that neither the Greek poets borrowed from other people their art of railing, neither needed the Romans to take it from them. . . .

"The Superiority of Persius to Juvenal and Horace"

Herein then it is, that Persius has excelled both Juvenal and Horace. He sticks to his own philosophy; he shifts not sides, like Horace, who is sometimes an epicurean, sometimes a stoic, sometimes an eclectic, as his present humor leads him; nor declaims, like Juvenal, against vices, more like an orator than a philosopher. Persius is everywhere the same; true to the dogmas of his master. What he has learnt, he teaches vehemently; and what he teaches, that he practices himself. There is a spirit of sincerity in all he says: you may easily discern that he is in earnest, and is persuaded of that truth which he inculcates. In this I am of opinion, that he excels Horace, who is commonly in jest, and laughs while he instructs; and is equal to Juvenal, who was as honest and serious as Persius, and more he could not be. . . .

Will you please but to observe, that Persius, the least in dignity of all the three, has notwithstanding been the first, who has discovered to us this important secret, in the designing of a perfect satire, that it ought only to treat of one subject; to be confined to one particular theme; or, at least, to one principally. If other vices occur in the management of the chief, they should only be transiently lashed, and not be insisted on, so as to make the design double. As in a play of the English fashion, which we call tragi-comedy, there is to be but one main design; and, though there be an under-plot, or second walk of comical characters and adventures, yet they are subservient to the chief fable, carried along under it, and helping to it; so that the drama may not seem a monster with two heads. Thus the Copernican system of the planets makes the moon to be moved by the motion of the earth, and carried about her orb, as a dependent of hers. Mascardi, in his discourse of the *Doppia favola,* or double tale in plays, gives an instance of it, in the famous pastoral of Guarini, called *Il Pastor Fido;* where Corsica and the Satyr are the under parts; yet we may observe that Corsica is brought into the body of the plot, and made subservient to it. 'Tis certain that the divine wit of Horace was not ignorant of this rule, that a play, though it consists of many parts, must yet be one in the action, and must drive on the accomplishment of one design; for he gives this very precept, *sit quodvis simplex duntaxat et unum* [that it must be appropriately simple and single]; yet he seems not so much to mind it in his Satires, many of them consisting of more arguments than one; and the second without dependence on the first. Casaubon has observed this before me, in his preference of Persius to Horace; and will have his own beloved author to be the first who found out and introduced this method of confining himself to one subject. I know it may be urged in defence of Horace, that this unity is not necessary because the very word *satura* signifies a dish plentifully stored with all variety of fruit and grains. Yet Juvenal, who calls his poems a *farrago,* which is a word of the same signification with *satura,* has chosen to follow the same method of Persius, and not of Horace. And Boileau, whose example alone is a sufficient authority, has wholly confined himself, in all his satires, to this unity of design. That variety which is not to be found in any one satire is, at least, in many, written on several occasions. And if variety be of absolute necessity in every one of them, according to the etymology of the word, yet it may arise naturally from one subject, as it is diversely treated in the several subordinate branches of it, all relating to the chief. It may be illustrated accordingly with variety of examples in the subdivisions of it; and with as many precepts as there are members of it, which altogether may complete that *olla,* or hotchpotch, which is properly a satire.

Under this unity of theme, or subject, is comprehended another rule for perfecting the design of true satire. The poet is bound, and that *ex officio,* to give his reader some one precept of moral virtue; and to caution him against some one particular vice or folly. Other virtues, subordinate to the first, may be recommended under that chief head; and other vices or follies may be scourged, besides that which he principally intends. But he is chiefly to inculcate one virtue, and insist on that.

From A Parallel of Poetry and Painting
(1695)

"The Imitation of Nature in Poetry and Painting"

To imitate Nature well in whatsoever subject is the perfection of both arts; and that picture, and that poem, which comes nearest to the resemblance of Nature, is the best; but it follows not that what pleases most in either kind is therefore good, but what ought to please. Our depraved appetites and ignorance of the arts mislead our judgments, and cause us often to take that for true imitation of Nature, which has no resemblance of Nature in it. To inform our judgments and to reform our tastes, rules were invented, that by them we might discern when Nature was imitated, and how nearly. I have been forced to recapitulate these things because mankind is not more liable to deceit than it is willing to continue in a pleasing error, strengthened by a long habitude. The imitation of Nature is therefore justly constituted as the general, and indeed the only rule of pleasing, both in poetry and painting. Aristotle tells us that imitation pleases because it affords matter for a reasoner to inquire into the truth or falsehood of imitation by comparing its likeness or unlikeness with the original; but by this rule every speculation in Nature, whose truth falls under the inquiry of a philosopher, must produce the same delight, which is not true. I should rather assign another reason: truth is the object of our understanding, as good is of our will; and the understanding can no more be delighted with a lie, than the will can choose an apparent evil. As truth is the end of all our speculations, so the discovery of it is the pleasure of them; and since a true knowledge of Nature gives us pleasure, a lively imitation of her, either in poetry or painting, must of necessity produce a much greater: for both these arts, as I said before, are not only true imitations of Nature, but of the best Nature, of that which is wrought up to a nobler pitch. They present us with images more perfect than the life in any individual, and we have the pleasure to see all the scattered beauties of Nature united by a happy chemistry, without its deformities or faults. They are imitations of the passions which always move, and therefore consequently please: for without motion there can be no delight, which cannot be considered but as an active passion. When we view these elevated ideas of Nature, the result of that view is admiration, which is always the cause of pleasure.

"Invention"

The principal parts of painting and poetry next follow. Invention is the first part, and absolutely necessary to them both; yet no rule ever was or can be given how to compass it. A happy genius is the gift of Nature: it depends on the influence of the stars, say the astrologers; on the organs of the body, say the naturalists; it is the particular gift of Heaven, say the divines, both Christians and heathens. How to improve it, many books can teach us; how to obtain it, none; that nothing can be done without it, all agree—*Tu nihil invita dices faciesve Minerva.* [You will neither do nor say anything on which Minerva does not look with favor.]

Without invention a painter is but a copier, and a poet but a plagiary of others. Both are allowed sometimes to copy and translate, but, as our author tells you, that is not the best part of their reputation. *Imitators are but a servile kind of cattle,* says the poet; or at best, the keepers of cattle for other men: they have nothing which is properly their own; that is a sufficient mortification for me, while I am translating Virgil. But to copy the best author is a kind of praise if I perform it as I ought; as a copy after Raphael is more to be commended than an original of any indifferent painter.

Under this head of *invention* is placed the disposition of the work, to put all things in a beautiful order and harmony that the whole may be of a piece. The compositions of the painter should be conformable to the text of Ancient authors, to the custom and the times; and this is exactly the same in poetry: Homer and Virgil are to be our guides in the epic; Sophocles and Euripides in tragedy; in all things we are to imitate the customs and the times of those persons and things which we represent: not to make new rules of the drama, as Lope de Vega has attempted unsuccessfully to do, but to be content to follow our masters, who understood Nature better than we. But if the story which we treat be modern, we are to vary the customs, according to the time and the country where the scene of action lies: for this is still to imitate Nature, which is always the same though in a different dress.

As in the composition of a picture the painter is to take care that nothing enter into it which is not proper or convenient to the subject; so likewise is the poet to reject all incidents which are foreign to his poem, and are naturally no parts of it: they are wens, and other excrescences, which belong not to the body, but deform it. No person, no incident in the piece or in the play, but must be of use to carry on the main design. All things else are like six fingers to the hand when Nature, which is superfluous in nothing, can do her work with five. A painter must reject all trifling ornaments; so must a poet refuse all tedious and unnecessary descriptions. A robe which is too heavy, is less an ornament than a burden. In poetry, Horace calls these things *versus inopes rerum, nugæque canoræ* [impoverished verses, sounding trifles]. These are also the *lucus et ara Dianæ* [sacred groves and rocks of Diana] which he mentions in the same *Art of Poetry;* but since there must be ornaments, both in painting and poetry, if they are not necessary, they must at least be decent; that is in their due place, and but moderately used. The painter is not to take so much pains about the drapery, as about the face, where the principal resemblance lies; neither is the poet, who is working up a passion, to make similes which will certainly make it languish. My Montezuma dies with a fine one in his mouth, but it is ambitious, and out of season. When there are more figures in a picture than are necessary, or at least ornamental, our author calls them *figures to be let,* because the picture has no use of them: so I have seen in some modern plays above twenty actors, when the action has not required half the number. In the principal figures of a picture, the painter is to employ the sinews of his art, for in them consists the principal beauty of his work.

From *Preface to the Fables*
(1700)

"Chaucer"

It remains that I say somewhat of Chaucer in particular.
In the first place, as he is the father of English poetry,
so I hold him in the same degree of veneration as the
Grecians held Homer, or the Romans Virgil: He is a
perpetual fountain of good sense; learned in all sciences;
and therefore speaks properly on all subjects. As he knew
what to say, so he knows also when to leave off; a
continence which is practised by few writers, and scarcely
by any of the Ancients, excepting Virgil and Horace. One
of our late great poets is sunk in his reputation because
he could never forego any conceit which came in his way;
but swept like a drag-net, great and small. There was
plenty enough, but the dishes were ill-sorted; whole pyra-
mids of sweet-meats, for boys and women; but little of solid
meat, for men. All this proceeded not from any want of
knowledge, but of judgment. Neither did he want that
in discerning the beauties and faults of other poets, but
only indulged himself in the luxury of writing; and perhaps
knew it was a fault, but hoped the reader would not find
it. For this reason, though he must always be thought a
great poet, he is no longer esteemed a good writer: and
for ten impressions which his works have had in so many
successive years, yet at present a hundred books are
scarcely purchased once a twelve month: for as my last
Lord Rochester said, though somewhat profanely, "Not
being of God, he could not stand."

Chaucer followed Nature every where; but was never

so bold to go beyond her. And there is a great difference
of being *Poeta* [a poet] and *nimis Poeta* [too much the
poet], if we may believe Catullus, as much as betwixt a
modest behavior and affectation. The verse of Chaucer, I
confess, is not harmonious to us; but 'tis like the eloquence
of one whom Tacitus commends, it was *auribus istius tem-
poris accommodata* [suited to the ears of those times];
they who lived with him, and some time after him,
thought it musical; and it continues so even in our judgment if compared with the numbers of Lydgate and
Gower, his contemporaries. There is the rude sweetness of
a Scotch tune in it, which is natural and pleasing, though
not perfect. 'Tis true, I cannot go so far as he who published the last edition of him; for he would make us
believe the fault is in our ears, and that there were really
ten syllables in a verse where we find but nine: but this
opinion is not worth confuting; 'tis so gross and obvious
an error that common sense (which is a rule in every
thing but matters of faith and revelation) must convince
the reader, that equality of numbers in every verse which
we call heroic, was either not known, or not always
practised in Chaucer's age. It were an easy matter to
produce some thousands of his verses which are lame
for want of half a foot, and sometimes a whole one, and
which no pronunciation can make otherwise. We can
only say that he lived in the infancy of our poetry, and
that nothing is brought to perfection at the first. We must
be children before we grow men. . . .

He must have been a man of a most wonderful comprehensive nature, because, as it has been truly observed
of him, he has taken into the compass of his *Canterbury
Tales* the various manners and humors (as we now call
them) of the whole English nation in his age. Not a single
character has escaped him. All his Pilgrims are severally
distinguished from each other: and not only in their inclinations, but in their very physiognomies and persons.
Baptista Porta could not have described their natures
better than by the marks which the poet gives them. The
matter and manner of their tales, and of their telling, are
so suited to their different educations, humors, and call-

ings, that each of them would be improper in any other mouth. Even the grave and serious characters are distinguished by their several sorts of gravity: their discourses are such as belong to their age, their calling, and their breeding; such as are becoming of them, and of them only. Some of his persons are vicious, and some virtuous; some are unlearned or (as Chaucer calls them) lewd, and some are learned. Even the ribaldry of the low characters is different: the Reeve, the Miller, and the Cook are several men, and distinguished from each other as much as the mincing Lady Prioress and the broad-speaking gap-toothed Wife of Bath. But enough of this: there is such a variety of game springing up before me, that I am distracted in my choice, and know not which to follow. 'Tis sufficient to say, according to the proverb, that here is God's plenty.